Literary Criticism and the Gospels

Literary Criticism and the Gospels

The Theoretical Challenge

Stephen D. Moore

Yale University Press
New Haven and London

Designed by James J. Johnson and set in Galliard type by
Brevis Press, Bethany, Connecticut. Printed in the United
States of America by BookCrafters, Inc., Chelsea, Michigan.

Library of Congress Cataloging-in-Publication Data

Moore, Stephen D., 1954–
    Literary criticism and the Gospels : the theoretical challenge
/ Stephen D. Moore.
    p.   cm.
    Bibliography: p.
    Includes index.
    ISBN 0–300–04525–5 (alk. paper)
    1. Bible. N.T. Gospels—Hermeneutics.   2. Bible as
literature.   3. Narration (Rhetoric)   4. Reader-response
criticism.   5. Structuralism.   I. Title.
BS255.5.M585   1989
226'.066—dc 19   89–30951
                                                             CIP

The paper in this book meets the guidelines for permanence
and durability of the Committee on Production Guidelines for
Book Longevity of the Council on Library Resources.

10 9 8 7 6 5 4 3 2 1

For Jane

Contents

Contents / ix

Acknowledgments

Heartfelt thanks to Robert Fowler and Richard Hays for reading and critiquing the manuscript; to David Wisdo for philosophical counsel; to Sean Freyne and Werner Kelber for frequent affirmation; to Gary Phillips for vital conversation; to Alan Culpepper for bibliographic aid; to the members of the Literary Aspects of the Gospels and Acts Group of the Society of Biblical Literature, and the Role of the Reader in the Interpretation of the New Testament Seminar of the *Studiorum Novi Testamenti Societas*, whose voices fill these pages; to John Collins for an unexpected favor; to Yale Divinity School, whose provision of a Henry R. Luce Postdoctoral Fellowship enabled, among other things, the writing of this book; and to Chuck Grench and Carl Rosen of Yale University Press, whose efficiency expedited its appearance.

Early versions of chapters 2, 7, and 8 appeared in *Forum, The Journal of the American Academy of Religion,* and *Neotestamentica* and are revised and included with permission. The diagram in chapter 4 appears by permission of Cornell University Press. Biblical quotations, unless otherwise stated, are from the Revised Standard Version.

Introduction: Prodigal Scholars and the Literary Swerve

"[T]his thy son . . . hath devoured thy living with harlots."
—Luke 15:30 (AV)

It is an exciting and confusing time for biblical studies. Vying with the venerable historical critical methods for a say on the biblical texts are a host of younger methods, or rather, groups of methods, that are putting new questions to the texts, rephrasing old questions, and getting new answers. Several clusters of criticism are evident. A variety of feminist criticisms strenuously demystify traditional biblical criticism. Third World voices, faint as yet, begin to gather volume. Other exegetes peer over disciplinary fences, or climb over altogether, to become cautious or avid readers in the social sciences or in literary theory and criticism. A profound crossdisciplinary restlessness has been catalytic in the emergence of several of these clusters—the social and literary clusters in particular, the feminist to a lesser degree. The spectacle of so many biblical scholars, many of them old enough to know better, climbing over the neighbors' fences has elicited bemused headshaking in some of their colleagues and outright disapproval in others. These vagrant scholars seem to some like irresponsible offspring, who, having received the share of property that has fallen to them, choose to take their journey into a far country to squander their living on improper theories and practices. But the parable of the Prodigal, as ever, admits another allegorical reading. The last time biblical scholars reeled under the heady influence of a variety of imported critical methods was when the historical criticism of the Bible took its first shambling steps in the eighteenth and nineteenth centuries in a world utterly transformed by modernity: scientific historical method, reasonable objective certitude, and newly flowered philological method all seemed to lie about for the picking.[1] (Present day elder sons who condemn recent prodigals conveniently forget

---

1. Cf. Kümmel, *Investigation*, esp. parts 2–4, and Frei, *Eclipse*.

xiii

that they themselves are descendants of those earlier prodigals who first "joined themselves to citizens of other countries," making respectable women of their harlots.) Willing exiles in that far country, biblical scholars have lived riotously for nearly two centuries. It has been murmured of late, however, that a great famine has arisen in that land and that historical criticism is in dire want.[2] Many are now coming to themselves in that strange country and have begun the journey back to parent disciplines long forgotten to offer themselves as hired servants or apprentices: "How many of my father's hired servants have bread enough and to spare, but I perish here with hunger!" (Luke 15:17).

Whereas Germany was the original locale in which alien methods were first applied to biblical study, the principal locale this time around would seem to be North America. It is not that biblical scholars never once peered over the fence in the interim; in their different ways Julius Wellhausen, Hermann Gunkel, and Rudolf Bultmann did (to name only the colossi). It is just that very many more are peering over the fence today than at any time in the past. Neither is it that non-American biblical scholarship is everywhere unidisciplinary. For example, with respect to the single trajectory I intend to cut through the current crossdisciplinary phenomenon—which concerns methods of gospel study appropriated from nonbiblical literary theory and criticism—South Africa must be regarded as a significant center of activity.[3] (Israel, in similar fashion, has become an important locus for crossdisciplinary literary work on the Hebrew Scriptures.[4]) The inroads made by the so-called literary approach, however, have been exceedingly modest in Great Britain (outside of the University of Sheffield) and scarcely less modest in France and West Germany, although a steady stream of structuralist and semiotic biblical work does continue to flow from both these countries and from Scandinavia,[5] the

2. The last fifteen years have seen a flood of titles that agonize over historical criticism or triumphantly proclaim its demise ("Will the Historical-Critical Method Survive?"; *The End of the Historical-Critical Method*; "Historical Criticism in the Dock"; etc.).

3. Due to the efforts of J. P. Louw and others, discourse analysis had a formative impact on much South African New Testament scholarship during the 1970s, which helps explain the school-like distinctiveness of the journal *Neotestamentica* or Petzer and Hartin, eds., *Perspective*.

4. The Israeli narratologist Meir Sternberg assumes credit for "developing 'the literary approach' to the Bible" (*Poetics*, 2). Sternberg and Perry's influential "King through Ironic Eyes" appeared in 1968. But what of Auerbach, *Mimesis* (1946); Frye, *Anatomy of Criticism* (1957); or Alonso-Schökel, *The Inspired Word* (1965)?

5. Scandinavian New Testament scholarship, like South African, has had an association with discourse analysis. See Olsson, "Decade," and the Coniectanea Biblica New Testament Series.

Netherlands, and so forth—a stream that has just as steadily reduced to a trickle in the Anglophone world.[6] But despite the persistence of that stream, Germany is possibly the least enthusiastic overall this time around, so far as the literary approach is concerned.[7] Indeed, the new literary criticism of the New Testament—specifically, the nonstructuralist types with which we shall deal—might claim with some justification to be a peculiarly American style of New Testament scholarship.

This book surveys the new literary criticism of the Gospels and Acts. I say "new" because, of course, literary criticism has been a component of biblical criticism almost since its inception, although it has not been a style of literary criticism calculated to spark recognition in "one who represents this field in secular scholarship" (Frye, "Analogies," 301). Indeed, another representative of the secular arm goes so far as to state that "the biblical scholar's definition of 'literary criticism' is virtually the opposite of the literary critic's definition," for a "purely literary criticism . . . would see the Bible, not as a scrapbook of corruptions, glosses, reductions, insertions, conflations, misplacings, and misunderstandings" (few biblical scholars see it quite that way any more, actually); instead, the "literary critic assumes unity in the text" (Gros Louis, "Considerations," 14–15).[8] The new literary criticism of the Bible, which has invested heavily but not exclusively in the idea of textual unity,[9] is a thriving area. Already the literature defies systematization. Books and articles applying nonbiblical literary methods in a single-minded manner issue forth steadily, though more frequently the new methods are used to supplement older methods and give them renewed edge. In response to the groundswell of interest a large number of "literary" seminars have made their appearance in our professional societies,[10] and a number of major publishing projects are

---

6. Three resources in such studies are: Crossan, comp., "Basic Bibliography"; Johnson, comp., *Bibliography*; and Miller, comp., *Structuralism*, 448–65. For more recent examples, see the journal *Sémiotique et Bible*.

7. Mainstream German scholarship's singularly cool attitude toward literary theory is in part the legacy of a controversy incited by Erhardt Güttgemanns and his "generative poetics" group (see Güttgemanns's journal *Linguistica Biblica* [1970–]). Semiotics, semantics, and textlinguistics still account in large part for West German literary-biblical work. One exception is Theissen's *Galilean,* an example of "narrative exegesis" (174) in the form of a historical novel.

8. The negative definition of pure literary criticism is a citation from an unspecified work of Northrop Frye.

9. See chapters 3 and 8 for my reservations concerning this assumption.

10. The Society of Biblical Literature, the *Studiorum Novi Testamenti Societas,* the Catholic Biblical Association, and the Westar Institute have more than fifteen seminars and working groups between them applying literary criticism to the Bible.

under way in addition. More remarkably, however, the Bible has become a hot property in secular literary study; significant numbers of critics and theorists have wrestled seriously with it.[11] I hope that this book can also be of some interest to such critics and their readers. (Those unfamiliar with the basic elements of biblical scholarship might find themselves mystified at times despite the Glossary, but a profession whose stronger members read Derrida in the French will, I hope, take such humdrum puzzlement in their stride.)

In New Testament studies—our main concern here—the new literary approach is an easily recognizable but variegated one that seems to go under a bewildering variety of names. "This new movement in Biblical interpretation," one practitioner tells us, "is Biblical Literary Criticism (also called Rhetorical or Composition Criticism)" (Stock, *Discipleship*, 10). Another introduces a similar book as "a study in literary, or narrative, criticism" (Kingsbury, *Matthew as Story*, vii), while the jacket of a third book, with pronounced similarities to the first two, explains that it draws on "a contemporary literary-critical method called narrative analysis (or reader-response criticism)" (Edwards, *Matthew's Story*). Formulations such as these could be multiplied, and the ease with which they blur or erase methodological differences prompts me to respond with a map—and a map is what this book is—that differentiates the main features of the critical landscape (too sharply, if anything)—and locates the main fault lines in the process. For topography is only part of the task. The other part is seismography, an equally propitious science when much of what seemed firm ground up to recently has begun to quake, faintly as yet, under our feet.

Much recent literary criticism of the Gospels has been of a decidedly popular sort (e.g., the last three books listed). The relative accessibility of this work is greeted with a sigh of relief by those who were reduced to yawns or groans by biblical structuralism, semiotics, and discourse analysis. Indeed, it seems to me that approaches centered on plot and character, and more lately on readers and reading (together, the main foci of the present book) have largely displaced structuralism, at least in North America, as the preferred way of appropriating literary and cognate studies for gospel research.[12] The advantages of accessibility hardly need spelling out.

---

11. The better known names read like a *Who's Who?*: Robert Alter, Mieke Bal, Roland Barthes, Harold Bloom, Jacques Derrida, Northrop Frye, René Girard, Geoffrey Hartman, Frank Kermode, Julia Kristeva, Louis Marin, J. Hillis Miller, Walter Ong, Michel Serres, George Steiner, and Meir Sternberg.

12. Structuralism has had a more significant impact on biblical criticism than on Anglo-

Furthermore, several popular literary works on the Gospels have displayed significant methodological innovation (I review some of these in chapters 2 and 4). Such accessibility, however, is often the incidental result of an inadequate grasp of the complexities of literary theory. *How are we really faring as literary critics?* Those of us with crossdisciplinary leanings are unavoidably acquainted with the opinions that more traditionally minded colleagues tend to have of our attempts to apply literary criticism to the Bible. Given, as we noted earlier, that nonbiblical literary critics have tended to greet our traditional versions of literary criticism with head-scratching puzzlement, how might *they* view our new attempts at a literary approach? What kind of survey of, or introduction to, the new literary criticism of the Bible, centered on the Gospels, might a literary critic or theoretician produce? (It is the less traditional literary critic that I have in mind.) A biblical scholar by training, I have perhaps read enough literary theory and criticism to have internalized a strategy of surveying that I firmly associate with that other discipline—a strategy irresistibly drawn to salient facets of what those being surveyed leave *unsaid* about their situations: what they presuppose, suppress, or otherwise overlook. (Such myopia being an enabling condition of all discourse, all that can be claimed for this book is a set of spectacles different from those normally worn by biblical scholars.) This criticism of criticism, or *metacriticism*—a thriving subfield within recent literary studies, with a penchant for virtuoso feats of one-upmanship (Johnson analyzes Derrida's analysis of Lacan's analysis of Poe, etc.)—has tended to work best when the surveyor has also had his or her own ax to grind.[13] This book lays little claim to analytic virtuosity, although I do have a rather large ax in hand, as will be seen. Metacriticism being the reading of reading,[14] I have little opportunity to

American literary criticism. Structuralism has generally been more at home with myth, folk tale, and other premodern literary genres than with the modern novel, though there have been notable exceptions, and has been singularly unsuccessful with poetry. After a lukewarm affair with structuralism that lasted until about the mid-1970s, Anglo-American literary criticism found itself increasingly attracted to, or forced to confront, poststructuralism and deconstruction. Biblical structuralism, which reached its zenith around the same time, has since declined steadily in North America. Paradoxically, structural exegesis of the New Testament has only discovered its distinctive voice in the 1980s, as witnessed by Patte, *Paul's Faith* and *Matthew's Faith* (the results of a decade-long simplification of Greimasian theory to a point where it retains its explanatory power but is comprehensible to nonspecialists), and Malbon, *Narrative Space* (an equally innovative appropriation of Lévi-Strauss).

13. One thinks of such works as de Man, *Blindness and Insight* (if not the archetype of this genre, then certainly its most influential product), Culler, *Structuralist Poetics,* and Eagleton, *Literary Theory.* The earlier reference was to Johnson, "Frame."

14. All criticism, it is sometimes argued, is the reading of antecedent readings. See my chapters 7 and 8.

engage the Gospels directly—not until chapter 8, at any rate.[15] Moreover, to read critically over the shoulders of others is to be absorbed in methodology and hermeneutics; hence, I cannot always do justice to the exegetical findings of the books and essays surveyed. The reader is urged to peruse these often provocative works for himself or herself.

Neither do I engage in a full-scale apologia for the new literary criticism of the Gospels. That being said, there *are* some potential misunderstandings that I should like, if possible, to deflect.[16] First, a sizable number of New Testament scholars view the literary approach as an illegitimate and facile transposition of methods appropriate to the modern novel to (mainly) first-century documents. This is a viable concern, one that I wrestle with specifically in chapter 6—though I have occasion to ask there also, from the standpoint of the burgeoning field of orality-literacy research, whether mainstream gospel scholars have *themselves* grasped the depth of the chasm that separates them from early Christianity. But the point to be made here is a much more general one. Over the last three decades, the theory of narrative has displaced the theory of the novel on the international scene as a central preoccupation of literary theory (cf. Martin, *Recent Theories,* 15–56). Over roughly the same period, narrative theory has become an interdisciplinary project (23, 26–27), making important inroads in fields as diverse as anthropology, historiography, psychology, and, of course, theology and biblical studies.[17] The literary study of the Gospels and Acts, in consequence, need by no means be chained to the novel.

A second misunderstanding concerns the seriousness of the literary trajectory in current biblical studies. It is often assumed to be light exercise—"fluff," as one colleague puts it—preoccupied with relatively unimportant facets of the biblical texts. But secular literary critics are not nearly as prone as they once were to thrill to a well-turned image or phrase. Instead, current literary criticism, hugely muscled from long, strenuous

15. Cf. Frei, *Eclipse,* vii: "This essay falls into the almost legendary category of analysis of analyses of the Bible." Methodological introductions to the new literary criticism of the Bible have abounded, but extended metacritical surveys of extant work in the field are exceedingly rare. The major survey to date of extant literary critical gospel work is Poland, *Literary Criticism,* which situates Frei, Via, Crossan, and Ricoeur in relation both to Bultmann's theological hermeneutics and to Anglo-American New Criticism. Poland's survey is excellent as far as it goes, which is to 1980.

16. For a complementary piece of apologetic, which attempts to head off a different set of misunderstandings, see Culpepper, *Anatomy,* 8–11.

17. On the relationship between the narrative trajectory in recent biblical studies and in recent theology, see Fackre, "Narrative Theology," which subdivides narrative theology in terms of "canonical story" (built on literary analysis of the Bible), "life story," and "community story."

workouts with Heidegger, Derrida, and de Man, Freud and Lacan, Saussurian semiology and Barthesian semioclasty, Foucault, French Nietzscheanism (Deleuze, Lyotard et al.), French feminist theory (Cixous, Irigaray et al.), various Marxisms (the Frankfurt School, Althusser, Jameson), and various Pragmatisms (Rorty, Fish), is eager for Herculean labors. The following claim is not altogether unrepresentative of the rising generation: "The new subject of literary study includes society and culture and sexuality and the unconscious, all considered as *texts*. Literary study as now conceived extends beyond the poems of Donne and the novels of Henry James and the narrow, fetishizing . . . notions of the work of art as . . . icon" (Krupnik, "Introduction," 3). Sadly, this book has nothing to say on sexuality and little to say on the unconscious. Nevertheless, if it is not apparent to my reader by the time he or she reaches chapter 8 that the literary trajectory has very serious implications for biblical study, I shall have failed in one of my aims.

The preceding observations might have fed the suspicion (also a common one among biblical scholars, and the reverse side of the "light exercise" objection) that theoretical iron pumping has been mainly remarkable for its lack of interesting results. Consider the case of biblical structuralism. As Leander Keck admitted in 1980, historical critics could feel threatened by it, because it proposed "a consistent, alternate way of reading texts," one which did not seem to need historical criticism ("Survive," 120). A retaliatory scenario soon developed that suggested that historical criticism had just as little need of structuralism. In this scenario, the structuralist was assigned the role of the historical exegete's slow-witted, if well-meaning, younger brother. The structuralist would lumber along, laden down with some massive Greimasian or Lévi-Straussian apparatus to arrive at some conclusion where, almost invariably, the unencumbered historical exegete would be waiting, having already attained it by means of a few economical strides. Witness Christopher Tuckett's assessment:

> Provided that we bear in mind the methods, aims and limitations of structuralism, and provided too that we can develop a healthy scepticism about the value of complex charts and a battery of neologisms, we can learn from this discipline and accept its value for us. Its scope will however be a limited one. We should not expect new meanings of a text to emerge from structuralist analyses. . . . A structuralist approach which suggests meanings in a text which nobody has ever seen before might be rather suspect. (*New Testament*, 162–63)

Raymond Brown wastes fewer words: "I must admit that rarely do I discover from the semiotic analyses what I have not recognized through careful textual exegesis" ("Infancy Narrative," 661). Brown's suspicions are as well founded as they are widely shared, promoting the corollary suspicion that *all* literary theory might well be in need of the same "healthy skepticism" so as not to let it get between the exegete and the text. But theory actually has less in common with some cumbersome apparatus that can be strapped on or discarded than with some vital internal organ to which we seldom give thought. Without an implicit (and for that matter complex) theory or matrix of theories, we would not even know what a text was, much less how we should go about interpreting it. All too often "[h]ostility to theory . . . means an opposition to other people's theories and an oblivion of one's own" (Eagleton, *Literary Theory,* viii). Like Eagleton, but in a different register, I too attempt "to lift that repression" in this book to "allow us [better] to remember" (ibid.). More specifically, I attempt to show that literary theory as it has developed since structuralism is not nearly as *confirming* of our conventional exegetical wisdom (putting it mildly) as structuralism inadvertently tended to be.

My decision to focus my survey on the Gospels is based on the fact that the Gospels have drawn the lion's share of literary critical attention to date, whereas the attention given to Acts, Revelation, and the Epistles has been slight in comparison.[18] However, I do not try to survey everything in gospel studies that might come under the aegis of the literary swerve. My principal *methodological* omissions have been structuralist exegesis, discourse analysis, rhetorical criticism (which, however, seldom draws on nonbiblical literary theory or criticism), and studies in the literary imagination of the Bible,[19] whereas my principal *topical* omission has

18. On Acts see Barthes, "Acts 10–11"; Brawley, "Paul"; Darr, *Characterization*; Kurtz, "Narrative Approaches"; Leitch, *Stories,* 109–13; Levinsohn, *Textual Connections*; Parsons, *Departure*; Petersen, *Literary Criticism,* 81–92; Praeder, "Ancient Novel"; "Narrative Voyage"; and "Parallelisms"; Tannehill, "Acts 3–5"; *Narrative Unity,* vol. 2; and "Tragic Story"; Tyson, *Death*; Walworth, "Narrator"; and cf. Pervo, *Profit*. On Revelation see Barr, "Elephants"; "Oral Enactment"; and "Symbolic Transformation"; Beardslee, *Literary Criticism,* 53–63; Güttgemanns, "Semiotik"; Hellholm, "Apocalyptic Genre"; McGinn, "Revelation"; Schüssler Fiorenza, *Justice* and "Visionary Rhetoric"; and cf. Derrida, "No Apocalypse" and "Apocalyptic Tone." Attempts to apply modern literary theory to Paul's letters include Cronjé, "Galatians"; Hays, *Faith* and *Echoes*; Heil, *Romans*; Heiny, "2 Corinthians"; Johanson, *1 Thessalonians*; Lategan, "Galatians"; Louw, *Romans 1 and 2*; McKnight, ed., "Reader"; Marks, "Pauline Typology"; Patte, *Paul's Faith*; Petersen, *Rediscovering Paul*; Schenk, *Phillipperbriefe*; Spencer, *Literary Style*; and cf. Goulder, "Pauline Epistles"; Plank, *Irony*; Seeley, "Poststructuralist"; and Talbert, *Reading Corinthians*.

19. Rhetorical criticism of the Gospels is well represented by Dewey, *Public Debate,* and Robbins, *Jesus*; and cf. Kennedy, *Rhetorical Criticism,* 97–140; Mack and Robbins, *Persuasion*; and Wuellner, "Rhetorical Criticism." Studies in the literary imagination of the

been the multimethodological body of parables work (much of it structuralist) that extends from the mid-1960s to the present.[20] Instead I center on two "younger" sets of approaches—*narrative criticism* and *reader-response criticism*—whose impact on gospel studies will, I suspect, reach its zenith in the 1990s—and on *poststructuralism,* looming up menacingly behind them, which, I further suspect, adumbrates the unprecedented interrogation of text and method that lies in store for biblical scholarship as it wends its way a little uncertainly out of the twentieth century and into the twenty-first. Frankly, rather than squeeze everything into the ark, I prefer to try to rock it instead.

The format I mainly adhere to is that of analytic discussion of representative books and essays in the literary criticism of the Gospels, gradually leading into an interrogation of some of the grounding assumptions of biblical studies in general. And rather than offer a *disinterested* descriptive overview of the field (not that there may be any such thing), I attempt to alter the reader's perception of the gospel narratives instead, and indeed of the critical task itself, especially in the later chapters of the book. I try to counterbalance the inevitable selectivity of this plotted account by concluding with an inclusive bibliography.

Two umbrella terms capture the foci of this book: *story* and *reader.* A preoccupation with story seems to be a salient feature of the new gospel criticism. Contrast David Aune's recent definition of literary criticism in the gospel context: "Literary criticism deals with the interpretation and evaluation of a literary work through the careful examination and analysis of the work itself on the basis of both internal factors (e.g., genre, structure, content, style, sources) and external factors (e.g., historical setting, social setting, biographical data, psychological information)" (*Literary Environment,* 19). This does amount to a succinct and comprehensive definition of the "older" literary criticism of the Gospels (and the Bible generally). But what immediately leaps to the eye in light of more recent developments is the lack of any explicit mention of *plot* (perhaps plot is a facet of structure for Aune). Much of the new literary criticism is deeply attentive to the ways in which a gospel's plot unfolds. This is the topic of chapter 1 and particularly of chapter 2, while more complex and more ambitious ways of dealing with gospel narrative is the topic of chapters 3 and 4. Indeed, some literary critics of the Gospels have tended to bracket

---

Gospels (and other biblical works) have included Beardslee, *Literary Criticism*; Frye, *Great Code*; Jasper, *Literary Imagination*; and Wilder, *Rhetoric* and *Myths*.

20. The omission has not been total, however; in chapter 8 I assess the poststructuralist trajectory in parables studies, as represented by Crossan.

the main preoccupation of gospel scholarship of the last three decades—the individual theologies of the evangelists—in order to center their attention on the narrative features of the texts. This raises the perplexing question of how exactly the older and newer foci intersect, if they intersect at all (a question addressed in chapter 5). A convenient label for the complex of related approaches surveyed in chapters 1 through 5, and a term now passing into common currency, is *narrative criticism*. I should stress that the term, as used in this book, refers to a form of *biblical* criticism. It seems to be a coinage of gospel scholars, as we shall see, and its usage underscores a point I elaborate, namely, the new literary criticism of the Gospels is an enterprise that differs significantly from anything to be found in nonbiblical literary criticism.

Our second umbrella term, *reader,* is focal to part 2. In New Testament studies, as we shall see, the more recent preoccupation with readers and reading is largely an extension of (or variation on) narrative criticism. Typically, for example, the successive responses that an unfolding plot sequence anticipates or elicits in a reader become the object of detailed analysis. "Reader-response criticism" in the context of the Gospels is thus the topic of chapter 6. Finally, chapters 7 and 8 allow the general swerve toward reading—the obsession with the problematics of reading that has characterized literary theory of the 1970s and 1980s and of which reader-response criticism is but a single manifestation—to take the measure of biblical exegesis in full, or as fully as space allows. For the question that ultimately confronts us in the 1990s, as we begin to forge ever more serious relations with literary theory, is an extension of the more specific one posed earlier, How are we faring as literary critics? Contemporary literary theory challenges and empowers us to phrase that question more inclusively: How are we faring as professional readers of the Bible? How are we faring as *biblical* critics?

PART I
Gospel Criticism as Narrative Criticism

Here are some articles of faith I could subscribe to: That . . . the primary concern of criticism is with the problem of unity . . . the kind of whole which the literary work forms or fails to form, and the relation of the various parts to each other in building up this whole.
—Cleanth Brooks, "The Formalist Critics"

Literary criticism . . . asks us to look at a gospel holistically.
—Joseph Tyson, *The Death of Jesus in Luke-Acts*

The following study will emphasize . . . unity. . . . This unity is the result of a single author working within a persistent theological perspective, but it is something more. It is a *narrative* unity, the unity appropriate to a well-formed narrative.
—Robert Tannehill, *The Narrative Unity of Luke-Acts*

[I]t would be unfortunate, it seems to me, to seek "unity" at any price, and in that way to *force* the work's coherence—which is, of course, one of criticism's strongest temptations, one of its most ordinary (not to say most common) ones, and also one most easy to satisfy, since all it requires is a little interpretive rhetoric.
—Gérard Genette, *Narrative Discourse*

[U]nity is in the good will of [the] reader.
—Harold Bloom, *Kabbalah and Criticism*

1
Reading for the Story I: Unregistered Border Crossings in Gospel Criticism

This is a book about books and essays, a map of secondary literature. What better way to bear in on our topic, then, than by way of some comments on a review of a book on a gospel? In an unusual discussion of J. A. Fitzmyer's 1,642 page commentary on Luke, C. H. Talbert recently argued that it is a monument to an era of Lukan scholarship now past, one that spanned the years 1954 to 1974.[1] Although there are references in Fitzmyer to works later than 1974, Talbert uses 1974 as a watershed "because in that year lectures by Paul Minear, later published as *To Heal and To Reveal* . . . signaled a new methodological departure, and because in that year the Luke-Acts seminar of the [Society of Biblical Literature], which was to give expression to a new way of doing Lucan studies, began. At the risk of oversimplification, one may attempt a summary of two distinct approaches to Luke, with 1974 as roughly the dividing line" ("Review," 337). He proposes four points of difference. First, in the earlier approach the units studied are roughly equivalent to the pericopae of a traditional Gospel Parallels. (Presumably, Talbert is referring specifically to the commentary format here.) After 1974 the focus is on larger thought units within the gospel. Second, the earlier approach built itself on a scrutiny of every divergence between Luke, Mark, and Matthew. The later preference has been for a close reading of the continuous gospel text. Third, the earlier approach sought to build a history of the gospel tradition, extending to the pregospel stages of transmission and to the historical Jesus in addition. The later trend is centered more on the message of the text in its canonical form. Fourth, while the preoccupation and dialogue of Lukan scholars in the pre-1974 period was mainly with the Conzelmann

1. In 1954 Conzelmann, *Die Mitte der Zeit*, ushered in a new era in Lukan scholarship.

school, in the later period it is mainly with Greco-Roman literature and modern literary criticism.

Fitzmyer's two-volume commentary epitomizes the earlier approach on all four points, for Talbert. He does not mention his own recent commentaries on Luke-Acts.[2] Not surprisingly, these exemplify the post-1974 approach as Talbert outlines it—though he does not himself dialogue with "modern literary criticism." Despite the inevitable polemics of Talbert's overview, however, there is still much to recommend it. What I find particularly arresting is that in contrast to the familiar appeals for a new way of reading the Bible not fixated on sources and history, Talbert proclaims that a quiet revolution has *already* occurred in the Lukan arena. But what kind of coup was it and what sort of territorial realignments did it effect? Here the cartographer must draw his or her lines carefully. I suggest that the new approach described by Talbert is essentially that of *composition criticism* (though he does not use that term), a method aligned with *narrative criticism* but in the last analysis clearly distinguishable from it. An elucidation of the similarities and differences facilitate the discussions that follow.

Where Composition Criticism Ends and Narrative Criticism Begins

A good example of the newer tendencies cited by Talbert is Robert O'Toole's *Unity of Luke's Theology* (1984). O'Toole explicitly states that his method is *composition criticism,* a holistic variation of redaction criticism in which the work itself (in this case, Luke-Acts), viewed rigorously and persistently in its entirety, becomes the primary context for interpreting any part of it.[3] O'Toole builds little on Markan or Matthean variants. Instead, themes (e.g., "God Continues to Bring Salvation to His People,

2. *Reading Luke* and *Acts.* Despite their different publishers, *Acts* is a companion volume to *Reading Luke* (so *Acts,* 4).

3. The term composition criticism, coined by Ernst Haenchen (*Weg,* 24), antedates the developments in Lukan studies covered by Talbert. However, Luke did become a favored site in the 1970s for a gradual shift from a preoccupation with gospel sources and the precise relationship of each gospel to its fellows to a preoccupation with the individual Gospels as compositional units when Acts began to acquire the role of primary control in the interpretation of Luke, a role which Mark had hitherto filled. Talbert is certainly correct to view Minear as a seminal figure in this development (see, e.g., Minear, *To Heal,* 83ff.). Although American Lukan studies has played midwife in the birth of composition criticism, the movement from redaction criticism to composition criticism (a halting, uneven movement, still in progress) has been a fully international one, has encompassed all four Gospels, and has been facilitated by a cautious but far-reaching holistic turn in biblical studies in general.

Israel, Who Are Now the Christians") and words (e.g., the vocabulary used in the Jesus-Peter, Stephen, Paul parallels) considered to be major vehicles of Luke's theology are selected and traced through the two-volume narrative.

O'Toole's book can be instructively compared with a 1985 article by Robert Tannehill, "Israel in Luke-Acts: A Tragic Story." Tannehill's reputation within the New Testament guild is that of a literary, or narrative, critic. "This study," Tannehill begins, "is part of an attempt to understand Luke-Acts as a unitary narrative in which the episodes receive their meaning through their function within the larger whole" (69). Tannehill's description of his strategy would not seem at all amiss in O'Toole's opening pages. Indeed, O'Toole draws an explicit parallel between his method and that of literary criticism: "Obviously, redaction criticism, which considers how an author modified his source(s), proves extremely useful in studying Luke's gospel where we know the sources he used, but it would be much less useful in Acts. . . . Therefore, the use of composition criticism, *which like literary criticism analyzes the whole of an author's work,* seems often to be the better method" (11, emphasis added). A comparison of these two studies, at first glance so similar in their holistic emphases, enables us to trace the border between narrative criticism and its nearest neighbor.

There is little in Tannehill's study that might startle a more traditional scholar. He is especially on the lookout for reliable indications of the overarching purpose of Luke-Acts. He finds such indications in previews of future events and reviews of past events that interpret the overall course of the story, in Old Testament quotations that express a divine purpose to be realized, in accounts of the various commissions given to Jesus, the Twelve, Paul, and so forth, and in statements by reliable characters within the story (e.g., Jesus, Peter, Stephen, Paul) that interpret events and disclose God's purpose. When Tannehill examines the use of these four devices in Luke 1–2, he finds an emphasis on the view that Jesus means redemption for Israel, that is, for the Jewish people. However, in Acts the Jews reject the Word, to which Paul responds by turning to the Gentiles. "So it seems that the expectation most emphasized in Luke 1–2 is largely *not* fulfilled in the following narrative" (72). The explanation Tannehill proposes is that the reader is being prepared in these early chapters to experience the story of Israel and its Messiah as a *tragic* story. Characters may have for themselves, and arouse in the reader, expectations of good fortune (as in Luke 1–2), while the actual outcome may be frustration of these expectations. And the more strongly such expectations are aroused, the more tragic their nonfulfillment will appear. In Luke-Acts, moreover, the downward turn of the plot for Israel is prolonged and complicated through recurrent awakening of hope and recurrent failure of fulfillment.

The dearth of references to Mark or Matthew in Tannehill's article matches Talbert's description of the current paradigm of Lukan studies. Also, Tannehill's intent to instate Luke 1–2 as a fully coherent prelude to Luke's story seems a logical extension of recent developments in Lukan studies: "since Paul Minear's article 'Luke's Use of the Birth Stories,' it should no longer be possible to ignore the many points of contact between the birth stories and the rest of Luke-Acts" ("Tragic Story," 73).[4] What is to prevent us from taking Tannehill's study to be an instance of composition criticism, like O'Toole's? Are there significant methodological differences between the two? One obvious difference turns out not to be particularly significant. Tannehill has occasion to refer in his footnotes to some literary critics and structuralists. This is possibly the main reason a casual reader might suppose that he or she was reading a piece of literary criticism. On closer examination, however, one finds that the nonbiblical critics cited contribute little to Tannehill's method. The most significant difference between O'Toole and Tannehill is rather one of focus. O'Toole's composition criticism represents the latest refinement of a method that descends from Henry J. Cadbury, Martin Dibelius, Hans Conzelmann, and Ernst Haenchen. But O'Toole still stands squarely in the Conzelmann-Haenchen tradition by reason of an overriding preoccupation with Luke's theology. Throughout, his goal is to paraphrase Luke's theological, christological, ecclesiological, soteriological, and ethical message, so far as it can be deduced from the narrative format. Tannehill, in contrast, is far more interested in Luke's story. "Unity of theological perspective is something different from the unity of story," as he tells us in an earlier article; "[w]e are only beginning to rediscover each gospel as a story which, like any other story, is meant to be read as a whole" ("Reading," 67). And reading whole, for Tannehill, means first of all attending to the plot (which we define provisionally as the arrangement of events within the story). Plot and theology are clearly interrelated. O'Toole is in some measure attentive to the plot—he frequently paraphrases narrative strands—but only in so far as it discloses theological perspectives. Tannehill is mainly intent on disclosing the plot of Luke-Acts (or an important facet of it), but in so doing he puts Luke's theological understanding of Israel in fresh aspect.

4. Cf. Minear, "Birth Stories." Similar approaches are taken by Brown, *Birth*, 241–43; Tiede, *Prophecy,* 22ff.

Despite the overlap, however, gospel criticism has switched tracks here for a new destination. Whereas composition criticism extends the tradition of redaction criticism by reason of an overriding interest in the evangelists' theologies, narrative criticism represents a break with that tradition in the sense that the focus is no longer primarily on theology.

Immigrant Concepts in Narrative Criticism

In the 1970s, narrative criticism's shoots sprouted and were nurtured in the Markan Seminar of the Society of Biblical Literature. Other anabolic stimuli included structuralism, then a new arrival on the American biblical studies scene, the availability of a publishing outlet in the experimental journal *Semeia*, founded in 1974, and the patronage of certain established scholars, notably Norman Perrin.[5] Most of all, it was a profound disgruntlement with the hegemony of historical criticism that impelled emergent narrative criticism. Throughout the 1970s, perhaps because of its ties with the Markan Seminar, effectively its center and forum, narrative criticism focused almost exclusively on the Gospel of Mark.

In 1980, the tenth and final year of the seminar, David Rhoads presented a paper on "Narrative Criticism and the Gospel of Mark" (published in 1982), which surveyed the nonstructuralist literary work on Mark of the 1970s. Here for the first time the approach is programmatically labeled *narrative criticism*.[6] For Rhoads, this is a broad area of inquiry, its principal foci being "plot, conflict, character, setting, narrator, point of view, standards of judgement, the implied author, ideal reader, style, and rhetorical techniques" ("Narrative Criticism," 412).[7]

Two interrelated ideas undergird the study of these areas. First, there is the idea that we came across in connection with Tannehill, namely, the gospel text should be approached as a coherent integrated whole. For

5. See Perrin's seminal "Evangelist as Author," which calls for a "general literary criticism" of the Gospels that would draw on extradisciplinary resources; also his *Jesus*: "the principles involved in the hermeneutical process are the same for any texts, sacred or secular, ancient or modern, literary or popular" (2).

6. The term is used occasionally in earlier studies such as Petersen, *Literary Criticism*, though not in Rhoads's consistent and definitive way.

7. *Narrative criticism* would hardly evoke this exact range of associations in a nonbiblical literary critic and is to that extent a unique usage of New Testament literary critics. The term is only beginning to gain currency in New Testament studies generally and is used far less frequently in literary criticism of the Hebrew Bible/Old Testament. Narrative criticism has been applied fairly intensively to Mark since about 1977; only since about 1983 has it been seriously applied to John, Matthew, or Luke. Acts and Revelation largely await their turn, as noted in the introduction.

Rhoads, the shift to literary criticism involves a corollary shift from "fragmentation" to "wholeness": "We know how to take the text apart to analyze it; adding narrative criticism to our study is an opportunity to reaffirm the original achievement of Mark in creating a unified story" (413).

Concern for the integrity of the gospel text in its received form is also a feature of composition criticism. Composition criticism, however, is best viewed as a logical extension of redaction criticism. In the 1960s, redaction critics such as Norman Perrin were already realizing that minute examination of the changes introduced by the evangelists in their sources must gradually lead to questions about "the arrangement of the material, the movement of narrative in which the material is now set, and the like. This is composition, but it is also a good indication of the theological purpose of the author" (Perrin, *Redaction Criticism*, 65). Perrin anticipated a day when composition criticism might need to be distinguished from redaction criticism "as redaction criticism now has to be distinguished from form criticism" (67). But with narrative criticism a significant displacement occurs, "the theological purpose of the author" no longer being at the center. This becomes clearly apparent when we come to the principal focus of narrative criticism as Rhoads understands it.

Closely allied to the idea that Mark's *text* has its own integrity and deserves to be read as it stands is the idea that Mark's *story-world* too has "autonomous integrity" ("Narrative Criticism," 413). Mark tells a story that generates a world of persons, places and events, and that has its own internal consistency and validity independent of its resemblance or non-resemblance to the real world of Jesus' or Mark's day. Indeed, Rhoads would define narrative criticism precisely in terms of this idea:

> narrative criticism works with the text as "world-in-itself." Other approaches tend to fragment, in part because their purpose is to put elements of the text into contexts outside the text; so, for example, biblical scholars may identify the feeding of the five thousand as an historical event in Jesus' time or as an oral story emerging from the early church or as vehicle for a theological truth . . . or as a story which reveals the author's intentions, or as instructions to Mark's community. *Narrative criticism brackets these historical questions and looks at the closed universe of the story-world.* (Of course, knowledge of the history and culture of the first century is a crucial aid to understanding Mark's story-world, but that is a different matter from using elements of a text to reconstruct historical events.) (413, emphasis added)

In one sense, ideas such as these push the holistic emphases of composition criticism, which had gained momentum by the late 1970s, to their
logical climax. But it would be a mistake to think that narrative criticism
arose naturally out of composition criticism, as composition criticism arose
out of redaction criticism. Narrative criticism's text-theory, as Rhoads ex-
pounds it, is an imported one; nothing in the theologically oriented gospel
criticism dominant in the preceding decades explains it adequately. Instead, Rhoads' conceptions of the text and of the critical task have marked
affinities with those of the New Criticism, which was the dominant mode
of Anglo-American literary criticism from the late 1930s through the 1950s.[8]
What was new about the New Criticism was its rejection of extrinsic
approaches to the literary text—biographical, historical, sociological,
philosophical—and its advocacy of an intrinsic criticism: "The natural and
sensible starting-point for work in literary scholarship is the interpretation
and analysis of the works of literature themselves. . . . But, curiously
enough, literary history has been so preoccupied with the setting of a
work of literature that its attempts at an analysis of the works themselves
have been slight in comparison with the enormous efforts expended on
the study of environment" (Wellek and Warren, *Theory,* 139).[9] (Uncanny
echoes of this verdict, uttered in 1942, have resounded in the biblical arena
over the past two decades.) The New Critics' answer, in a gesture reminiscent of Kant's in his *Critique of Judgment,* was to reconceptualize the
poem (shorthand for the literary work of art) as an autonomous, internally
unified organism, the bearer of a meaning that must be validated first and
foremost by the context of the work itself. Rhoads makes a parallel claim
for the Markan text.[10]

Rhoads's affiliation with the New Criticism goes beyond this claim,
however. A fundamental New Critical tenet was the inseparability of form
and content.[11] Form was not to be thought of as instrumental, the vehicle
for ideational or propositional content or cultural or historical reality,

8. Poland, *Literary Criticism,* 65–105, provides a fine discussion of the New Criticism.
Among the many introductions by secular critics, two in particular stand out: Berman,
Reception, 26–82, for its stereoscopic situating of the New Criticism; and Wellek, *Modern
Criticism,* 6:144–292, for the author's eyewitness role in relation to it.

9. Though Wellek and Warren were not New Critics in the full sense, their theory
was supportive of the New Critical agenda.

10. Rhoads's claim was anticipated in the field of Hebrew Scriptures in Muilenburg's
1969 manifesto "Form Criticism and Beyond," which is similarly colored by Anglo-American
formalism; e.g., "The literary unit is . . . an indissoluble whole, an artistic and creative unity,
a unique formulation" (369).

11. The classic expression is Brooks, "Heresy of Paraphrase."

separable from the literary text and independent of it. Rather, the meaning of the text was indissolubly bonded with its form. In "Narrative Criticism," Rhoads says nothing directly of form and content. Yet, if an example were sought of how form might be said to "mean," one could do no better than to continue the citation from that article, begun above. Having shown how traditional scholarship might interpret the feeding of the five thousand in Mark (historically or theologically, i.e., in terms of some historical or theological content), he gives a form-related interpretation of the same event: "The feeding of the five thousand is a dramatic episode *in the continuum of Mark's story.*" Within that continuum, each element has its place: "Jesus, Herod, the centurion—dramatic characters. The exorcisms, the healings, the journeys, the trial and crucifixion—vivid events in the narrative world of Mark's story, each element important and integral." Whatever Mark's gospel may yield in terms of history or early Christian theology, first and foremost it is "a closed and self-sufficient world, with its own integrity, its own past and future, its own set of values, its own universe of meaning" (413–14).[12]

The distinction between composition criticism and narrative criticism can now be rephrased as two distinct ways of locating the primary meaning of the biblical text. For composition critics, the meaning resides in the text's theological (or ideational) content. This content is separable in principle from the narrative form; narrative is the vehicle of theology. Narrative criticism, in contrast, is a *formalist* criticism; the meaning of the biblical text is located in the details of its structure. What the text says cannot legitimately be extrapolated from how it is said.

Nowhere in "Narrative Criticism and the Gospel of Mark" (or elsewhere, seemingly) does Rhoads acknowledge the similarities of the views he advocates with those of the New Critics. It is not that Rhoads has leaned exclusively on the New Criticism; he does draw heavily on other areas of literary study also. I would argue, however, that Rhoads's views of the text and of the critic's task are essentially New Critical views. Is he himself aware of this? He does refer in passing (413) to Hans Frei's *Eclipse of Biblical Narrative* (1974), certainly a major conduit through which New

---

12. The inseparability of form and content in Mark is explicitly declared in Rhoads and Michie, *Mark,* 4, 62. Cf. Beardslee, *Literary Criticism,* 2: "Participation in the form is itself an essential part of the reading of a literary work." This conviction has especially colored literary criticism of the parables; see, inter alia, Crossan, *In Parables,* 13 (the parables "articulate a referent so new and so alien to consciousness that the referent can only be grasped within the metaphor itself "), and Scott, *Symbol-Maker,* 11 ("We cannot state what a parable means, for it has no meaning separate from itself ").

Critical ideas have flowed into gospel scholarship.[13] Frei himself, however, scarcely acknowledges New Critical influences on his book.[14] Whatever can be said of Frei, the following explanation would seem to fit Rhoads. Early literary critics of the New Testament who drew on the New Criticism (e.g., Beardslee, *Literary Criticism* [1971], Crossan, *In Parables* [1973]) tended to make their debts explicit, but since the late 1970s, the tendency among literary critics of the Gospels has been to voice their holistic convictions with no hint of their affiliative origins.[15] The impression being fostered among biblical students and scholars in consequence is that secular literary criticism, as it pertains to literary narrative, is a discipline preoccupied with the unity of texts and the autonomy of story-worlds— an impression well wide of the mark, except in the sense that these have been among the concepts most contested in recent years. Pronounced dead for more then twenty years, the New Criticism has shown phoenix-like powers of resilience (cf. Bové, "Variations"). Nevertheless, the views of literary text and meaning that it canonized should be seen by biblical critics for what they are: the legacy of a particular movement whose golden age is now long past, and not the whole of literary criticism or its definitive concerns.[16]

The metonymic characterization of literary criticism as a holistic activity has been correlated to a tendency to assume that the gospel texts are unified. Were we to recognize that concepts like textual unity have been at the storm center of recent critical debate, the following story, which we tell again and again, might not run quite so smoothly: historical criticism has gone down the primrose path of fragmentation, and although it has

13. On Frei and the New Criticism, see Poland, *Literary Criticism*, 122, 132–37. What also flowed through Frei's *Eclipse*, were, of course, the ideas of Auerbach's *Mimesis*, though this is less important to our situating of narrative criticism. Note Petersen's verdict on Auerbach: "[he] missed the major point of literary concerns in contemporary biblical studies, namely the . . . question of textual integrity" ("Biblical Studies," 35).

14. One possible reason being that prior to the "French invasion" of the 1960s and 1970s—structuralism, and hard on its heels, deconstruction—certain New Critical tenets had been so deeply internalized in Anglo-American literary criticism that they seemed to require little acknowledgment or justification (Cain, *Crisis*, is excellent on this).

15. See, inter alia, Fowler, *Loaves*; Kingsbury, *Story*; Rhoads and Michie, *Mark*; Tannehill, *Narrative Unity*; Tyson, *Death*; and cf. Staley, *First Kiss*, 29.

16. Culler puts it nicely: "Once upon a time it might have been possible to think of criticism as a single activity practiced with different emphases. The acrimony of recent debate suggests the contrary: the field of criticism is contentiously constituted by apparently incompatible activities. Even to attempt a list—structuralism, reader-response criticism, deconstruction, Marxist criticism, pluralism, feminist criticism, semiotics, psychoanalytic criticism, hermeneutics, antithetical criticism, *Rezeptionsästhetik* . . .—is to flirt with an unsettling glimpse of the infinite that Kant calls the 'mathematical sublime'" (*On Deconstruction*, 17).

certainly succeeded in accumulating some vital data along the way, it has now moved into a cul-de-sac. Meanwhile, secular literary critics have known what biblical literary critics have only lately come to realize, namely, a literary text must first of all be read on its own terms, as a unit. One then sets out to disclose the full extent of the unity that the historical critics have overlooked. I propose a rather different metanarrative, however, in which secular literary critics and theoreticians seem to side with the preholistic tradition of gospel scholarship against the holistic tenor of more recent work (see chapters 3, 4, and 8 below).

Returning to Rhoads's article, it should be noted that he includes the approach to Mark "as a story which reveals the author's intention" in his list of extrinsic approaches, which it will be narrative criticism's business to bracket ("Narrative Criticism," 413). Here again one detects a New Critical undercurrent. One of the factors marked for excision by the New Critics was the so-called intentional fallacy—the notion that the meaning of a literary work is identical with its author's intention.[17] By 1960 the author had slipped well off center in Anglo-American literary criticism, as it became "virtually taboo to speak of the [poetic] text as an act of communication among real people in a real world" (Lanser, *Narrative Act,* 46). Now, not only would one be hard put to find a narrative critic who brackets the biblical author's intention in this way, but one can safely assert that Rhoads himself does not do so. On the first page of Rhoads and Michie's *Mark as Story,* which appeared in the same year as "Narrative Criticism" (1982), we learn that "the [Markan] writer has told the story in such a way as to have certain effects on the reader. . . . The author . . . developed the characters and the conflicts, and built suspense with deliberateness, telling the story in such a way as to generate certain emotions and insights in the reader." Sentences like these abound in *Mark as Story* and, indeed, in the current story-and-reader approach to the Gospels generally: the text produces specifiable effects on the reader, which implicitly originate in an author's intentions. Narrative criticism, even where it shades over into reader-responses criticism, tends to hold strongly (if implicitly) to the view that the gospel text has a primary, recoverable meaning: what its author intended. This is its unbroken link with traditional biblical criticism.

Most of the works cited by Rhoads in his survey of Markan narrative criticism fail to accord with his definition of it. Few indeed could be said

---

17. Wimsatt and Beardsley had thrown down the gauntlet in "The Intentional Fallacy" (1946).

to bracket historical and theological questions in order to deal with the text as "world-in-itself." Not surprisingly, Rhoads's programmatic definition of narrative criticism fits his own *Mark as Story* far more closely than most of the Markan works he lists in his extensive concluding bibliography. (Notable exceptions on that list, which better accord with Rhoads's own orientation, are the studies by Norman Petersen and Robert Tannehill.)[18]

Narrativist studies of a marginal kind (those mainly preoccupied with gospel theology and *Sitz im Leben*) can be successfully mined for what they yield on plot, character, style, and so forth—Rhoads's essay is just such a mining operation. However, this book needs to draw far sharper lines. Because significant numbers of gospel exegetes are now looking with interest to narrative criticism or beginning tentatively to appropriate it, I would do better to center on unreservedly narrativist gospel readings. How do such readings proceed, and what exactly is at stake in them?

---

18. Petersen, "Mark 4:1–8:26"; *Literary Criticism*; "Biblical Studies"; and "When Is?"; and Tannehill, "Disciples"; "Narrative Christology"; and *Mirror*.

2

Reading for the Story II: Postcritical Targums on the Gospels

[W]e remain more determined by narrative than we might wish to believe.
—Peter Brooks, *Reading for the Plot*

[D]escriptions of reading stories seem themselves to be governed by aspects of story.
—Jonathan Culler, *On Deconstruction*

Narrative criticism is a story-preoccupied gospel criticism. Being preoccupied with story means, most of all, being preoccupied with *plot* and *character*. Some briefing on the technical usage of these terms facilitates the ensuing discussions.

Plot and Character

Utilizing insights that go back at least to Aristotle, we can define a plot as a set of events linked by temporal succession and causality. A description of an event-set not linked by succession—that is, a description of simultaneous events—would not constitute a plot in any conventional sense of the term; plot requires some change in a state of affairs. Ordinarily, plots move "from a stable beginning through complications to another point of equilibrium at the end" (Martin, *Recent Theories,* 81). But plots are not constituted by temporal linkage alone. Events must also be linked causally. In E. M. Forster's well-known example, "The king died and then the queen died of grief" is a plot, but "The king died and then the queen died" is not (*Aspects,* 93). The causal connections between events need not be fully stated in a plot; indeed, they seldom are. In consequence the reader must supply them. Our desire to impose maximum plot-coherence on a set of narrated events is an innate and powerful one; we pose as many connections as we can. Indeed, "readers will tend to assume that even 'The king died and the queen died' presents a causal link, that the king's death has something to do with the queen's," unless otherwise instructed (Chatman,

Story, 45–46).[1] The desire for coherence is especially well attested in gospel scholarship. One thinks of the perplexity that Mark's young man sans linen cloth (14:51–52) has occasioned over the years, not to mention his baffling conclusion (16:8).[2]

Plot and character are inseparably bound up in the reading experience, if not always in critical thought. Each works to produce the other. Characters are defined in and through the plot, by what they do and by what they say. The plot in turn comes into view as characters act and interact. Characters are further defined by what the narrator and fellow characters say about them. For example, by the time the adult Jesus emerges on the scene in Matthew or Luke, a crucial body of information concerning him has already been transmitted to the reader through a range of reliable speakers (narrator, angel, Baptist, etc.).[3] Characters "can be dynamic (when they change and grow) or static (when they do not); they can be consistent (when the predicates associated with them do not result in seeming contradictions) or inconsistent; and they can be round or flat, that is, complex or simple, multidimensional or unidimensional, capable of surprising us or incapable of it" (Prince, *Narratology,* 72–73). Characterization in the Gospels tends toward the "flat" and "static" end of the spectrum. Gospel characters are plot functionaries first and foremost; that is why the seemingly redundant figure of Mark's fleeing youth provokes unrest in commentators. These, however, are not uniformly simple constructs. Mark's Jesus is a complex character with many and varied traits, while the disciples in Mark are also complex in that they display conflicting traits.

Commentary by Any Other Name

Narrative criticism is attentive first and foremost to the plot-generative interaction of characters within the story-worlds of the Gospels. The dis-

1. Causal linkage is what distinguishes a minimal plot from a minimal narrative. A narrative requires two or more events in temporal sequence as does a plot—but that is all it requires. Thus "The king died and the queen died" is a minimal narrative. Is it a plot? Chatman would say yes; Forster, no. See further Leitch, *Stories,* 130; Prince, *Narratology,* 1–4; and Rimmon-Kenan, *Narrative Fiction,* 135 n. 12.

2. Mark seems to have gotten more baffling: "Mark's Gospel, once so clear, stable, and slightly boring—'and then Jesus said, and then he went, and then he did'—has become in the last few years a strangely modernist document filled with interruptions, reversals, and uncanny nonendings" (Tracy, *Plurality,* 13).

3. See, e.g., Matthew 1:1–17, 20–23; 2:6, 15b, 17–18, 23; 3:11–12; Luke 1:32–33, 35, 42–44, 46ff., 68ff.; 2:10–11, 26, 29–32, 34–35, 38.

tillation of the particular gospel's theology, the quest for *Sitz im Leben,* and the quest for the historical Jesus are given second place or bracketed altogether. What would happen if this intense story-attentiveness were extended to entire gospel narratives—as has already in fact occurred? The outcome would be a new genre of biblical criticism: the narrative commentary.

The advent of biblical commentaries clothed in such unconventional guise begs the question, What is a biblical commentary to begin with? A 1982 issue of the journal *Interpretation,* devoted to this very question, presented some very traditional answers: the commentary "must show the structure of the New Testament author's thought. It must reflect the social and historical setting within which it was produced," and so forth.[4] But what if theological or historical exposition is no longer to be the definitive thing for a small but growing band of scholars, who will persist nonetheless in presenting us from time to time with unit-by-unit expositions of entire biblical books? The answer to the problem of definition, perhaps, is that the biblical commentary, however experimental, will still be recognizable as commentary by reason of its formal organization. Whatever its privileged themes or emphases, biblical commentary will continue to denote a detailed or summary, but more or less sequential, exposition of all the major sense units in a biblical text, or a continuous section of a biblical text.

But how substantial must the continuous section be in order for the exposition to qualify as a commentary? Raymond Brown's *Birth of the Messiah,* for example, in part a verse-by-verse elucidation of Matthew 1–2 and Luke 1–2, tends to correspond to conventional expectations that the term *biblical commentary* elicits, whereas a verse-by-verse elucidation of Luke 1:1–4 (e.g., Richard Dillon's "Previewing Luke's Project from His Prologue [Luke 1:1–4]") tends not to so correspond—or does it? Conventional expectation is an extremely pliable yardstick. For example, what if Dillon's article were expanded to book-length (does our uncertainty partly derive from its being an article)? The polls would undoubtedly show an increase in the percentage of those for whom it could then qualify as a bona fide commentary on Luke 1:1–4. But what if it were an elucidation of a single verse only, or even of a single word (the difficult *kathexes* of

4. Editorial, 341, paraphrasing Krentz, "Commentaries," in the same issue. That theology and history are the complete stock-in-trade of biblical commentary is an assumption that none of the six contributors to the issue think to question, nor does Lohfink, "Kommentar." For a different style of appraisal, employing philosophy, literary criticism, and linguistics, see Kieffer, "Kommentieren."

Luke 1:3, which has been the subject of a number of articles over the years)? What does seem certain is that with every reduction in length of the text being elucidated, the classification *commentary,* if applied, loses more and more of its generic sense and reverts more and more to its nongeneric everyday sense (a series of explanatory observations). As things presently stand, the exposition of a substantial block of continuous text seems to be the salient formal trait that sets the commentary off from the monograph or other genres of biblical scholarship.

Stories of Jesus

The first story-centered commentary on an entire gospel, to my knowledge, was Werner Kelber's *Mark's Story of Jesus* (1979), the first of four volumes in a *Stories of Jesus* series.[5] This is a nontechnical series; its format excludes footnotes and scholarly digressions. Despite these limitations, however, the first and fourth volumes (Kelber on Mark and Edwards on Matthew) display significant methodological innovation.

Mark's Story of Jesus pioneers a close, sequential, story-attuned reading of the entire text of Mark. A critical method and a critical vocabulary absolutely characteristic of narrative criticism receive expression in the opening paragraph:

> Both in study and in worship the Gospel of Mark has generally been treated as a collection of short stories. Articles and monographs single out specific aspects of the Gospel, commentaries are prone to break up the narrative flow, and translations are deeply influenced by this piecemeal approach. Reading only sections of Mark in worship likewise fractures our vision, perpetuating habits of hearing and reading which are detrimental to a total comprehension. Because we have focused on the individual stories *in* Mark we have not really come to the know the story *of* Mark. This book is designed to introduce the reader to a single coherent story, Mark's story of Jesus' life and death. From a literary perspective the reader is therefore advised to approach the Markan story as he or she would any other story: to read the whole story from beginning to end, to observe the characters and the interplay among them, to watch for the author's clues regarding the plot, to discern the plot development, to identify scenes of crisis and

---

5. For an early literary commentary on Mark 1–4, see Gros Louis, "Mark" (1974), a product of the "Bible as Literature" approach that antedates narrative criticism.

recognition, and to view the story's resolution in the light of its antecedent logic. (11)

Kelber's strategy can be instructively compared with that of Talbert's *Reading Luke* (1982). In Talbert's view, Fitzmyer's magisterial commentary on Luke exemplifies the "pre-1974" approach to Lukan commentary. Talbert's own method, he tells us, is not the "word-by-word, phrase-by-phrase, verse-by-verse method of traditional commentaries." Rather, the thrust is in "understanding large thought units and their relationship to Lukan thought as a whole" (*Reading Luke*, 2). The word *thought* is significant here. In chapter 1 we saw that to make thought the focus as opposed to story is distinctive of composition criticism as opposed to narrative criticism; indeed, it is on the evangelist's unfolding theological viewpoint (his "thought") that Talbert's subsequent reading is centered.[6] (Interestingly, he cites part 3, "Argument and Structure," of C. H. Dodd's *Interpretation of the Fourth Gospel* as the closest parallel to his method.) As such, I find Talbert's claim that he investigates Luke "with a type of redaction criticism heavily influenced by nonbiblical literary criticism" (*Reading Luke*, 2) a puzzling one. There are no references to works of nonbiblical literary criticism in this commentary and no signs that he has any familiarity with the area. Composition criticism (and it is under this rubric that Talbert's method fits) is best accounted for not in terms of direct borrowing from literary criticism but as an outgrowth of tendencies already apparent in redaction criticism.

Rather, it is Kelber's book that represents "a type of redaction criticism heavily influenced by nonbiblical literary criticism." Closely bonded with redaction criticism's preoccupation with the evangelist's theological viewpoint is a preoccupation with the evangelist's specific situation (*Sitz im Leben*) and that of his target audience, which fine-tuned that viewpoint and prompted its written expression. The opening paragraph of Kelber's introduction, quoted in its entirety above, invites the reader to read Mark as he or she would any other story—sequentially and as a unit. But the final paragraph of the introduction issues quite a different sort of invitation: "The Roman-Jewish War and the destruction of the temple provide a broad historical backdrop for the Gospel of Mark, and the reader may keep these events in mind in reading the gospel. There may be a connec-

6. The story/thought distinction, while not epistemologically watertight, is useful as a rule of thumb enabling differentiation of works that at first glance are deceptively similar— Talbert, *Reading Luke,* Tannehill, *Narrative Unity,* or Tyson, *Death* (the latter two works privilege story, Tannehill's in particular). Narrative criticism and composition criticism, however, may not always be prised apart so easily (see Karris, *Luke,* for a case in point).

tion between the loss of a national center and Mark's writing the story of
Jesus. In any case the story he tells appears to be both meaningful and
intelligible when read against the background of Israel's searing tragedy"
(14). In the opening paragraph Kelber's reader is urged to read Mark as
he or she would any other story, with attention to the internal world of
the story and to the interplay of characters within that world—to read
Mark in and for itself, as it were. The interplay of characters in the plot,
it is implied, is what the story is about. But by the time he or she reaches
the final paragraph of the introduction the reader is being asked to perform
a different sort of reading: he or she should read Mark as a kind of allegory
of the situation that occasioned it. (Clearly, I am playing fast and loose
with the letter of Kelber's text here, but it is an allegorical reading of just
this type that he goes on to perform.)

Is it possible to read both ways at once? The *mirror* model of Mark,
urged in Kelber's opening paragraph, alternates with a *window* model in
the subsequent analysis. The goal in Kelber's substantive chapters is predominantly one of moving behind the ostensive plot, deciphering the
allegory, seeking out the historical plot, which for Kelber concerns the
central figures of the Jerusalem church who abandoned Jesus on the cross,
opting for the "Kingdom in power" instead, as they thought. They remained stalled in Jerusalem after the resurrection, never reaching the goal
of Galilee. Now Jerusalem has been destroyed with its temple, an event
that confirms what the ministry of Jesus had shown: that Jerusalem is not
the place of the Kingdom. The Jerusalem church stands opposed to the
will of Jesus and of God, and so the disciples have missed their way into
the Kingdom.[7] Kelber's reading seems to imply that this is the story that
counts, the story that presides, ventriloquist-like, over the speech and
action of the surface story. Or switching metaphors we can say that the
gospel's meaning is ultimately gleaned in Kelber's analysis by mapping its
elements, allegory-like, onto a set of historical events. Is the mirror model
set up in the book's opening paragraph shattered in the subsequent analysis? Or might the mirror/window opposition (implicit in Kelber's project,
but made explicit in my account of it to interrogate its results) itself be
an inept one? A theoretically recharged Kelber, engaged in "Hermeneutical
Reflections on the Gospels" (1987) nearly a decade after *Mark's Story of
Jesus*, might well have been reflecting on the problematic of the latter when
he wrote:

7. *Mark's Story*, 60–70, 73ff., 82–96. Kelber's negative thesis on the Markan disciples,
related to that of Weeden, *Traditions*, has met with its share of rebuttal (see, e.g., Donahue,
Discipleship, 24–27).

a categorical distinction [may not] be drawn between the gospels as mirrors vis-a-vis windows. Precisely because they participate in the ongoing discourse of tradition, narrative gospels contain traces of absent others, which, while integrated into their respective gospel worlds, may serve as windows for those who know the scope of the tradition. When viewed from these perspectives, therefore, opposites such as . . . literary versus historical readings, and mirror versus window views of language dissolve into the single overriding reality of interpretation. (127; see further chapter 8 below)[8]

The final volume in the *Stories of Jesus* series, Richard Edwards's *Matthew's Story of Jesus* (1985), extends the reach of the budding narrative commentary genre.[9] Like Kelber on Mark, Edwards's reading of Matthew is also one that follows "the development of the plot or the flow of the narrative" (*Matthew's Story*, 9). However, Edwards's approach to consecutive analysis is more rigorous than that of earlier commentators:

Rather than view the work as a completed or finished whole, I intend to examine the narrative from the point of view of a reader who begins at the beginning. This approach is less concerned with an outline and more interested in the way the narrator anticipates or recalls ideas or subjects in the progress of the story. . . . Since reading is a cumulative process that extends over a period of time, the sequence of information and its relation to earlier portions of the story will be my primary concern. (Ibid.)[10]

In other words, Edwards approaches the gospel as event rather than as object—an event set off by the creative involvement of a reader swept up

8. The mirror-window analogy, crafted initially by Krieger, *Window*, 3–4, has often been adduced to distinguish biblical literary criticism from historical criticism; see, inter alia, Culpepper, *Anatomy*, 3–4; Karris, "Windows"; and Petersen, *Literary Criticism*, 19.

9. The intervening volumes, Edwards, *Luke's Story*, and Kysar, *John's Story*, show less assimilation of nonbiblical literary criticism and are in general less adventurous. Contrast Blackwell, *Passion*, a rather more interesting attempt at literary commentary despite the limitations of an equally popular series format. Blackwell's controlling premise is that to understand Mark's passion story one must understand it "not as the historical communication of truth but rather as the imaginative communication of truth" (14). The method used is quasi-structuralist.

10. Edwards, however, does not take equal account of all the major sections of Matthew, least of all Jesus' lengthy discourses. Kingsbury, *Matthew as Story*, a more detailed, and less reader-oriented, exposition of Matthean plot, has also been accused of neglecting the discourses—though he has since atoned for that neglect; see Kingsbury, *Story*, 2d ed., 105–14, and "Sermon."

in the forward flow of the plot. Here we are fully into the area where narrative criticism shades over into reader-response criticism.

The Critic as (Re)Teller of Tales

Robert Tannehill's *Narrative Unity of Luke-Acts* (1986) is the most ambitious example to date of a New Testament narrative commentary.[11] Tannehill's introduction clarifies his focus: "A complete literary analysis of Luke-Acts would involve much that I have ignored. I have chosen to focus on major roles in the narrative. . . . I will be standing on the borderline between character and plot, understanding character in terms of role, which is character in action and interaction within an unfolding plot" (1). The immediate focus, then, is character and plot. Beyond that, Tannehill is interested in "the overarching purpose which unifies the narrative" and that is disclosed by close attention to the plot. The purpose in question is "the unifying purpose of God behind the events which are narrated, and the mission of Jesus and his witnesses represents that purpose being carried out through human action" (1–2).

Tannehill's methods differ from those of Kelber and Richard Edwards (the more plot-centered of the other literary commentators) in at least two respects. First, Kelber and Edwards (the latter especially) work with the construct of a hypothetical reader, who comes to the text for the first time, and who reads it from beginning to end. Both critics, Edwards in particular, are concerned with mapping the unfolding responses of this reader construct. Tannehill, in contrast, states explicitly that his discussion "represents part of what might be said after reading a second, third, or fourth time. It is not confined to what is happening when reading for the first time, with much of the text still unknown" (6). Bound up with this strategy is a second factor. To read with the construct of a first-time reader, as Edwards and Kelber do, is to read the text in sequence. Tannehill prefers to jump back and forth a little. In a strict consecutive reading, the chapters of the critic's text correspond to successive portions of the gospel text. Although Tannehill's overall organization is loosely sequential, his central chapters are organized more by the gospel's themes than by its unit-by-unit progression. These chapters concern Jesus in his interaction with the

11. Tannehill does not use the term *narrative commentary,* though it would encapsulate *Narrative Unity* nicely. The term is a very recent one and is traceable to two of Robert Funk's Westar Institute ventures: the Bible, Narrative, and American Culture Seminar and the Literary Facets Seminar. On the possibilities and problems of narrative commentary, see Culpepper, "Changing Paradigms," and Moore, "Narrative Commentaries."

groups that appear repeatedly in the narrative: the oppressed and disenfranchised, the crowds, the authorities, and the disciples.

> Isolating and following the developing relations between Jesus and significant groups in the narrative, a task that, to my knowledge, has not been previously attempted in such breadth and detail, helps me to clarify some continuities and progressions that would be less clear if I simply followed the order of the material in Luke, as the standard commentary does. A great deal is going on at once, and it is easy for the discussion to become fragmented. The text is like a rope with multiple strands. The continuity of each strand is not easily seen since it winds around other strands. (5)

Tannehill's holistic emphasis leads him to relax the consecutive approach, thus departing from the norm of traditional commentary. By thematic organization, balanced by close attention to the continuities of the plot, he hopes "to avoid the 'flattening' effect of much commentary in which a narrative's main interests and emphases are lost in the host of details discussed" (ibid.).

Tannehill's commentary, which carefully footnotes its debts to mainstream scholarly opinion or just as carefully takes issue with it, demands attention even from more traditional Lukan scholars. In this painless format, one that demands the least assimilation by the uninitiated of unfamiliar terms and concepts, narrative criticism seems but a heartbeat away from redaction and composition criticism. Nevertheless, the narrative commentary, a fledgling genre that has fully hatched only with Tannehill's book,[12] does mark a new relationship between the commentator and the gospel text—or more precisely, the recovery of a very old relationship.

The form that gospel commentary has taken through much of the present century is comprehensively illustrated by Fitzmyer:

> Having set forth the Synoptic relationship of [a] passage, I have always tried to explain its form-critical character. . . . These two questions . . . are, however, only preliminary and serve only to clear the air for the discussion of the *meaning* of the passage as a unit in its relation to the Gospel-part in which it is found and to the Gospel as a whole. The attempt to arrive at its meaning may require a discussion of the passage's structure, theological preoccupation, and essential message. All of these aspects of the passage are treated in a section

12. Tannehill cites no antecedents for his story-centered commentary. Although there are antecedents there is no reason to suppose that they have significantly influenced him.

called "COMMENT," which is then followed by "NOTES," in which
minor problems raised by individual words or phrases, textual criticism, philological analysis, or history are treated in detail. (*Luke [I–
IX]*, viii)

The end result is a comprehensive, easily consulted resource. However,
Tannehill complains that the classic approach to commentary results in a
flattening effect, the contours and emphases of the narrative being lost in
a host of details. Tannehill prefers to sacrifice some of the detail in order
to let the continuity, integration, and forward movement of the story
emerge. In so doing he produces a critical text that is itself akin to a well-
plotted narrative. Earlier we defined a plot as a set of events linked by
temporal succession and causality. Narrative commentary in the mode of
Tannehill is essentially a retelling of a gospel designed to draw maximal
attention to its plotted qualities of flow or forward movement (the aspect
of temporal succession), and to the integration and interrelation of its
parts (causality, in the broad sense). To highlight the connections the
narrative commentator amplifies them, putting even stronger emphasis on
connections that are explicitly stated and positing connections that are
either implied or obscure. The evangelist's narrative is paraphrased, not
by means of discrete statements of propositional content as in the verse-
by-verse commentary, but by means of a second plotted narrative, the
commentator's own, that explicates the primary narrative for the reader
by augmenting it. Commentary thus regains a targumic form.[13]

The narrative critic is faced with trying to deal critically with the
narrative thought of the evangelists without distorting it. A partial and
possibly unconscious consequence of that attempt, it seems, is that the
narrative critic's text (e.g., Tannehill's, or those of the contributors to the
Stories of Jesus series) becomes itself, in large part, a plotted narrative text.
The features the narrative critic prizes in the gospel text—centeredness on
event and participant, continuity and interconnectedness, conflict, suspense, and resolution—become salient features of his or her own text.
The interpretation of narrative becomes interpretation as narrative, and
gospel commentary becomes a postcritical targum.

Narrative commentary, as practiced particularly by Tannehill, takes
the story-centered method to its limit. The very features that define a

---

13. The targums were Aramaic translations of the Jewish scriptures that appeared in
the last centuries B.C.E. and early centuries C.E. Paraphrase was the hallmark of targumic
rendering, the barrier between translation and exegesis becoming an extremely permeable
one.

story—events and actors, sequence and interconnections—become the focus of attention. Does it follow, then, that narrative commentary treats the essential features of a gospel narrative? Paradoxically, that may not be the case (even if we accept for now that narrative can have essential features). And beyond that question an even more interesting one arises. Harold Bloom puts it very bluntly: "criticism frequently has a stronger apparent presence than the poem upon which it comments. Indeed the criticism can seem to have more unity, more form, more meaning. Is it just that the critic has become more than adequate to the poem, or is it perhaps that the critic's illusions about the nature of poetry [or narrative] are governing the nature of his commentary"? (*Kabbalah*, 121).

3

Points of View in/on a Gospel

[The narrator] symbolizes the epistemological view familiar to us since Kant that we do not apprehend the world in itself, but rather as it has passed through the medium of an observing mind.
—Kate Friedemann, *Die Rolle des Erzählers in der Epik*

[D]esiring immediacy . . . doomed to the mediate.
—J. Hillis Miller, *The Disappearance of God*

Enter the Narrator

Plot and character have figured prominently in our story. We have heard the gospel text spoken of in terms of its narrative or narrative world, a world of characters, settings and actions, which must be interpreted and made to cohere. But that is only half the story. To speak solely in such terms is implicitly to equate the narrative text with a play; there too an autonomous world of characters, settings, and events is encountered that requires a similar sense-making effort from its audience. The more one moves in the direction of that implicit equation, the more one misses the crucial, indeed the generic, difference between dramatic narrative and written narrative.[1] In drama (as in opera, film, ballet, mime, etc.) events are seen and heard as in the real world, that is, "directly." In written narrative, graphic or acoustic symbols (i.e., words, read in silence or aloud) are all that our senses encounter. The rest must be supplied from imagination.

To shift the emphasis a little, in written narrative, character, setting, and event are mediated to a reader, and they are mediated by a narrator.[2] The narrator is the one who tells the story, and because the story-world is filtered through the narrator, everything about it bears traces of the narrator's selectivity and evaluation. The term *point of view* has long been used in literary criticism to denote the complex, shifting relationship be-

---

1. Stanzel, *Theory*, 4–21; Martin, *Recent Theories*, 109–111, 173.

2. Readers au fait with current critical theory will note that the opposition on which I base my argument, i.e., direct, immediate perception vs. mediated, indirect perception, is one that begs a deconstructive dismantling, as do certain other oppositions used in the preceding chapters (intrinsic/extrinsic, text/reader, etc.; see chapters 7 and 8).

tween tale and teller, between the narrative world and how it is relayed.[3] At one moment the narrator may speak in his or her own voice (e.g., Matthew 1:22; Mark 13:14; Luke 1:1–4; John 2:21) to shape the reader's interpretation of the story; at another he or she may cede these explanatory functions to a reliable speaker within the story: an angel, Jesus, a heavenly voice, or even a Gentile soldier (Matthew 27:54 = Mark 15:39) or a demon (e.g., Mark 1:24; 3:11; 5:7). Or again he or she may nuance his or her phrasing so as to covertly stamp his or her own view of what is being told upon the telling (e.g., when the gospel narrator refers to Jesus as "the Lord"). The narrator channels his or her description of an event through the physical perception of a character (e.g., Luke 1:11), or his or her presentation of a character can penetrate beneath the surface to reveal thoughts, feelings, and motivations (e.g., Matthew 9:3; Mark 10:21a; Luke 1:29; John 13:28–29), or alternatively the perspective given can be an external one, the character being presented strictly from the outside (e.g., the presentation of Jesus in all four Passion narratives). Point of view denotes the rhetorical activity of an author as he or she attempts through the medium of a narrator (or more precisely, by an act of narration), and from his or her position within some socially shared system of assumptions, beliefs, and values to impose a story-world upon a reader (or listener).

Point of View in Mark

To understand better how point of view functions in a gospel we turn to Norman Petersen's "'Point of View' in Mark's Narrative" (1978). Petersen's work of the late 1970s was another catalyst in the emergence of narrative criticism (see especially his *Literary Criticism*). This work also builds on holistic terrain, but what distinguishes Petersen from other narrative exegetes is his perspicacity on the precise relationship of narrative criticism to historical criticism.

In light of the vigorous application of French structuralism to biblical texts in the 1970s in North America, it is surprising that an influential tradition far closer to hand went neglected—an Anglo-American tradition centered on the study of point of view in literary narrative, of which Wayne Booth's *Rhetoric of Fiction* (1961) is regarded the classic expression. Peter-

3. Celebrated studies of point of view include: Booth, *Rhetoric*; Cohn, *Transparent Minds*; Genette, *Narrative Discourse*, chaps. 4 and 5; Lanser, *Narrative Act*; Stanzel, *Theory*; Uspensky, *Poetics*; and cf. Bal, "Narrating." Those entirely new to the area should begin with Petersen, "Mark's Narrative" or Culpepper, *Anatomy*, 13–50.

sen's "'Point of View' in Mark's Narrative" was the first published study
of a New Testament text to center on point of view.[4]

It is not on Booth that Petersen draws, however. Drawing on Boris
Uspensky's *Poetics of Composition* (1970) instead, he attempts a systematic
analysis of the narrator's role in Mark. He schematizes the narrator's point
of view in terms of its ideological, phraseological, spatiotemporal, and
psychological dimensions. These four dimensions (or planes) interpene-
trate throughout the narrative, one or another of them being foregrounded at any given time. Ideologically, everything in Mark is evaluated
by one point of view, which the narrator and Jesus share. Indeed, in Mark
only two ideological viewpoints are possible: the divine or the human.
The distinction between them receives explicit expression in Mark 8:33,
when Jesus accuses Peter of thinking in human terms. Even demons and
other opponents (e.g., 1:24; 14:61) are made vehicles for the narrator's
ideology; it permeates every facet of the narrative. In the plotting of the
episodes and the details of characterization, the pervasiveness of Mark's
ideology can especially be seen. He has created "a world of values as well
as of events" ("Mark's Narrative," 108). The phraseological plane pertains
more to the explicit level of verbal expression such as speeches put on the
lips of characters and scriptural quotations by the narrator. Jesus' speech
in particular sifts and subordinates the points of view of all the other
characters, as does the narrator's own speech as it frames their actions and
speech. A salient feature of the narrator's speech is commentary—direct
addresses to the reader (e.g., 5:41; 7:3–4; 13:14) that interpret or explain
aspects of the story-world, bridging the distance between it and the reader.
The titles of Jesus (Son of God, Son of Man, etc.), with the points of
view implicit in them, are likewise phraseological phenomena. Spatially,
the Markan narrator "hovers over every episode, able to see them all from
a distance, in both space and time, yet free to descend at will into the
action of an episode, locating himself as an invisible observer even in the
most private councils, be they in houses, boats, banquets, synagogues, or
'court rooms.' Indeed, the narrator is 'with' Jesus even when no other
actors are present or capable of knowing what Jesus experienced (1:10–11;
6:46–48; 7:33–34; 14:35–36)" (112). In contrast, the narrator's temporal

---

4. The path had already been broken by Boomershine, "Storyteller," 284–314, and
Tannehill, "Disciples" (which deals obliquely with point of view). More recent studies include
Culpepper, *Anatomy,* 13–50; Dewey, "Disciples"; du Rand, "John"; Fowler, *Reader* and
Loaves, 157–79; Hedrick, "Narrator"; Kurtz, "Narrative Approaches"; Resseguie, "Central
Section"; Rhoads and Michie, *Mark,* 35–44; van Aarde, "Mt. 22:1–14"; and cf. Kingsbury,
Christology; Staley, *First Kiss.*

position in relation to the story-world is relatively fixed, lying at a time just prior to the parousia (cf. Mark 13). And finally, on the psychological plane, the narrator has the ability to penetrate the surface of his characters (e.g., 2:6–7; 5:29–30; 6:20), narrating their thoughts, emotions, motivations, and sensory experiences. One character shares this omniscient ability: Jesus (e.g., 2:8; 12:15). But the narrator also has the capacity to reveal Jesus' own "inner life" (e.g., 5:30; 10:21). En route, Petersen digresses to ponder the generic implications of the Markan narrator's nonrealistic spatial and psychological abilities (or omniscience), concluding that "Mark's rhetoric is the rhetoric of fiction"—such nonrealistic rhetorical devices being characteristic of narrative fiction—"and it provides the most compelling evidence that his gospel is a bona fide literary composition" (115). The latter point requires special comment as it is the real theme of Petersen's essay.

Points of View on Mark

Petersen's strategy is to draw on the tradition of point-of-view criticism— a tradition not particularly associated with a holistic agenda—not simply to show how point of view functions in Mark, but to show it with the aim of isolating evidence that will prove that Mark is a carefully integrated narrative.[5] "By following the various aspects of point of view in it, we can learn to read it as a narrative rather than as a redaction" ("Mark's Narrative," 97).

Petersen has some very interesting observations to make on the long-established view that Mark combines disparate units of tradition. He invokes Karl L. Schmidt's description of Mark in *Der Rahmen der Geschichte Jesu* (1919) as "a virtual collection of traditional pearls arrayed sequentially on a very fine authorial string" ("Mark's Narrative," 104). But, for Petersen, Schmidt failed to press home the implications of his position and left the question hanging of whether, or to what extent, Mark should be regarded as a narrative. If the metaphor of the string of pearls were pressed, could not each pericope in Mark be said to have a separate, anonymous narrator? William Wrede had demolished the illusion that Mark's text represented the real world of events, but "Schmidt suggested the haunting possibility

---

5. Tannehill similarly culls key techniques of plot analysis from structuralism in his "Narrative Christology" and uses them to further his ongoing demonstration of the literary unity of Mark—a concern evocative of American formalism but quite alien to biblical structuralism of the 1970s. These related strategies of Petersen and Tannehill reflect a widespread pattern in narrative criticism (see chapter 4).

that *the impression of narrative created by Mark's text is also an illusion*" ("Mark's Narrative," 104).[6] According to Petersen, redaction criticism has simply assumed that Mark's text is a narrative, without having ever proved it: "source and form criticism knocked our textual Humpty Dumpty off the wall and failed to reconstitute him with their evolutionary theory, since the latter produced only an anonymous community product, not Humpty Dumpty. Redaction criticism, on the other hand, has attempted to reconstruct . . . not Humpty Dumpty but his theology" (*Literary Criticism,* 20). Petersen's overriding preoccupation in "Mark's Narrative" and in the chapter on Mark of his *Literary Criticism,* is one of completing redaction criticism's unfinished business and proving that Mark is indeed a narrative. Thus, the article is an attempt to show that Mark's point of view is consistent throughout, indicating a single narrator and a bona fide narrative. He wants to find a firm level of integrity in Mark in the wake of fifty years of fragmentation. Paradoxically, he finds that William Wrede's demolition in *The Messianic Secret* (1901) of the illusion that Mark's text refers directly to the real world can be made to contribute to this end. Mark's text does not accurately depict history, certainly, yet "it may coherently depict *his story*" ("Mark's Narrative," 104). Critical measurement of Mark against a historical paradigm has shattered the precritical integrity it enjoyed. That integrity can be restored, it is implied, only if the critical paradigm of history is replaced with a postcritical paradigm of story.

The Ghost of Fragmentation Past

Petersen thus alerts us to the fact that the narrative integrity of a gospel is something that cannot in the least be taken for granted. This alert is especially timely in the current research climate, where the quest for theological unity in the Gospels (intensifying as redaction criticism turns a slow corner from a primary emphasis on the evangelists' modification of their sources to an emphasis on their compositional creativity) is coupled with the quest for narrative unity in the Gospels. Consider the following programmatic statement that introduces Tannehill's *Narrative Unity of Luke-Acts*: "The following study will emphasize the unity of Luke-Acts.

6. Cf. Petersen, *Literary Criticism,* 22–23. Petersen's concern that historical criticism threatens Mark's status as a narrative is extremely puzzling. Given the minimalism that characterizes narratological definitions of narrative ("the king died and then the queen died" might fulfill the requirements) there seems to be little question that Mark is a narrative. Petersen's real question is surely whether or to what extent Mark is to be regarded an integrated narrative. (This is what I take him to mean, though I retain his own term, *narrative,* in summarizing his position.)

This unity is the result of a single author working within a persistent theological perspective [the unity with which redaction and composition critics are preoccupied], but it is something more. It is a *narrative* unity, the unity appropriate to a well-formed narrative" (xiii).

James Dawsey's *The Lukan Voice: Confusion and Irony in the Gospel of Luke* (1986) is like a photographic negative of Tannehill's *Narrative Unity*, though both are literary readings of Luke. Tannehill is well aware that Luke-Acts is not a seamless weave but is imperturbably confident nonetheless that the evangelist is in full control of his materials:

> our expectations of narrative unity, shaped perhaps by the modern novel, are not always fulfilled in Luke. Much of Luke shares the episodic style of the synoptic gospels in general, in which individual scenes may be vivid but their connection into story sequences is often unclear. The neglect of clear causal connections among episodes (indications that one event leads to the next) is striking when we compare the synoptic gospels with modern narrative. Our narrator is quite capable of making such connections, as major portions of Acts attest, but chose to leave the Jesus tradition in its looser form. Despite the episodic style of large portions of Luke, it traces the unfolding of a single dominant purpose. This unifies the gospel story and unites Luke with Acts, for this purpose is not only at work in the ministry of Jesus but also in the ministries of Jesus' witnesses. Luke-Acts is a unified narrative because the chief human characters (John the Baptist, Jesus, the apostles, Paul) share in a mission which expresses a single controlling purpose—the purpose of God. (*Narrative Unity,* xiii)

Furthermore, "the author has carefully provided disclosures of [this] overarching purpose which unifies the narrative" (1). But is the author's disclosive purpose successful? Does he manage to bring his recalcitrant materials to heel? Not surprisingly, the heuristic grid that Tannehill proceeds to lay on the text is rigged in the author's favor.

Dawsey brings a very different grid to Luke. It is almost as though he had decided to let whatever source-induced disunity there is in Luke unravel itself and gamble on being able to posit an authorial intention that would pull it all back together again. Essentially this is a study in Lukan style but with an unusual twist: "While the technique of giving story characters identifiable patterns of speech is readily associated with such modern-day geniuses as Mark Twain and William Faulkner, it is in fact an old storyteller's device used by, among others, Petronius, Aristophanes, and Homer. It is not so surprising, therefore, to find that the Lukan author distinguished among the voices of the characters in his story, and that when he spoke through them he spoke a very different language than when he spoke through his narrator" (15). The first chapter analyzes the narrator's voice, the second that of Jesus, for specific speech traits. On the basis of features such as the narrator's use of short sentences, the lack of variety in his use of connective particles, and the small number of syllables in his average word, Dawsey concludes that the narrator's voice is of an oral type. Moreover, "the narrator's language has as its locus the community of faith"; it belongs and is directed to that community (32). Dawsey bases this on the extensive use of Septuagintal formulae in Luke, interpreted as indicators of a specialized language of worship. Analysis of Jesus' speech yields rather different results. Jesus "speaks the simple language of common people" (41). The evidence for this is mainly presented in one of the three appendixes to the book that buttress the arguments of its first two chapters. There, "212 instances of the popular standard of Jesus' speech" are listed. Also, on the basis that Jesus' sayings in Luke are for the most part pronouncements with little persuasory intent, Dawsey concludes that his speech is more prophetic than didactic. "While the narrator speaks a language of worship, Jesus speaks a language of prophecy" (41).

But this is only the beginning. With the stylistic findings in place, Dawsey engages in a more general review of Jesus' speech that builds on the earlier analysis but is now oriented more to content: what sort of understanding is ascribed to Jesus in Luke, both of himself and of his mission? The narrator's viewpoint on Jesus is similarly analyzed, and the two viewpoints compared. The comparison yields a series of antitheses. For example, Jesus calls himself a prophet in Luke before his crucifixion and appropriates the title Christ only after his resurrection. The view thus ascribed to Jesus, Dawsey thinks, is one of consummation through suffering: "The Christ is not the Christ until he dies on the cross and is raised. ... Until such a time he is a prophet" (49). The narrator, in contrast, does not call Jesus a prophet at all: "To the narrator, from the beginning, Jesus was the Christ" (88). This is tied to a further theme: "the Lukan Jesus makes no attempt to keep his identity a secret." The narrator, however, "holding throughout that Jesus was the Christ, appropriates the idea of secrecy into his account" (89). They also understand Jesus' death differently. In Jesus' view, most of his generation have rejected him. But in the narrator's view Jesus is not so much a rejected messiah as a misunderstood one. To explain Jesus' death "the narrator then finds it necessary to build up the betrayal theme and emphasize the complicity of Satan" (87). Satan is of much lesser consequence in Jesus' thought because his power has already been broken (Luke 10:18, etc.).

Based on a painstaking and heavily statistical analysis of Lukan style, Dawsey's reading amplifies every chord of residual disharmony in the Lukan composition, arising from the forced cohabitation of disparate source materials. It is instructive to see how easily such data is accumulated when one goes to the gospel text with one's antennae adjusted to pick up contradictory voices instead of a noncontradictory authorial voice. The question then is, having loosed a cacophony of voices and viewpoints, can Dawsey instigate closure by subjugating this cacophony to a controlling authorial voice and viewpoint?

For Dawsey, Jesus' view throughout, as gleaned from his own speech, is highly consistent, and "seems to hearken back to a very early theology" (103), one which the Lukan author endorses but which the narrator misunderstands (the narrator being the Lukan author's very special creation). "In a sense, the author sided with Jesus against his own narrator" (110). But why bother to create such a narrator in the first place? The vital clue, for Dawsey, is to be found in the narrator's prologue (Luke 1:1–4). He contrasts the prologue, "written in high Attic style to a 'most excellent Theophilus,' so that he might 'know the truth concerning the things of which [he] has been informed,'" with Jesus' statement in 10:21 that God has hidden his secrets from the wise and understanding and revealed them to mere babes (147). "There is an immense irony at play in this portrait of a narrator who . . . sets out to pass on to the most excellent Theophilus, in his educated, cultic language, a knowledge of the things that the wise and understanding cannot see" (149). And the purpose of the irony?

> one can imagine a variety of settings and ways in which the Third Gospel could have been read or presented in the early Church so that the ironic stance of the narrator would have allowed the community to be confronted again with the saving humiliation of Jesus. For example, through the narrator, a proud church might have relived its own tendency to exalt Jesus, and therefore its denial of the suffering Son of God. . . . And at every point, Jesus would have confronted the community, saying, "If any one would come after me, let him deny himself and take up his cross daily and follow me" (Lk 9:23).

It might be, then, that the narrator's misunderstanding of Jesus was the bridge that allowed for full participation in the story and led to decision. The meeting of Jesus and his community would have become impossible when the community became so immersed in the character of the narrator that it could be confronted by the incongruity between its words and Jesus' words. . . . As the distance between the hearers' view and Jesus' view was laid bare through the narrator, Jesus appeared. (155)

A number of key tactical moves underpin Dawsey's arguments throughout. Jesus' speech is analyzed in strict isolation from that of the narrator and vice versa. The differences discovered between the two voices are explained, not as incidental effects of the author's editing, but as calculated effects of the author's intention[7] (most conservative biblical scholars would begin to back away from Dawsey at this point). Self-consistent and opposing viewpoints are constructed for Jesus and the narrator on the basis of the stylistic evidence, and the author's viewpoint is said to coincide with that of Jesus and to diverge from that of the narrator. Finally, he is able to assign profound meaning to this divergence by the reconstruction of an audience with a profoundly subtle response. The lynchpin of Dawsey's reading, therefore, and the feature that takes it where Henry J. Cadbury and other analysts of Lukan style would not have thought to go, is the attribution to the narrator of a theology that the Lukan author does not endorse. In literary critical parlance, Luke's narrator is an unreliable narrator. This term, coined by Wayne Booth, is neutral on the question of historical reliability, but instead denotes a custom-made narrator whose ideology and perceptions deviate from those of its author-creator (*Rhetoric*, 149ff., 304–309). Dawsey, who amply footnotes his debts to *Lukan* scholarship, fails to mention the currency of this concept in nonbiblical literary criticism (it is very widely used). Indeed, though he makes full use of the concept of the unreliable narrator, he does not use the term. More importantly, he does not mention, if he knows, that the unreliable narrator is generally assumed to be a modern device. To my knowledge, the view of Scholes and Kellogg, that the unreliable narrator is "quite uncharacteristic of primitive or ancient narrative," has never been seriously contested: "The author of an *apologia* is expected to be presenting himself in the best possible light, and thus is to be taken *cum grano salis*," but the full-fledged unreliable narrator is a product of the modern novel (*Nature*, 264). Does Dawsey realize just how revolutionary his casting of the Lukan narrator as unreliable is? He presents us with a narrative technique and a matching audience response almost two millenia out of time.

The lesson is plain for redaction critics and narrative critics alike. The

7. See, e.g., 32, 41, 103, 124, 183.

more one is willing to home in on the crevices and interstices that result in the Gospels (the Synoptic Gospels in particular) from the conflation of source material, the more bizarre the authorial intention one will need to hypothesize to fill in those widened cracks. Contrast the quite unremarkable intention that Tannehill ascribes to the Lukan author. But how closely has Tannehill read the text? Not with the painstaking closeness of Dawsey, certainly. Where Dawsey goes awry is not in his scrupulous attention to the cacophony of viewpoints in Luke, but in his attempt to impose coherence on that discordance at any cost. Rigorous attention to contradictions and disjunctions does indeed knock our textual Humpty Dumpty off the wall, as Petersen would say. And redaction, composition, and narrative criticism have duly stepped in to reconstitute Humpty Dumpty with a totalizing authorial intention, each in its own way.[8] But Dawsey's maverick study inadvertently suggests that the ghost of fragmentation is not so easily laid to rest.[9] Dawsey is no form or source critic, certainly, but the ghost that he raises is that of the form and source critical paradigm of the fragmentary and agglomerate text—the text that is not "a well-formed narrative." It seems to me that that ghost is summoned all too easily to unsettle the paradigm on which composition and narrative critics have come to rely: a monologic gospel text in which conflicting perspectives are synthesized, canceled, or harmonized by the assignation of some masterful overriding purpose—or, as the arch-New Critic Cleanth Brooks might have put it (for it is the ghost of American Formalism that the more recent paradigm summons up), a literary text that exhibits a successful "unification of [contradictory] attitudes into a hierarchy subordinated to a total and governing attitude" ("Heresy," 189).[10]

8. Composition criticism extends the thrust of redaction criticism, arguing that the evangelist's theological vision imposes a high degree of unity on the text. Narrative criticism's argument is analogous, though it locates the unity more in the evangelist's crafting of his story.

9. In contrast to Dawsey's inadvertent challenge to the unity of Luke(-Acts), see the calculated challenge of Parsons, "Making." Parsons bears in on his topic from five different angles: authorial unity, theological unity, narrative unity, generic unity, and canonical unity. Parsons' project, which he describes as "loosening the hyphen in Luke-Acts," has its roots in his *Departure*.

10. Even as Brooks's *Well Wrought Urn* (1947) made its appearance, gospel scholars were on the brink of discovering that the evangelists were composers as well as compilers. New Criticism had nothing to do with this. Neither does current gospel criticism, even at its most holistic, closely approximate New Criticism; what separates them are their respective objects of analysis: the modern poem on the one hand, ancient narrative on the other. Remarkably, however, even as gospel scholarship has edged closer to American Formalism as it has moved through redaction criticism, composition criticism, and narrative criticism, American literary criticism over the same time period, rocked by structuralism and especially

The Critical Unconscious

[T]he book is part of the theological network that is now unraveling.
—Mark C. Taylor, *Erring*

What is really at stake in such debate, other than the rise and demise of paradigms? What does Tannehill's imperturbable confidence, or my own equally imperturbable skepticism, regarding the Lukan author's mastery over his creation actually mean? Does it all reduce to differences in toilet training, as one colleague helpfully suggested to us at a recent meeting of the Literary Aspects of the Gospels and Acts Group? I am certainly prepared to entertain that possibility,[11] but I suspect that our narratological differences of opinion can also be read as displacements of theological differences. From time to time, critics such as J. Hillis Miller have offered incisive theological readings of selected narrative theories. Here Miller cites Samuel Taylor Coleridge, whose influence on New Critical organicism was considerable: "Aesthetic wholeness in a narrative, he [Coleridge] says, must be copied from the wholeness of a universe which circles in time around the motionless center of a God to whose eternal insight all times are co-present" (*Repetition,* 23). Coleridge writes:

> The common end of all *narrative,* nay, of *all,* Poems is to convert a *series* into a *Whole.* . . . Doubtless, to his [God's] eye, which alone comprehends all Past and Future in one eternal Present, what to our short sight appears strait is but part of the great Cycle—just as the calm Sea to us *appears* level, tho' it indeed [be] only a part of a *globe.* Now what the Globe is in Geography, *miniaturing* in order to manifest the Truth, such is a Poem to that Image of God, which we were created with, and which still seeks Unity or Revelation of the *One* in and by the *Many.* (Coleridge, "Letter," 128).

"The concept of the organic unit of the work of art," concludes Miller, "cannot be detached from its theological basis" (*Repetition,* 24; see further Miller, *Disappearance*). Roland Barthes is yet more specific; for him, the modern concept of the author has displaced the concept of God. Hence his oft-quoted dictum: "a text does not consist of a line of words releasing

---

by poststructuralism, has edged closer to gospel criticism in its pre-1950s period—one dominated by form criticism in which the concept of the author (in the full sense) took a back seat, along with the concept of textual unity. For different reasons, the concept of the author is weakened in structuralism and poststructuralism, and that of textual unity in poststructuralism.

11. Note too Holland's homology, "*Unity* is to *text* as *identity* is to *self*" ("Unity," 815).

a single 'theological' meaning (the 'message' of the Author-God)" ("Death," 147). Is it, then, entirely fortuitous that the purpose unifying Luke-Acts is (in Tannehill's account of it) that of the author and of God simultaneously? The word *purpose* first occurs in *Narrative Unity* midway through the opening page: "Despite the episodic style of large portions of Luke, it traces the unfolding of a single dominant purpose." One assumes that Tannehill is referring to the author's purpose here; the preceding sentence had stated that the narrator (the author's voice within the narrative)[12] "is quite capable of making [causal] connections, as major portions of Acts attest, but chose to leave the Jesus tradition in its looser form." But as the succeeding sentences make clear, the purpose of God (as Luke-Acts represents it) is the unifying force to which Tannehill is referring: "Luke-Acts is a unified narrative because the chief human characters (John the Baptist, Jesus, the apostles, Paul) share in a mission which expresses a single controlling purpose—the purpose of God. The individual episodes gain their significance through their relationship to this controlling purpose of God" (xiii). Thus, by a sleight of hand, the unifying purpose of the author of Luke-Acts passes over into the unifying purpose of God—here, a character in the narrative ("God functions as a character in the plot, though hidden from human view" [29]).[13] Indeed, the attributes of mastery, potency, and omniscience that *Narrative Unity* implicitly attributes to the Lukan author are subtly transferred to God throughout the book.[14] Or was it only by analogy with God that the author acquired those attributes in the first place? The symbiotic union of author and deity in *Narrative Unity* suggests that it might accurately be read, not only as a critical commentary, but also as a displaced doxology; for the author (prime mover) whose encompassing plan it celebrates is ultimately a dual-natured one, not only human but divine.

Synergistic with the "theological unconscious" of modern secular criticism is a more encompassing "political unconscious,"[15] which has been

12. The implied author of Luke-Acts is, of course, closely identified with its narrator: "[w]e can begin with the assumption that the values and beliefs affirmed by [one] are also those of the [other]" (*Narrative Unity,* 7). But they are not equal partners. Ultimately it is the implied author who is the prime mover in the story-world; the narrator is merely "an instrument used for getting the story told," a "voice telling us all that we learn" (ibid.). The term *author* as used in my discussion of *Narrative Unity* is shorthand for this amalgam of implied author and narrator.

13. If this is so, then the author of Luke-Acts is doubly hidden in Tannehill's account, subsumed in God, or eclipsed by him.

14. The theme that it is God's purpose that shapes the story is frequently reiterated (20–22, 29–31, 40–41, etc.).

15. The term is especially associated with Frederic Jameson (see *Political Unconscious*).

probed by various analysts. Take, for example, Michel Foucault's etiology of the power of authors in our era:

> Texts, books, and discourses really began to have authors (other than mythical, "sacralized" and "sacralizing" figures) to the extent that authors became subject to punishment, that is, to the extent that discourses could be transgressive. In our culture . . . discourse was not originally a product, a thing, a kind of goods; it was essentially an act—an act placed in the bipolar field of the sacred and the profane. . . . Historically, it was a gesture fraught with risks before becoming goods caught up in a circuit of ownership.
>
> Once a system of ownership for texts came into being, once strict rules concerning author's rights, author-publisher relations, right of reproduction, and related matters were enacted—at the end of the eighteenth and the beginning of the nineteenth century—the possibility of transgression attached to the act of writing took on, more and more, the form of an imperative peculiar to literature. ("Author," 148; cf. Foucault, *Archaeology,* 221–22).

Returning to Tannehill, we submit that if his confidence in Luke's power to rule is at base the confidence of faith (Luke's dominion over his story-world being symbiotic with that of God), the corollary assumption that there is a realm of meaning in Luke-Acts, or a deposit of meaning that is Luke's inalienable possession (to switch to a more contemporary "mercantile" register), is a function of Tannehill's sociocultural situation and that of the guild to which he belongs. Foucault later cautions: "if we are accustomed to presenting the author as a genius, as a perpetual surging of invention, it is because, in reality, we make him function in exactly the opposite fashion. One can say that the author is an ideological product, since we represent him as the opposite of his historically real function. . . . [S]ince the eighteenth century, the author has played the role of the regulator of the fictive, a role quite characteristic of our era of . . . individualism and private property" (159).[16] Now, it is not that Luke need hold exclusive rights to the semantic resources of his text; Tannehill is prepared to accept the possibility that Luke's monopoly might have to be a limited one:

16. Cf. Barthes, "Death," 142–43: "The author is a modern figure, a product of our society insofar as, emerging from the Middle Ages with English empiricism, French rationalism and the personal faith of the Reformation, it discovered the prestige of the individual. . . . It is . . . this positivism, the epitome and culmination of capitalist ideology, which has attached the greatest importance to the 'person' of the author."

> Reading a narrative is an imaginative process. . . . This imaginative
> process includes a realm of free play. There are a large number of
> possible connections and significances which the text may suggest but
> not necessarily emphasize. Some of these will no doubt depart from
> the author's conscious intentions, but no author can completely con-
> trol what readers will find in the text. If these discoveries or inventions
> do not obscure the text's main emphases, the author and other inter-
> preters would do well to be tolerant. (*Narrative Unity*, 3)

But would the anonymous author of "Luke-Acts" really have been as
thrifty with his (or conceivably, her) significations as we, the self-appointed
trustees of his estate, undertake to be on his behalf ? And if the answer is
"hardly," as it would seem to be, what then are we to make of this "Luke"
("Mark," "Matthew," "John") whom we have anachronistically dressed in
a business suit and appointed chief executive over our hermeneutical affairs? If he is not simply to be regarded as a historical figure inefficiently
managing our scholarly discourse in absentia, from some remote point
antecedent and external to it, who or what is he in addition? A rhetorical
(tropic) figure *in* our critical discourse?[17] A symbolic figure in our critical
(theopolitical) unconscious—Tannehill's, mine, that of the guild collectively? These questions await consideration. And though I may already
have played too roughly with Robert Tannehill (to whom I am strongly,
if strangely, indebted), or played unfairly with him—for though I speak
rather frankly of my own beliefs later on, it is not in order to subject them
to a theoeconomic analysis—I cannot resist legitimating that (serious) play
and the questions I have raised with one final quotation from *Narrative
Unity*: "There is a subversive process of detecting connections, a 'hermeneutics of suspicion' which seeks to uncover significant connections which
the author might not acknowledge. These connections reveal cultural limitations, unconscious or concealed drives. . . . Such subversive interpretation is also necessary; no human work can be exempted from it" (3–4).

Gospel Critics Who Are Men or Women of Action

Let us resume our estimate of the price currently being paid for a rein-
tegrated gospel. But despite my own hesitancy regarding that price, I
believe the "formalist moment" in gospel studies is—or was—a timely and
indispensable one. It enabled us to read the Gospels in an important new

---

17. Foucault might interject: "Where has [this discourse] been used . . . and who [has
been permitted to] appropriate it for himself " ("Author," 160).

way, and every discussion in this book presupposes it. Holistic criticism has taken firm root within our discipline, no longer a tender shoot but a sturdy plant. Are we now ready for still tougher comestibles? Might holistic criticism not seem a little too soothing now, lacking intellectual bite?

These questions will be opened up in due course. But for now, redirecting our attention to the discussion that opened this chapter, a rather different problem is raised by plot-centered gospel criticism. It can be argued (within certain limits) that mediacy of presentation is the generic trait of oral and written narrative. In written narrative, in contrast to scenic narrative (theatre, film, etc.), all that is sensibly present to a reader is the written sign; everything else must be imagined. Whether in written or oral narrative everything is mediated through the voice of a narrator. In the critical handling of written narrative this fundamental generic trait (mediacy as opposed to immediacy) receives greater or lesser attention.[18]

It receives least attention from theoreticians and critics who take plot to be narrative's essential feature. The question they pose to the text is primarily a drama-related one: What happens? This question has elicited a good deal of plot-based structural narratology (though the structuralist question more precisely is: What *can* happen in a narrative? Cf. Propp, Greimas, Todorov, Bremond et al.). In recent New Testament studies, the dramatic question helps to explain the narrative commentaries that center almost exclusively on plot and on the cognate category of character. It also helps to explain why plot and character loom so very large in current literary criticism of the Gospels generally.[19]

Critics who center on the action-linked features of written narrative— those features it shares with theatrical and televised drama and film—tend, consciously or unconsciously, to pay little attention to the special features of the written medium, most notably, point of view. In general, the model of the narrative text that has predominated in the literary criticism of the Gospels has been a drama-related one, founded on the sibling categories of plot and character. In one sense, the preoccupation with plot and character needs no explaining. People and their actions fascinate all of us. However, to transfer this preoccupation directly to criticism is to risk overnaturalizing the narrative text, thereby eliding its peculiar written

18. Here I take my lead from Martin, *Recent Theories*, 109–111.
19. Books preoccupied with plot and character include: Blackwell, *Passion*; Edwards, *Luke's Story*; Gros Louis, *Literary Interpretations* (both vols.); Kelber, *Mark's Story*; Kingsbury, *Story*; Kysar, *John's Story*; Navone and Cooper, *Story*; Nuttall, *Luke*; Rhoads and Michie, *Mark*; Stock, *Discipleship*; Tannehill, *Narrative Unity*; Tyson, *Death*; and cf. Barr, *New Testament*; Kort, *Story*; and Theissen, *Galilean*.

traits: the absence to the senses of the persons and things described, the centrality of the narrator as mediator, and so forth. Perhaps too the preoccupation with plot and character is residual of former historical concerns: in the text-centered approach of narrative criticism, the older question of "What happened?" is rephrased as "What happens?" Of course, in some instances the question posed by the narrative critic to the text is a historical one as well as a dramatic one. For example, in Kelber's *Mark's Story of Jesus* the question "What happens in the story?" was subordinated to the question "What happened to provoke the story?" Thus, occasionally in narrative criticism, and regularly in redaction criticism, gospel narratives are read as symbolic dramas.

A second style of narrative criticism—one that also minimizes the difference between scenic and written narrative—discusses the action-linked features of narrative (plot, character, setting) separately from the features that mediate them: the role of the narrator and point of view, as well as the role enjoined on the reader. While this has been an extremely productive approach for narrative criticism, it does involve some misapprehensions. It attempts (unsuccessfully, as we shall see) to treat action, character and setting (the dramatic, filmic elements in narrative) in abstraction from the ubiquitous narrating voice that frames, filters, and shapes them, especially by the manipulation of point of view.

Other literary critics of the Gospels have taken mediacy itself as their point of departure. Their work has tended to take one of three forms. The first is the study of point of view in the Gospels. (There has been no monograph to date fully devoted to point of view in a gospel.) The second approach to mediacy arises in the domain where narrative criticism intersects with reader-response criticism. Here the emphasis is still as much on the narrator as on the reader, specifically on the rhetorical techniques employed by the narrator to elicit particular forms of involvement in the reader. And there is a third approach to mediacy longer established than the first two and less beholden to nonbiblical literary criticism. This is the study of style and literary technique in the Gospels, which (in literary critical terms) is yet another aspect of the narrator's framing of the action.[20]

---

20. I do not deal with this area directly since it is associated more closely with rhetorical criticism than with narrative criticism. Studies of style and literary technique that do intersect with narrative criticism include: Dawsey, *Lukan Voice*; Dewey, *Public Debate*; and Rhoads and Michie, *Mark*, 44–55. For general stylistic and rhetorical studies of, or pertinent to, the Gospels and Acts, see the bibliographies in Robbins, *Jesus*, and Kennedy, *Rhetorical Criticism*.

4

The Narrative Mechanics of a Gospel

The What and the How of Mark

New Testament critic David Rhoads and literary critic Donald Michie collaborated in 1982 to publish *Mark as Story,* a deceptively simple-seeming book. There is one important difference between *Mark as Story* and anything that preceded it in narrative criticism. Earlier works investigated individual facets of Markan narrative (e.g., point of view), or limited combinations of such facets (e.g., plot, character, and the role of the reader).[1] *Mark as Story* presents us for the first time with a descriptive poetics of a gospel.

Poetics had been mainly associated with the analysis of lyric poetry until the 1960s but has since been linked with narrative prose, thus recovering more of its original Aristotelian sense of "a general theory of literary works." As narrative theory, poetics searches for the general principles that manifest themselves in narrative discourse. As descriptive poetics it deploys such theory to describe, for example, the workings of a single narrative text, which is what Rhoads and Michie do in the case of Mark.

Rhoads and Michie distinguish between the content of a narrative, its story, and the form of a narrative, its rhetoric: "The story refers to 'what' a narrative is about—the basic elements of the narrative world—events, characters, and settings. Rhetoric refers to 'how' that story is told in a given narrative in order to achieve certain effects upon the reader.

---

1. E.g., Tannehill, "Disciples" and "Narrative Christology," combines an interest in plot, character, and the reader (so too Kelber, *Mark's Story*); Dewey, "Disciples," combines character, the role of the reader, and point of view.

Thus we can distinguish between 'what' the story is about and 'how' the story is told" (4). As content and form, the "what" and the "how" are nonetheless inseparable, Rhoads and Michie are careful to assure us. "Only for purposes of analysis" are they separated, and even then the "fragmentary analysis" (of character or style, for example) is countered by interpreting each feature in the context of the whole narrative. The organization of the book follows on from the separation of the "what" and the "how," story and rhetoric. The first substantive chapter ("The Rhetoric") examines how the story is presented, that is, the role of the narrator, point of view, standards of judgment, style, narrative patterns, and so forth. The succeeding chapters ("The Settings," "The Plot," "Characters") examine the story, or the narrative what.

The three story chapters are interlinked. Not only do the settings in Mark (e.g., the Jordan, the desert, the sea, mountains, the Way, Jerusalem, the temple) supply atmosphere; "they also create conflicts and reveal character" (65). The sea, for example, is a place of chaos and destruction, which occasions a revelation of Jesus' power (the storm calming) evocative of the creative power that brought order out of primeval chaos and that parted the Red Sea. Also, it is a place of testing that reveals the disciples' lack of faith. The second story chapter, on plot, centers on conflict. Against the background of the establishment of God's rule, Jesus engages in conflict with the supernatural forces of evil, the threatening forces of nature, the hostile religious authorities, and his own incorrigible followers. These different strands of conflict intermesh constantly, "yet each . . . has its own direction, content, ambiance, and resolution" (73). The final story chapter examines the narrator's characterization of Jesus, the disciples, the authorities, and the minor characters. The Markan Jesus, for example, is found to be a remarkably complex figure, possessed of numerous traits, who develops in the course of the action and who evinces a gamut of reactions from those around him. The disciples are also complex, but because they display conflicting traits: loyalty, cowardice, courage, obtuseness, fascination with Jesus, self-centeredness, and capacity for sacrifice.

The book also attempts to integrate its two foci, rhetoric and story. Discussion of the rhetoric frequently previews plotting and characterization. For example, the discussion on point of view echoes Petersen in arguing that only two mentalities are possible in Mark: "The tightness and consistency of the Markan narrative in this regard is really quite extraordinary: the protagonist Jesus establishes the values, attitudes, and actions involved in thinking the things of God, and the characters either exemplify that teaching or . . . illustrate the contrary"—or again, as in the disciples' case, vacillate between the two poles (44).

Prominent features of literary technique in Mark are also examined: repetition, "two-step progression," the "extraordinary number of questions, mostly rhetorical" that characters pose within the story, irony, and so forth. It is argued of Markan irony, for instance, that though it manifests itself in numerous ways, these are uniformly rooted "in the nature of the rule of God as differentiated from what most characters in the story expect" (60). Indeed, Mark's story overall is structured by ironic contrasts: "The rule of God is hidden; the identity of the anointed one is secret; those disciples whom Jesus thought were on the inside turn out to be blind like those on the outside; Israel's leaders are blind to the rule of God; the rule of God overturns all worldly expectations; the most important are the least; the greatest become slaves; those losing their lives are saving them; and the king rules from a cross" (61). A concluding chapter centers on the Markan reader, and attempts "to weave some pieces of the fabric of [the] study together by discussing the reader's overall experiences of [the] story" (137).

Mark as Story, then, is a descriptive poetics of Mark. This systematic and relatively comprehensive account of the narrative mechanics of the gospel has no real precursors in literary exegesis, but it has since been paralleled on the Fourth Gospel by Alan Culpepper and on Matthew by Jack Dean Kingsbury. How did Rhoads and Michie happen on the story-rhetoric model that empowers their systematizing venture? The answer *Mark as Story* suggests—implicitly, for it is not much given to self-analysis—is that the model was close at hand and ready to be applied to biblical narrative in Seymour Chatman's *Story and Discourse* (1978). Chatman's book has greatly facilitated narrative criticism's emergence as a well-defined field of inquiry. In order to appreciate this, we first need to situate *Story and Discourse* in context.

Atop a Two-Storey Model

Story and Discourse emerged from the structuralist study of narrative that thrived in the late 1960s and early 1970s. This narrative poetics (or narratology) was less concerned with interpreting individual narratives than with developing general theories that would stand to narrative as linguistics stands to language—that is, which would make explicit the system of narrative (its constituent parts, techniques, conventions, etc.) that enables individual narratives to function intelligibly. One strand of this (mainly

French) tradition was of particular interest to Chatman: "Taking poetics as a rationalist discipline, we may ask, as does the linguist about language: What are the necessary components—and only those—of a narrative? Structuralist theory argues that each narrative has two parts: a story (*histoire*), the content or chain of events (actions, happenings), plus what may be called the existents (characters, items of setting); and a discourse (*discours*), that is, the expression, the means by which the content is communicated" (*Story*, 19). The narrative model that Rhoads and Michie take from structuralism via Chatman is thus a two-storey model: every narrative is a structure with a content plane (called *story*) and an expression plane (called *discourse*, which Rhoads and Michie aptly reterm *rhetoric*).

This structuralist, dualist model acquired an entirely new significance in Chatman's work. An American himself, he used it to fuse together two traditions of narrative study hitherto largely independent of one another: a French tradition centered on plot, character, and narrative time and an Anglo-American tradition centered on point of view. More precisely, Chatman let the French model of story and discourse organize his book and determine the matters to be treated—What constitutes story? Answer: plot, character, and setting. How is story transmitted? Answer: through the activity of a narrator who manipulates point of view, comments overtly or covertly on the action, and so forth. Although the chapters devoted to plot and character drew heavily on the French theoreticians, those devoted to discourse drew heavily on the Anglo-Americans (Wayne Booth, in particular). This fusion of the two traditions resulted in a theory of narrative arguably more comprehensive than its competitors (principally Genette's *Narrative Discourse* [1972] and Stanzel's *Theory of Narrative* [1979]). Its importance for New Testament literary criticism was that it enabled the individual facets of gospel narrative to be interrelated and integrated more successfully than before, an obvious boon for a narrative criticism intent on displaying the unity of the gospel text.

The distance that this enabled narrative criticism to come in a very short time is illustrated in Norman Petersen's analysis of Mark in his *Literary Criticism for New Testament Critics*, a work that precedes *Mark as Story* by four years. Petersen also employs a dualist, two-story model of narrative, but his is derived from Russian Formalism, an extraordinarily innovative school of literary theory and linguistics that was active between 1914 and 1930. (This is in fact the same model as is used in *Story and Discourse*, except that there it has passed through French structuralism.) The Formalists distinguished *fabula* (story), consisting of the entire sequence of events referred to in a narrative in their causal, chronological order, from *sjužet* (plot), consisting of the sequence of events in the actual order in which they appear in the narrative. (To give a simple illustration, Luke 3:18–22 flashes forward in time to tell of John's imprisonment, then backtracks to give an account of Jesus' baptism.) For the Formalists, the handling of time (preeminently, the rearrangement of chronological order by means of flashback and flashforward) was central to the way in which a set of pretextual events (whether real or imagined) is translated into narrative.

This is precisely the understanding taken over by Petersen in his analysis of Mark: "*Narrative being a time art* in which writers orchestrate their reader's experience by relating story time, plotted time, and reading time [the time it actually takes to read the text], we will begin at the beginning of Mark and work through his book by commenting as we go on the orchestration of these three temporal features" (*Literary Criticism*, 50, emphasis added). This strategy does enable Petersen to argue his point—that is, Mark is a carefully plotted narrative—but it entails a rather narrow conception of narrative rhetoric. The French narratologists of the 1960s reworked the Formalist notion that narrative is essentially a "time art"— that is, the rearrangement of chronological time is its principal means of creatively rendering its subject matter.[2] For the French theoreticians, and for Chatman following them, temporal reordering is but one of a wide range of devices whereby story (*histoire*) is communicated as discourse (*discours*). (Discussion of narrative time thus occupies a mere twenty pages of Chatman's book.) The insight Chatman builds on is that everything in narrative discourse is selection, framing, arranging, filtering, slanting, that is, rhetorical. This is the insight that Rhoads and Michie take over in turn from Chatman, though, as we shall see, the edifice Chatman builds in *Story and Discourse* departs significantly from his groundplan, as does that of Rhoads and Michie following him. What the story-discourse model offered narrative criticism was the possibility of systematically accounting for a gospel's narrative in a way that would do justice both to the complexity of the narrative as an instrument of communication and to its unity as an integrated system.

From the Threefold Johannine Addresser to the Threefold Johannine Addressee

A descriptive poetics of the Fourth Gospel appeared hard on the heels of *Mark as Story* and independently of it: Alan Culpepper's *Anatomy of the*

2. Rimmon, "Comprehensive Theory," 35–36, is good on this.

Fourth Gospel (1983). Culpepper's book is as dependent on Chatman's *Story and Discourse* as Rhoads and Michie's is, but for different reasons. Both books were faced with the same problem: what should a relatively comprehensive narrative analysis of a gospel treat, and how should it be organized? Rhoads and Michie's approach to that problem was shaped, as we saw, by Chatman's model of story and discourse. Culpepper's approach is shaped more by Chatman's *narrative communication model* (*Story,* 151):

Narrative text

Real author	→	Implied author	→ (Narrator) → (Narratee) →	Implied reader	→	Real reader

I believe that Chatman's narrative communication diagram has subtly yet considerably shaped the way New Testament literary critics today conceive of the gospel text. The communication from the real (actual, historical) author to the real reader is conducted instrumentally through the personae within the box. Distinguished from the flesh-and-blood author is the *implied author.*[3] This term denotes the complex image of the real author that the reader infers as s/he reads—a selecting, structuring, and presiding intelligence, discerned indirectly in the text, like God in his/her creation. The author's generation of this textual second self is a profoundly rhetorical act (e.g., Luke 1:1–4). The *narrator* is also said to be immanent in the text as the voice that tells the story, a voice which may or may not be that of one of the characters. The principal New Testament examples of narrators who do participate in the story as characters are John of Revelation, and the "we"-narrator of Luke-Acts (see Acts 16:11ff.). The narrative voice is the instrument by means of which the story-world, and the image of its author-creator, is transmitted (a bearer of divine messages, if you will).[4] The *narratee* is defined as the narrator's immediate addressee (e.g., Theophilus in Luke-Acts), and the *implied reader* as the (generally more oblique) image of "the reader in the text": the reader presupposed or produced by the text as (in some theories) its ideal interpreter.

Having set himself the task of "understanding the gospel as a narrative text, what it is, and how it works," Culpepper presents an elaborated version of Chatman's communications diagram. The main difference between Culpepper's version of the diagram, and that reproduced above, is

3. A term of Booth's (*Rhetoric,* 70–76, 151).
4. Those perplexed about the precise distinction between narrator and implied author, a distinction often unclear in ancient narrative, should consult Bal, "Laughing Mice," 208–210, or Staley, *First Kiss,* 27ff. On the narratological personae generally, see Prince, *Dictionary.*

that *story* is put in the space between narrator and narratee as the content of the narrative communication. Such a model will enable a fresh understanding of "what the gospel is and how it achieves its effects" (3), and Culpepper goes on to show how his book will be organized around it. Chapter 2, the first substantive chapter, "is devoted to a discussion of . . . the narrator," along with a look at the real and implied author. "Chapters 3 through 6 are devoted to various components of the story, its time, its plot, its characters, and the implicit commentary [e.g., irony and symbolism] which makes it so intriguing." Finally, chapter 7 is an analysis of the gospel's audience, as implied and circumscribed by the text.

As a descriptive poetics of John, Culpepper's book invites comparison with Rhoads and Michie's poetics of Mark. Culpepper's is the more thorough account of the two: (1) Discussion of the narrator and the reader is a good deal more comprehensive than in *Mark as Story.* (2) Rhoads and Michie devote little over a page to narrative time, whereas Culpepper gives it an entire chapter. (3) Culpepper prefaces his chapters on plot and character with theoretical discussions ("What Is a Plot?," "Characterization in Contemporary Criticism," etc.), whereas Rhoads and Michie do not. (4) Culpepper privileges plot and character less than Rhoads and Michie do, resulting in a more even treatment of narrative features. (The particular strength of *Mark as Story,* however, lies in its excellent analyses of Markan plot and character. These interlinked analyses are the core of the book, and strongly influence the authors' handling of the chapters that precede and follow them.)

Culpepper finds that the narrator in John is a device that the author manipulates to guide the reader through the world of the story and to provide the proper perspective from which to view it. From the outset (1:1–18), the narrator extends his omniscient viewpoint to the reader, supplying an overview of the identity of Jesus and a preview of the action to follow. Distributed comments by the narrator later reinforce this initial exposition. The narrator is also able to provide inside views of Jesus' thoughts and emotions and those of the disciples, minor characters, and opponents (e.g., 4:27; 6:6; 12:6). These inside views function principally to establish character and to explain responses. The narrator's special abilities, however, are not confined to his omniscience; he is omnipresent also, able to be present in any location—or even in two locations simultaneously—in order to provide the reader with an unhampered view of the action. "While this freedom diminishes the narrative's verisimilitude, any threat which it poses is offset by the added authority it gives the narrator, and by implication the narrative" (26). Nonetheless, the shifting spatial location of the narrator must be carefully distinguished from the geo-graphical location of the evangelist. The narrator's temporal perspective, however, is a retrospective, interpretation-enabling one. Memory and scripture intertwine, memory provoking scriptural interpretation and the scripture overlaying memory and refocusing it "so that the story the nar-rator tells is set in a perspective no 'on the scene' reporter would have" (29). At its most comprehensive, the narrator's point of view on Jesus and his ministry is a combination of his twin perspectives on Jesus' "whence" and his "whither," his origin as the preexistent *logos* and his destiny as the exalted Son of God. This combined perspective conditions the gospel's entire characterization of Jesus. The narrator's relationship to Jesus is de-finable on other levels also; the narrator functions, for instance, as au-thoritative interpreter of Jesus' words (e.g., 2:21; 6:6; 6:71). The relation-ship overall is an exceedingly close one: "both Jesus and the narrator are omniscient, retrospective, and ideologically and phraseologically indistin-guishable," twin vehicles for the implied author's ideology (42–43).

Using Gérard Genette's categories, Culpepper discusses time in John in terms of order, duration, and frequency. Events occur in one order but can be narrated in another. For example, John is interspersed with retro-spections (*analepses*), many referring to events that long antedate the nar-rative events proper. These serve to anchor the story firmly within the history and scriptural heritage of Israel. Other retrospections refer to ear-lier events within the story itself, which properly begins at 1:19. Frequently these retrospections alert the reader to something that happened along the way, not reported at the time (e.g., 1:48; 4:38; 6:70). Manipulation of the order in which the reader hears of events is also accomplished by prospections (*prolepses*), which can refer to later events in the story, to events that begin in the story and continue past its ending (e.g., 14:16), or to events that are later than the final events of the story (e.g., 10:16). The first type serve mainly to build dramatic intensity, the second type link Jesus to the church, and the third type reflect and clarify the situation of the gospel's implied readers. Duration, Genette's second category, refers to the alternating speed of the narration. The narrator can devote a con-siderable span of text to a single event (e.g., word-for-word "repetition" of a discourse of Jesus), and then skip over or briefly summarize extensive time periods (e.g., a year elapses between the Passover of 2:14–3:21 and that of 6:4). What this amounts to is strategic emphasis of certain events and deemphasis of others—a key way in which a time period is plotted. The third category, frequency, refers to the way in which the narrative can repeatedly recount an event that happened only once or can recount once what happened frequently. John makes great use of repetition: "Jesus does a series of signs, has extended (and often repetitious) discourses, goes to the Jewish festivals in Jerusalem. . . . The interchange of these activities provides the material for the story, and the repetition of vocabulary, themes, activities, and settings serves to create the impression that these were characteristic of Jesus' ministry" (74).

Johannine plot "is a matter of how Jesus' identity comes to be recognized and how it fails to be recognized." His identity is progressively revealed by the repetitive signs and discourses, by metaphor and symbolic image, "but each episode has essentially the same plot as the story as a whole. Will Nicodemus, the Samaritan woman, or the lame man recognize Jesus and thereby receive eternal life? The story is repeated over and over" (88–89). The plot is thus a somewhat episodic one, integrated more by theme than by action development. Integration is achieved primarily through the reiterated theme of conflict between belief and unbelief as responses to Jesus, coupled with the participation this elicits in the reader, who is drawn into the company of those who recognize Jesus.

Johannine characterization, likewise, is entirely christocentric. Jesus is a static character in the Fourth Gospel; he does not change. "He only emerges more clearly as what he is from the beginning" (103). The functions of the other characters are to draw out various aspects of Jesus' character by supplying personalities and situations with which he can interact, and to illustrate a spectrum of alternative responses to him: rejection (e.g., the Jews), acceptance without open commitment (e.g., Nicodemus), acceptance of Jesus as a worker of signs and wonders (e.g., 2:23–25; 6:66), belief in Jesus' words (e.g., the Samaritan woman), commitment in spite of misunderstandings (e.g., the disciples), paradigmatic discipleship (e.g., the Beloved Disciple), and defection (e.g., Judas). Such characterizations are strategically oriented toward the reader, pushing him or her also toward a decisive response to Jesus.

Culpepper then turns to implicit commentary, a key device of Johannine rhetoric. This takes the form of strategic use of misunderstandings, irony, and symbolism. The misunderstandings of characters (e.g., 2:20; 3:4) enforce a sharp distinction between insiders and outsiders, those who understand Jesus and those who do not. They draw the reader into the inner circle and teach him or her how to read the gospel. Irony in John, like everything else, centers on the figure of Jesus: his rejection by those who eagerly expect the Messiah, the ignorance of these and many others of his origins and identity, his death at the hands of those to whom he had come to bring life, and so forth. Irony works as a powerful device drawing the reader to identify with the implied author's "superior" viewpoint on the story.[5] Varied use of symbols (e.g., light, water, bread) "also tell the reader that things are more than they seem to be" (199). Symbols have a profound unitive effect in John, according to Culpepper, interrelating different parts of the gospel by their recurrence, uniting the concrete with the abstract and the earthly with the heavenly.

An Agenda for Narrative Criticism

Culpepper's book is the most comprehensive account to date of the narrative mechanics of a gospel. The book's disparate lines of inquiry achieve a measure of overall integration, as we saw, by being subordinated to a governing view of the narrative text based on Chatman's narrative communication diagram. Rhoads and Michie used Chatman's story and discourse model to organize *their* multifaceted study of Mark. Neither Culpepper nor Rhoads and Michie have followed Chatman slavishly. Rather, the organizational strategies of *Mark as Story* and *Anatomy* presuppose those that underpin *Story and Discourse* and would not otherwise have been available to Culpepper or Rhoads and Michie without some breakthrough in general narrative theory on their part comparable to that of Chatman. Chatman's topics are dealt with in a different order in *Anatomy* and *Mark as Story*, but the list of topics treated (as reflected in a comparison of the tables of contents) is essentially the same in all three.

This brings us to a crucial aspect of the importance of *Story and Discourse* for emergent narrative criticism. In his preface Chatman writes:

> questions of balance and scope have been paramount, and I must justify presenting just this much [narrative] theory and no more. My primary concern has been to work out, as clearly as I could, the ramifications of the story-discourse dichotomy and to explain those insights, by myself and others, which it has prompted. So I have excluded many narrative topics that have interested literary scholars— invention, mimesis, the historical development of genres. . . . One cannot include in a single volume every interesting issue that impinges upon narrative, and it is perhaps better not even to mention them than to mention them only, without integrating them into the central

5. Johannine irony has attracted particular attention from literary-minded exegetes. See the excellent bibliography in Duke, *Irony*. Subsequent studies have included O'Day, "Narrative Mode" and *Revelation*, and Staley, *First Kiss*, 95–118. In addition, see chapter 8 below for a rather different handling of the topic.

discussion. I propose a reasonable and modern answer to the question "What is a narrative?" That is, "Which are its necessary and which its ancillary components, and how do they interrelate?" But I do not wish (nor am I able) to account for everything that can be found in narratives. (10)

Mark as Story and *Anatomy*, building on Chatman, establish something like a normative field of inquiry for narrative criticism and suggest the possible parameters of such a field. The largely disparate threads of inquiry that constituted the nonstructuralist narrative analysis of the Gospels of the late 1970s come together in these two books (Culpepper's in particular, though he himself makes no such claims) in the form of a set of closely related issues to be addressed—an agenda, if you will: "Our aim is to contribute to the understanding of the gospel as a narrative text, what it is, and how it works. . . . By 'how it works' I intend questions regarding how the narrative components of the gospel interact with each other and involve and affect the reader" (*Anatomy*, 5–6).

A Tale of Two Disciplines

Narrative criticism has strong affinities with narratology (this term is conventionally used of the work of Chatman, Genette et al.). But the differences are just as striking. Narratology is about theory, narrative criticism is about exegesis. Narratologists analyze texts mainly to develop theories. Narrative critics utilize theory mainly to explicate texts. Narrative critics to date have shown little interest in theory.[6] Jack Dean Kingsbury's *Matthew as Story* (1986) is a case in point: "One literary theorist, Seymour Chatman, has provided a useful outline for discussing the constituent parts of narrative, and David Rhoads has shown us with what profit this outline can be employed in investigating a Gospel such as that of Mark. The present investigation of Matthew's Gospel will also draw from Chatman's outline, and supplement it as well with the work of others" (1).[7] Kingsbury claims to discuss the method to be used "in some detail" in his first chapter. But as it turns out, less than a quarter of the first chapter is devoted to theory and methodology, the rest being largely a preview of the seven exegetical chapters to follow. The theoretical discussion, moreover, seems

6. Though see Staley, *First Kiss*, 27–47, and Funk, *Poetics*, especially. Funk probes biblical and other texts for signals related to plot, character, and narrative perspective, attempting to break new theoretical ground in the process.

7. Compare Staley, *First Kiss*, 21: "The model that we shall use in the following chapters is indebted to . . . Seymour Chatman."

inordinately dependent on Rhoads's "Narrative Criticism and the Gospel of Mark" (it obtains much of its theory second hand), and of the 103 works listed in Kingsbury's bibliography, only nine are works of nonbiblical literary theory or criticism. Like so many biblical scholars receptive to literary criticism, Kingsbury is simply not interested in the fine points of theory and method.

Critics such as Kingsbury, Tannehill, and Rhoads exemplify narrative criticism's independence from narratology. They use narratology to produce sustained interpretations of entire narrative works—something that is very much the exception in literary study, whether continental or Anglo-American. There are two points to be made here. First, narratology does not privilege or emphasize the unity of individual narrative works. When one thumbs through the work of contemporary narrative theorists (Bal, Chatman, Prince, Rimmon-Kenan, Stanzel et al.) one does not find sustained discussions of individual narratives.[8] Instead one finds a myriad of examples, ranging from phrase to paragraph length, culled from a wide spectrum of literature, modern and premodern, to illustrate whatever point happens to be under discussion. It is not with the unity of given narratives that these theoreticians are concerned, but with the unity of the narrative theories being advanced. In narrative criticism the priorities are reversed. It is with the unity of the given (biblical) narrative that the critic is concerned, and he dips at random into the reservoir of narrative theory.

Second, we should consider the exceptions that prove the rule, where narratology bases itself on the interpretation of a single text. Might such an enterprise exhibit strong affinities with narrative criticism? The best known example of this approach is Gérard Genette's *Narrative Discourse* (1972).[9] In contrast to fellow structuralists who opted for less challenging primary material (myth, folktale, and other varieties of prenovelistic narrative, including biblical narrative) Genette adopts Marcel Proust's *A la recherche du temps perdu* as his base-text. *Narrative Discourse* is an elegant dialectic of theoretical and descriptive poetics, description giving rise to

8. See Bal, *Narratology*; Chatman, *Story*; Prince, *Narratology*; Rimmon-Kenan, *Narrative Fiction*; Stanzel, *Theory*; and cf. Booth, *Rhetoric*.

9. Excluding Barthes' still better known *S/Z*, a quasi-narratological analysis of a Balzac novella, but one intent, among other things, on sabotaging narratology. (*S/Z* is about as unlike narrative criticism as can be imagined). Genette, *Narrative Discourse*, is a translation of "Discours du récit," a self-contained unit (67–272) within his *Figures III*. *Narrative Discourse* has been one of the works of literary theory most frequently cited in literary critical gospel studies of the 1980s (along with Booth, *Rhetoric*; Chatman, *Story*; Uspensky, *Poetics*; and two works by Wolfgang Iser—*Implied Reader* and *Act of Reading*—that figure prominently in chapter 6).

inductive theory, theory enabling further description, built on a firm refusal to give ultimate priority to either. But here, where we might expect to find close affinities between narratology and narrative criticism, the differences are particularly telling. (The salient characteristics of narrative criticism's text-theory, to the extent that we can speak of one, were listed in chapter 1 in our discussion of Rhoads' "Narrative Criticism.") The view of the gospel text which the narrative critics (Rhoads, Tannehill, Petersen, Culpepper, Kingsbury et al.) have urged is ultimately a comforting one. It reassures us that in the wake of a long history of fragmentation, exposure of internal contradictions and the like, it is now once again possible using the methods of literary criticism to see that the gospel narratives do after all possess wholeness and internal consistency. Genette's views on Proustian narrative, however, are calculated more to unsettle than to reassure. As Genette reads it, this celebrated work, "which seems so massively committed to representing a world and a character's experience of it,"[10] is fraught with repeated violations, both flagrant and subtle, of the conventions of representation to which it ostensibly subscribes. The traditional, humanistic, "comfortable" view of the *Recherche* is ruptured by Genette's repeated disclosure of anomalies, impossible combinations, and internal contradictions. This is a side of Genette—a poststructuralist side—that I have never come across in narrative criticism (which cites him frequently, as we noted) and that sets him at a far remove from the latter. Just how far is revealed in his concluding observations:

> readers will not find here a final "synthesis" in which all the characteristic features of Proustian narrative noted in the course of this study will meet and justify themselves to each other. ... [I]t would be unfortunate, it seems to me, to seek "unity" at any price, and in that way to *force* the work's coherence—which is, of course, one of criticism's strongest temptations, one of its most ordinary (not to say most common) ones, and also one most easy to satisfy, since all it requires is a little interpretive rhetoric.
>
> Now, if we cannot deny in Proust the will for coherence and the striving for design, just as undeniable in his work is the resistance of its matter and the part played by what is uncontrolled—perhaps uncontrollable. (266–67)

This last sentence encapsulates part of what was at stake in the debate staged above between Tannehill's *Narrative Unity* and Dawsey's *Lukan*

---

10. From Jonathan Culler's foreword to *Narrative Discourse*, 12.

Voice: the tension between what the evangelist might be said to control, or to be unable to control, in his narrative. Jacques Derrida, who casts an occasional shadow across the pages of *Narrative Discourse,* observes: "the writer writes *in* a language and *in* a logic whose proper system, laws, and life his discourse by definition cannot dominate absolutely. He uses them only by letting himself, after a fashion and up to a point, be governed by the system. And the [critical] reading must always aim at a certain relationship, unperceived by the writer, between what he commands and what he does not command of the patterns of the language that he uses" (*Grammatology,* 158).[11] In appropriating narrative theory, narrative critics regularly defuse it. An accusation often leveled at American literary critics is that they domesticate French theory when they import it. Chatman, for example, stands accused of taming Roland Barthes, upon whom he relies heavily (see, e.g., Scholes, "Review"). In narrative criticism this sort of domestication is more thoroughgoing; after all, the biblical studies guild is blissfully wedded to a notion with which literary critics have been ill at ease for more than four decades, namely, recovery of the literary author's intentions is a viable and central project of criticism.[12] Biblical scholars have always proceeded more cautiously than literary scholars, have devoted themselves for a far longer period to extrinsic (especially historical) methods of study, and have unquestionably derived a great deal more from such methods than their literary counterparts. The extrinsic methods were in their brightest bloom in literary studies during the final quarter of the last century and the first three decades of the present one. Indeed, the history of our discipline often seems like a delayed action replay of that other one—which would explain, for example, why American biblical criticism has only recently become preoccupied with the formal coherence of the text, an emphasis in its zenith in American literary criticism in the 1940s and 1950s. The constraints that define narrative criticism and that result from that time lag—foremost being the constraint (willingly accepted) of engaging in dialogue with traditional biblical scholarship, itself happily wedded to the most deeply traditional strands of nonbiblical literary scholarship—suggest both that narrative criticism will continue to

11. Cf. Derrida, *Dissemination,* 95–96, 129–30. Much of Derrida's oeuvre is an exploration of this "structural unconscious."

12. The debate on authorial intention is, of course, highly pertinent to biblical studies. Biblical scholars have occasionally tried to connect with the debate (e.g., Stendahl, "Classic"; Tuckett, *New Testament,* 175ff.; and Tyson, *Death,* 17–21), but have tended to gloss over its complexities. Contrast such treatments as Bagwell, *Interpretation*; Kermode, *Telling,* 201–20; and Newton-De Molina, ed., *Intention* (not to mention Knapp and Michaels, "Against Theory," or Derrida, *Margins,* 307–30, and "Limited Inc").

tone down the theory it imports, and that it will remain a distinctly different enterprise from anything found in the fields of nonbiblical literary study—though that need by no means constrain individual works of narrative criticism.

Although the term *narratology* is beginning to be applied to the style of gospel study under consideration, *narrative criticism* is a better term for it. Criticism, exegesis, commentary is what that method is essentially about. And since in the work of some of its practitioners (Kingsbury, Tannehill, Tyson et al.) it is clearly affiliated with composition criticism, both in its holistic preoccupation and its preoccupation with overarching authorial purpose, it is tempting to speculate that it is well on its way to becoming a fourth criticism in gospel studies. Narrative criticism is an alien in the assembly of form, redaction, and composition criticism, since the tracing of its genealogy takes us well outside the guild—but an alien making decided efforts to assimilate.

5

The Place of Gospel Theology in a Story-Centered Gospel Criticism

[A]re we not coercing the Bible into being "literature" by attempting to transfer [literary critical] categories to a set of texts that are theologically motivated?
—Robert Alter, *The Art of Biblical Narrative*

Narrative criticism's relationship to nonbiblical literary study seems clear. But what is its precise relationship to redaction criticism? What place, if any, can the individual theologies of the evangelists have in narrative criticism? If narrative criticism breaks with redaction criticism by substituting a paradigm of story for one of theology, does it forfeit the possibility of making any significant contribution to the theology-centered tradition of gospel study?

Redaction Criticism: A Subfield of Narrative Criticism?

To answer the questions posed above we should first demystify the expression "an evangelist's theology." A synonym that expresses the meaning of *theology* in this context and that strips it of extraneous connotations is an evangelist's *ideological point of view*,[1] denoting the systems of assumptions and convictions against which everything in the story (the set of persons, events, and places) is evaluated—or to put it another way, in terms of which everything in the story is presented. The advantage of this reformulation is that it enables us to relate redaction (and composition) criticism's field of inquiry quite precisely to that of narrative criticism. Ideological or evaluative point of view in the context of a gospel is not simply equivalent to what literary critics mean by the blanket term *point of view*, which we defined as a narrator's encompassing attempt to impose a story-world upon a reader (or hearer). Rather, it corresponds to only

1. I find varied support for such a synonym in Uspensky, *Poetics*, 8–16; Culpepper, *Anatomy*, 33; Bahktin, *Imagination*, 341; and Sternberg, *Poetics*, 37.

one of the four modalities of point of view distinguished by Boris Uspensky. To this extent it is possible to regard redaction criticism's principal field of inquiry (the theologies of the evangelists) as a subfield of a much larger project: a general descriptive poetics of the Gospels and Acts.

While it is not entirely inaccurate thus to phrase the relationship of redaction criticism to narrative criticism, it is distorting. For redaction criticism in the classic German mold, theology and *Sitz im Leben* are indissolubly bonded; thus the gospel story has, so to speak, an allegorical dimension. The details of its form are assumed to answer in part to some set of real events contemporary with, and of concern to, the evangelist. The components of the story—character, event, setting—are assumed to be molded to speak indirectly to that *Sitz*. But this external setting is only of secondary concern to the narrative critic who is mainly interested in the gospel's internal dynamics—specifically, its functioning as an instrument of narrative communication. (To complete our all too tidy schema, we might add that composition criticism's principal concern is with the gospel's internal functioning as an instrument of theological communication.) Narrative criticism's disinclination for historical research, coupled with (or resulting in) the fact that it has yet to prove itself to the guild at large, is enough to render dubious in the extreme any suggestion that narrative criticism might somehow supersede redaction criticism altogether (not that any narrative critic has thus far dared to make that suggestion). Indeed, as things presently stand, narrative criticism's status in the guild depends in large part on its willingness to show itself an able and congenial helpmate to redaction and composition criticism.

Actually, narrative criticism is admirably equipped to play the role of capable secretary and undertake a complementary investigation of a gospel's theology. The following rough schema suggests itself. Attention might be given first of all to the gospel narrator's explicit comments on characters and events in the story-world (e.g., the formulary citations of scripture in Matthew, the prologue in John), and on the task of narration itself (e.g., Luke 1:1–4; John 20:30–31). Attention might also be given to the narrator's implicit commentary, especially the use of irony, peculiar phrasing of the subject matter (e.g., *exodos* in Luke 9:34, *analēmpsis* in 9:51), and major use of symbols. The plot might be analyzed in detail to discern the major ideological factors that motivate its particular structuration. Based on the yield of the first three steps, the ideology of characters who appear subordinate to the overarching ideological viewpoint should be analyzed to further clarify it. Such ideology could be explicitly expressed (e.g., by Jesus, an angel, or some other reliable character), or merely implied in a character's speech or actions. The ideology of characters not in accord with the dominant point of view (e.g., the Marcan disciples) could also be analyzed to bring it into still sharper focus.

There is little in this rough schema that redaction critics have not tackled at one time or another (serious attention to plot being the major exception), and narrative critics have tackled all of it, albeit in piecemeal fashion. Redaction criticism's landmark concern—gospel theology—is thus well within narrative critical territory, despite the methodological disparities between the two. Although they are well positioned to do so, the story-centered critics have not as yet shown any inclination to mount a systematic investigation of the theologies of the Gospels and Acts, one which might significantly complement the efforts of the dominant, theology-centered school. The reason for their listlessness is that they prefer to attend to the evangelists' stories. But in centering on story instead of theology, do they diminish the power of the Gospels, reducing them to ordinary works of literature? The answer a story-centered critic might give is that to center exclusively on theology would be to lessen the power of these narratives yet more severely. But before I sink entirely into diatribe, two statements by Jack Dean Kingsbury and Robert Tannehill contrasting their own narrative-critical approach with the theological one are worth noting.

What Are Gospels About?

In his *Matthew as Story* (1986), Kingsbury usefully differentiates that book from his commentary, *Matthew* (1977), which was "a study in composition criticism" (vii). The earlier volume treated "the *thought* of Matthew in topical fashion," defining the center of that thought and then discussing "questions of christology (the figure of Jesus), of theology (the notion of the Kingdom of Heaven), and of ecclesiology (discipleship and the church of Matthew)" (ibid.). *Matthew as Story* is rather differently focused:

> To approach Matthew's Gospel as a unified narrative . . . is to concentrate on the very story it tells. When one reads the Matthean narrative, one temporarily takes leave of one's familiar world of reality and enters into another world that is autonomous. . . . This world, which possesses its own time and space, is peopled by characters and marked by events that, in varying degrees, are extolled or decried in accordance with this world's own system of values. By inhabiting this

world one experiences it, and having experienced it, one leaves and returns, perhaps changed, to one's own world. (*Story*, 2)[2]

The contrast in emphasis Kingsbury draws is between Matthew's thought and narrative world. Matthew's narrative world impels the imaginative participation and transformation of a reader. A comparable statement of contrast occurs in Tannehill's *Narrative Unity*: "A gospel story exercises influence in a much richer way than through theological statements, which might be presented in an essay. . . . Seeking for a Lukan theology within Luke-Acts tends to divorce theological themes from the larger purpose of the work. Instead, we should seek to understand Luke-Acts as a system of influence which may be analyzed in literary terms. The message of Luke-Acts is not a set of theological propositions but the complex reshaping of human life, in its many dimensions, which it can cause" (8). Tannehill seems to think of Luke-Acts in dynamic terms first and foremost and to fear that overemphasis on static, theological categories has reduced its rhetorical, story-based power.

Kingsbury and Tannehill are both arguing the insufficiency of an approach that would tear the theology or thought of a gospel away from its narrative moorings. Participation in the narrative form of a gospel is essential to its adequate interpretation.[3] In failing to recognize this, the theology-centered tradition has muted the rhetorical power of the gospels, their story-based capacity to reshape the reader or listener (the listener in the pew most of all, perhaps). Are redaction criticism and narrative criticism, then, to be differentiated in terms of form and content? Is redaction criticism an approach that centers on the content of a gospel and narrative criticism one that centers on its form? The question is complicated by the fact that content is conceived differently by each. Neither side is given to theoretical discussion of the issue, but the differences are not hard to discern.

For redaction critics (as for composition critics), a gospel's content is *ideational*—specifically, an overarching theological viewpoint, extrapolated from the narrative form, and reexpressed in propositional language. Certain literary exegetes have worked with quite a different understanding of gospel content. For them, content has been reconceived in strict and narrow terms as the set of story events, with those who enact and undergo them and the locations that form their setting, to which the given gospel

---

2. Cf. "A Comparison of Redaction Criticism to Literary Criticism" in *Matthew*, 2d ed.

3. Cf. chapter 1 above.

refers. This stricter notion of content entered narrative criticism by way of Chatman[4] and has become a tacit feature of much of its discourse. This notion needs to be recapitulated and reexamined, again with reference to Rhoads and Michie's *Mark as Story*.

Impelled by Chatman, Rhoads and Michie distinguish between the content of Mark, which they term its story, and the form, which they term its rhetoric. The story refers to what the narrative is about, which they take to be "the basic elements of the narrative world—events, characters, and settings" (4),[5] while rhetoric refers to how that story is told in a given narrative so as to achieve certain effects upon the audience. They then show how their analysis of Mark is organized in terms of this model. The first substantive chapter explores the rhetoric—"the role of the narrator, point of view, standards of judgement, style, narrative patterns and other rhetorical devices" (5)—and the three subsequent chapters explore the story, that is, setting, plot, and character.

It can be argued, however, that Rhoads and Michie have missed the real impact of their model. If story is to be understood strictly as the "what" of the narrative, and rhetoric as "how" that story is told, then everything in the narrative (which is all a "telling," after all) is rhetorical. To relegate the rhetoric to a single chapter runs counter to their initial definition of it. It should encompass not only the features they discuss in their "Rhetoric" chapter (point of view, style, narrative patterns, etc.) but plotting, characterization, and description of settings as well. This discrepancy between initial definition and subsequent application is also derived from Chatman's book. Chatman notes, for example, that Aristotle defined plot (*mythos*) as "the arrangement of incidents," and adds that for structuralist narrative theory (the theory on which Chatman is drawing) this "arrangement is precisely the operation performed by the discourse" (*Story*, 43). (Rhoads and Michie substitute the term *rhetoric* for Chatman's *discourse*, as we saw.) Yet Chatman treats the different aspects of this discursive arrangement (e.g., a narrator's reordering of chronological sequence) under the rubric of story rather than discourse (62ff.).[6] Story, in the structuralist sense, denotes "the narrative events, abstracted from their

4. It can also be found in its essentials in Frei, *Eclipse*, though Frei's impact on narrative criticism has been indirect. More than any other single work, *Eclipse* made narrative a theological and exegetical category to be reckoned with, but for practical tools narrative critics have turned not to narrative theologians such as Frei (his *Identity* notwithstanding, which demonstrated his approach to exegesis) but to secular narratologists and literary critics.

5. Cf. Culpepper, *Anatomy*, 7: "The story itself consists of characters, events, and their settings."

6. See Mosher, "Synthesis," 171, and cf. Leitch, *Stories*, 16–17.

disposition in the text and reconstructed in their chronological order, together with the participants in these events" (Rimmon-Kenan, *Narrative Fiction,* 3).[7] However, when we come to read or analyze a concrete narrative text, for example, Mark, everything in that text is encountered as discourse-rhetoric: "the events do not necessarily appear in chronological order, the characteristics of the participants are dispersed throughout ([i.e., *character,* the story element, becomes *characterization* in the text], and all the items of the narrative content are filtered through some prism or perspective [point of view]" (ibid.). Thus, were the logic of their story-rhetoric model to be fully deployed, it would seem that Rhoads and Michie's chapters on story ("The Settings," "The Plot," "Characters") necessarily pertain to Markan rhetoric as much as the chapter explicitly entitled "The Rhetoric."

The point is ultimately a simple one (narrative is ubiquitously rhetorical), but it has significant consequences for our conception of a gospel's content and for our attendant conception of its theology. In terms of the schema just outlined (an intensification of a narrative critical schema), a gospel's content is not ideational or theological. Instead, theology (more precisely, theological point of view) is viewed as part of the gospel's form; it is part of the narrative means (the "how") in terms of which the contentual set of events is formulated (framed, relayed, given shape, etc.). Reconceived with a rigor that narrative criticism demands but has yet to realize, the notion of form encompasses everything in the presentation of the contentual set of events to which the given gospel refers. Such presentational strategies include plotting, characterization, the filtering of story events through theocentric, christocentric, and other perspectives, the rearrangement of chronological sequence, the use of literary patterns and techniques, and so on.

Thus recontextualized, the evangelist's theology, as redaction critics have traditionally conceived of it, is seen no longer as the salient aspect of a gospel's content, but rather as a single aspect of its narrative form. However, rather than apportion theology a small holding in a much larger field of inquiry, narrative criticism might instead invite a radical rethinking of that phenomenon. The assumption that the Gospels and Acts express the theologies of the evangelists—a tacit assumption of redaction and composition criticism—is a strangely contradictory one. It implies that (logically if not temporally) the theology precedes the narrative in which it is expressed. Redaction and composition criticism would reverse this

---

7. The question of whether a story thus abstracted might correspond to a set of real events is bracketed in this formulation. The priority of story over discourse (in the structuralist sense) is a logical priority rather than a temporal one.

implied sequence, moving from narrative form to topical content (christology, ecclesiology, soteriology, etc.). Redaction and composition critics,
then, attempt to recover the theology of the evangelists; to do so they
paradoxically recast that narrative theology in a systemic and topical form
alien to it. But narrative criticism, with its imported dictum of the inseparability of form and content, implies a rather different understanding. An
evangelist's theology or thought—which we define minimally as a socially
shared system of theocentric convictions as reformulated rhetorically by
the evangelist—is not expressed in narrative. Narrative is not its vehicle
or instrument; it is narrative thought through and through. The mediation
of a set of events centered on Jesus of Nazareth by emphasis of certain
details and repression of others, by plotting, characterization, manipulation of point of view, deformation of chronological sequence, stylistic
nuance—the rendering of this enigmatic set of events as structured, coherent narrative is the evangelist's thought and that of his immediate tradition.[8] This is what it means to say that it is narrative thought.

This is one way of answering whether the story-centered methods
can deal adequately with the theology of a gospel. Narrative criticism's
retort, as I (rather freely) interpret it, would be that it is the theology-
centered tradition that falls short in dealing with the evangelist's thought:
it ruptures the latter's essential narrativity. If this is indeed the case, then
the resulting picture is paradoxical in the extreme: by putting story in
place of theology, the narrativist position (inadvertently) sets up the conditions for better describing that thought. But there is a final ironic twist
that complicates this sanguine ending.

Is Redaction Criticism More Literary than Narrative Criticism?

At the beginning of chapter 3 I noted that it can be argued—and probably
disputed—that the generic trait of all verbal narrative, whether oral or
written, is that it is mediated. What is supplied by one's sense of sight in
scenic narrative (theatre, film, etc.) must be supplied by one's imagination
in verbal narrative in response to a mediating narrative voice. I concluded
by noting that this generic trait can receive greater or lesser attention from
critics, and that it receives least attention from critics who take plot to be

8. The attempt to coherently render "the enigmatic set of events" (notably, the crucifixion) would date back to the events themselves. Just as surely, however, the traditions
circulating in connection with Jesus of Nazareth acquired an unprecedented degree of nar-
rativization with the advent of the written gospel, which is to say, an unprecedented heightening of a certain kind of coherence.

the salient feature of a narrative—which accounts for a large number of those doing literary criticism of the Gospels at present. (Here I have argued that specific plots can be studied only as instances of plotting, so that the operations of mediacy can not be circumvented in actuality. But rather than treat point of view as a category ancillary to plot—the current tendency among literary exegetes—plot should be placed unequivocally under the aegis of point of view, or, to be technically exact, under the more comprehensive category of discourse.) Others minimize the difference between scenic and written narrative in another way; they acknowledge the mediating features (voice, point of view) of the narrative that frame and shape the action-linked features (plot and character), but then go on to discuss the latter in abstraction from the former (e.g., Rhoads and Michie, *Mark as Story,* Culpepper, *Anatomy,* Kingsbury, *Matthew as Story*). Both styles of narrative criticism—the plot-centered style being very much more prevalent—put their practitioners in an odd position. Many of them are reacting against a tradition that abstracts a propositional or ideational content from the Gospels. Instead they assert the inseparability of an evangelist's thought and his narrative means. Indeed, some of them tend to reconceive of the gospel's content in terms not of thought but of story. But the paradox is that most of them attempt to abstract the story (plot, character, etc.) from the narrator's discourse that mediates it. They rely themselves, that is, on a separation of form and content, reenacting in a different register the very thing that many of them are reacting against.

Theology (theological or ideological point of view) has traditionally been distilled from the gospel's story, evoking a reaction that repeats the crime in which the story is distilled from the discourse that mediates it. When the situation is thus framed, the paradox is striking indeed. In this perspective, redaction criticism (preoccupied with theological point of view) seems more discourse-oriented, more true to the generic, verbal-narrative trait of mediacy, and to that extent more literary than much narrative criticism (typically preoccupied with action and character). Of course, the objection that can be raised against the theological fixation is that it is excessively abstract and ideational; it fails to do justice to the flow and integration of the story. One way in which the narrating discourse and the narrated action might be kept to the fore simultaneously is to consistently subordinate one's reading of the gospel to the following type of question: What kind of involvement in the plot does the narrator's discourse elicit at this moment or at that? This strategy is *reader-response criticism* (or one possible version of it) and is attended by its own special set of problems (see chapter 6).

"Sensible" Biblical Criticism: Criticism without Content

> What ought . . . to prohibit considering writing . . . as the simple empirical husk of
> the concept is the fact that this husk . . . is *coextensive* with the whole life of the
> discourse.
> —Jacques Derrida, *Dissemination*

One more complication can be factored into our discussion of form and
content. This pertains to the question, not of how best to conceptualize
a gospel's content relative to its form, but of how viable the opposition
of form and content might be to begin with. (By way of concluding these
chapters on narrative criticism, which testifies so insistently to the inseparability of form and content, I hope to wrest from that testimony its
logical, iconoclastic conclusion—thereby becoming more narrative critical
than the narrative critics themselves.)

Even should one opt to affirm the inseparability of form and content
in gospel narrative, one will have separated them conceptually nonetheless
in order to argue the grounds for one's decision. And such separation will
once again have reinforced an assumption that we cling to, namely, our
texts do in fact express a content, whether it is to be conceived of narratively, theologically, or narrative-theologically. The presupposition that
conventional usage of the terms form and content actively props up (and
I include my own usage up to now) is that a gospel possesses or presupposes some content (theology, christology, soteriology, ecclesiology, etc.,
or a pretextual story in its chronological order, comprised of characters,
events, and settings), which receives concrete expression in the narrative.
Form, as we customarily conceive of it, is content sensibly manifested—a
notion that is the narratological correlate of John 1:14 ("And the Word
became flesh").[9] Doubtless few of us would want to argue that some
formless content subsists beneath, behind, or even in the given narrative.
But the notion of formless content is nonetheless a tenacious one, feeding
the suspicion that there is some formless something, somewhere, to which
form might be said to be answerable—an author's intention, perhaps.
Might we not assume that the author knew what he or she wanted to
say—had some content in mind—and then decided how best to say it?
But as the adage goes, "How do I know what I mean till I see what I
say?" Perhaps the author only discovered what he or she wanted to say in

---

9. Staley has provided a remarkable if inadvertent corroboration of this: "analogous
to the classic dogmatic theologian who can uphold the humanity and deity of Christ in a
kind of creative tension without subsuming one under the other, so too, the New Testament
narrative critic must hold in tension both the story as it is discoursed and its ability to point
beyond and behind itself " (*First Kiss,* 118).

the process of actually saying it. This latter version has "the enormous merit of not positing, as the alternative version does, immaterial signifieds which somehow exist in the writer's mind even before signifiers are found for them."[10] (I shall not pretend that the author's intention can be excised quite so painlessly, but a more adequate discussion of it will have to await another time.) Form in the latter version is not answerable to, does not acquire its contours from, some primordial, unformed Content. Rather, form—for example, of a given gospel narrative—might be described as the verbal act of a particular author

> performed in response to—and thus shaped and constrained by—
> sets of multiple interacting conditions. For any narrative, these con-
> ditions would consist of (1) such circumstantial variables as the par-
> ticular context and material setting (cultural and social, as well as
> strictly "physical") in which the tale is told, the particular listeners or
> readers addressed, and the nature of the narrator's relationship to
> them, and (2) such psychological variables as the narrator's motives
> for telling the tale and all the particular interests, desires, expectations,
> memories, knowledge, and prior experiences (including his knowl-
> edge of various events, of course, but also of other narratives and of
> various conventions and traditions of storytelling) that elicited his
> telling it on that occasion, to that audience, and that shaped the
> particular way he told it. (Smith, "Narrative Versions," 226)

Impelled by the will-to-narrate-to-some-end (perhaps what we mean by intentionality), narratives acquire their forms only in relation to other forms. But what of their relations to brute, unformed, extralinguistic causal forces—that is, material reality? Taking the case of the Gospels once again, we can say that like historians and other kinds of storytellers, the evan-gelists would have shared with their audiences "general notions of the *forms* that significant action *must* take by virtue of [their] participation in the specific processes of sense-making which identif[ied them] as . . . mem-ber[s] of one cultural endowment rather than another" (White, *Tropics*, 86). Causal forces can only be comprehended under a description, and narrative is a form of description. Every form answers relationally to other forms, so that every narrative is a reformulated form.[11] But what or where

10. Sturrock, "Roland Barthes," 67. See further Barthes, "Death," 145; Descombes, *French Philosophy*, 95, 98; and de Saussure, *General Linguistics*, 110.

11. The version of content here espoused is thus an eminently "sensible" one: "'sensible language' directs itself against [a] Platonizing translation into the ideal" (Krupnik, "Intro-duction," 21).

then is content?[12] Content may not name an unformed mental sphere of meaning that precedes and orients an author's narrative. Indeed, far from formless content preceding form, form itself might just as easily be said to precede content: an interpreter faced with a form of narrative attempts to retrieve its content. But the content that interpretation thereby yields is a misnomer; as the interpreter's construal of that text, it is the response he or she forms to the form being interpreted. Content always names some form or other. So formless content neither precedes form nor issues from it. Conventionally, of course, content means "what the text is about." But that immanentist, univocal "what," suggesting some yet-to-be-discovered cache of meaning that exists prior to the act of interpretation, is but one further effect of content's compelling mystique. The propensity in each biblical scholar to speak and write as though we might one day stumble on those hidden chambers of content within our biblical texts, as we gradually hone our methods—coming ever closer to finding the concealed levers and seeing the secret doors swing open—bespeaks the "lingering strain of naive Platonism" that befuddles our critical thinking.[13] Hypostatized Content, invariant and discoverable, is the enabling fiction of our exegetical practice. Today, it is not our biblical texts that need demythologizing so much as our ways of reading them.

Let us digress briefly to reflect on some of the implications of our discussion for positions taken earlier in this chapter. Narrative is inescapably rhetorical. But narrative bereft of a primordial content with which to deal expressively requires even closer attention to its rhetoricity than that urged earlier. Thus, the adequacy of competing approaches to the Gospels is still measurable by the respective degrees of awareness they exhibit of the Gospels' ineluctable rhetoricity. But a corresponding attentiveness is now required to the illusory mystique attaching to concepts such as theological content (which turns out not to be content after all, but an aspect of form instead) or story (in the sense that narrative critics are now using the term). The challenge is to reformulate them as appropriate. A poststructuralist narrative criticism—one dubious of metaphysical inner-chambers in the Gospels—can be contrasted to the kind of narrative criticism

12. And what, for that matter, is *form*? "[F]orm is never anything but a process on the way to its completion. The completed form never exists as a concrete aspect of the work. . . . It is constituted in the mind of the interpreter as the work discloses itself in response to his questioning" (de Man, *Blindness,* 32). Form, like its sibling content, has had its own history of reification, hypostatization, etc. (cf. Derrida, *Margins,* 157ff., and *Writing,* 4ff.). Thus, there are yet further complications that could be factored into our discussion.

13. The quoted phrase comes from Smith, "Narrative Versions," 213, who employs it in a rather different context.

built on the structuralist narratology of Chatman and others. A gospel's narrative discourse, instead of being conceived as dealing expressively with the essential elements of a prediscoursed narrative world (à la Chatman, Rhoads and Michie et al.), can now be conceived as dealing transformatively with a range of alternatively discoursed narrative worlds. If we dispense with the *what* of structuralist narratology—the prediscoursed narrative-world-in-itself, said to be the content of the narrative—Chatman's two-storey model of story and discourse collapses to be replaced with a one-storey model of—what? ("Discourse-discourse" hardly has the same ring to it.) However we decide to rephrase it, narrative discourse (narrative form) comes to be seen as dealing reexpressively with other discourses. Because it is with other competing discourses that the given narrative is now seen to deal instead of with a malleable and inert "narrative world," it becomes evident that the given narrative also presupposes, submits to, affirms, negates, slants, filters, amplifies, or represses other elements of that general discursive matrix in which it is situated and constituted. Narrative discourse, then, is thrust into the forefront of our critical attention and activity instead of being allocated second billing after the "essential" elements of the story-world, as it tends to be in current literary criticism of the Gospels.[14] The question, "Do the theologies of the evangelists have any place in a story-centered gospel criticism?" can then be rephrased as "Does the theological discourse of the evangelists have any place in a discourse-centered gospel criticism?"—rephrased, that is to say, as a rhetorical question, in the double sense of a question expecting the answer yes and of a question concerning gospel rhetoric. But the practice of a discourse-centered gospel criticism—an uneasy alliance of poststructuralism, narrative criticism, and redaction criticism—exceeds my own capacities at present. Thus my reconstructive suggestions for narrative criticism are confined and counterposed in the main to a fixation with textual unity. And the discourse I feel best equipped to tackle here is less the discourse of the biblical narratives themselves than the discourse of their professional readers. A further explanation, however, is needed concerning why our discourse as biblical interpreters might be a problem.

Narrative is inescapably rhetorical—but so is criticism, and embar-

---

14. In thus drawing attention to discourse's aggressive/defensive aspects, I suggest a potential collaboration between the specific, ahistorical, apolitical understanding of discourse that has prevailed in structuralist narratology (Chatman et al.) and the general, historical, political understanding of it that has prevailed in French poststructuralism, especially in the work of Foucault. For some very different reflections on the project of a poststructuralist narratology, one that may be crucial to the future of narrative criticism, see Bal, "Tell-Tale."

rassingly so when it is deprived of a transcendent content before which it might efface itself. The following two questions have led me to come down hard on content (a concept which, after all, despite its idealist underpinnings, seems indispensable to critical discourse as we know it)[15]: What is at stake in the notion that our biblical texts express a certain content? Might it be the corollary notion that they contain invariant properties? The latter notion, unless I miss my guess, has a powerful hold on our collective exegetical psyche. Also to be pondered is the question that any challenge to this intuitive notion must provoke: If our texts do *not* contain such properties, what prevents interpretive anarchy in the academy (or in general)? But before reflecting on why or how it is that (professional) readers are so well-behaved, one must look at a group of model readers in action.

15. Our critical language is founded on (and founders on) concepts such as content (and form), but there is no other language readily available.

PART II
Gospel Criticism as Reading

[I] will approach the gospel's theology . . . in terms of the journey on which the reader is taken.
—Jeffrey Staley, *The Print's First Kiss*

[T]he study of a literary work should concern not only the actual text but also, and in equal measure, the actions involved in responding to that text.
—Wolfgang Iser, *The Act of Reading*

[R]eader-response criticism attempts to describe what a text *does* to a reader, i.e., what assumptions the reader is making, what expectations he or she is forming, what conclusions he is reaching.
—James Resseguie, "Reader-Response Criticism and the Synoptic Gospels"

To speak of the meaning of a work is to tell a story of reading.
—Jonathan Culler, *On Deconstruction*

The stories told by . . . Wolfgang Iser— indeed, by all so-called reader-response criticisms—belong to [the] category of narratives with a happy ending. The onset of deconstruction, however, has generated an alternative plot in which the reader is the agonist or anti-hero, manipulated by an uncanny text which puts in question his ill-starred quest for meaning.
—Elizabeth Freund, *The Return of the Reader*

6

Stories of Reading: Doing Gospel Criticism as/with a Reader

Adventures of the Reader

From being an observer in the wings or at best a minor participant, the reader gradually acceded to the role of protagonist in literary studies through the 1960s and 1970s. By the beginning of the 1980s one could scarcely pick up a literary journal without finding articles and book reviews (if not the entire issue) devoted to the continuing adventures of the "amazing reader in the labyrinth of literature."[1] During this time the amazing reader had many aliases and roles, engaging the text or emerging from it in guises such as the Implied Reader, the Informed Reader, the Narratee, and the Model Reader. The carnival also featured the Reader in the Text and the Flesh-and-Blood Reader, the Competent Reader and the Literent, the Encoded or Inscribed Reader, the Subjective Reader, Superreader, the Newreaders, and the willful Misreader. The carnival is now largely packed up and gone, but it has left a new sense of what it means to be a reader— and a critic—in its wake.[2]

1. The title of an article by Robert Rogers.
2. The following introductions to reader-response criticism are recommended: Culler, *On Deconstruction*, 64–83; Freund, *Return*; Mailloux, *Conventions*, 19–65; Suleiman, "Varieties"; and Tompkins, "Introduction." Ray, *Meaning*, is an excellent (if difficult) discussion of a wide range of reading theories, while Holub, *Reception Theory*, discusses *Rezeptionsästhetik*, reader-response criticism's German counterpart. (Culler, Freund, Ray, and Tompkins each map the field from poststructuralist perspectives.) Introductions by New Testament critics include: Fowler, "Who Is?" (possibly the best starting point for those entirely new to the field); McKnight, *Reader* and *Postmodern Use*; Lategan, "Current Issues"; Lategan and Vorster, *Text*, 67ff.; and Schenk, "Rollen." Cf. Brown, "Reader Response," and Croatto, *Hermeneutics*. Tompkins, ed., *Reader-Response*, 233–72, remains the best bibliography, as far as I know, though for a complementary list with a German as opposed to an American bias see Schmidt, "Bibliography."

It should not be supposed, however, that reader-response criticism is, or ever was, a conceptually unified criticism; rather it is a spectrum of contrasting and conflicting positions. Along the spectrum some have been concerned with how actual readers read, others with the factors (institutional, sociocultural, linguistic) that delimit reading in the first place. Others still have centered on the notion that the text projects an image of its audience, immanent in the text and coextensive with it, as fictional a construct as any of its characters. To read any text is necessarily to engage, in and through its rhetoric (however overt or subtle), a projection of the reader that that text requires. This projection is proffered as a *role*, one which can be taken on or rejected but which can not be circumvented. To read any literary text, in this view, is always in some sense to read through its reader construct, to dialogue with it, and through it to dialogue with its author construct (the image of the author that the text puts forth). Recent literary exegesis of the Gospels, attentive to the strong roles of reading that these texts enjoin, has found this reader-in-the-text approach especially congenial.[3] Indeed, if the hypothetical reader (or hearer) is thought of as one exposed to the text for the first time, then we have a working definition of reader-response criticism in the New Testament context. New Testament reader-response criticism is a more narrowly focused and more unified phenomenon than its nonbiblical counterpart.

The rediscovery of the reader entails a genuine paradigm shift in literary studies, signifying a full turn of the circle of possible critical emphases: "The classicist poetics is focused on the norms (rules) of literary genres and forms, i.e., on the literary 'codes'; the Romantic 'expressionist' criticism centers on the concept of the creative personality of the poet, i.e., on the 'encoder'; for the twentieth century . . . [the text] is the prime focus of attention [as in the New Criticism, Russian Formalism, classic structuralism, etc.]; finally, our time has discovered the last, up to now

---

3. Recent reader-oriented gospel exegeses, most of which center on the intratextual reader, include: Anderson, "Matthew," "Sermon," and "Triple Stories"; Bassler, "Parable"; Beavis, "Trial"; Burnett, "Characterization" and "Prolegomenon"; Culpepper, *Anatomy*, 203–228; Darr, *Characters*; Dewey, "Disciples"; Edwards, "Matthew's Portrait" and *Matthew's Story*; Eslinger, "Wooing"; Fowler, *Loaves, Reader*, "Reading Matthew," "Rhetoric," and "Thoughts"; Horton, "Pregnancy"; Keegan, *Interpreting*, 115–27; Kingsbury, "Reflections"; Kotzé, "John"; Petersen, "Reader" and "When Is?"; Phillips, "Hard Saying" and "History"; Plunkett, "Samaritan"; Praeder, "Parallelisms"; Resseguie, "Reader-Response"; Rhoads and Michie, *Mark*, 137–42; Scott, "Accounting," "Praise," "Mismanage," and *Word*, 45–56, 79–81; Staley, *First Kiss*; Stock, *Discipleship*, 205–8; Tannehill, "Disciples"; van Iersel, *Reading Mark*; and cf. Adam, "Sign," and Wittig, "Multiple Meanings." Finally, see Detweiler, ed., "Reader Response"; de Villiers, ed., "Reading"; Fisher and Jobling, eds., "Ethics"; and McKnight, ed., "The Reader."

sadly neglected component of literary communication—the reader ('decoder')" (Doložel, "Eco," 181).[4] Author, text, reader: with some reduction we can say that literary critics have been preoccupied with each of these moments in turn. And what of biblical criticism? It seems we are witnessing an age of the text in biblical studies, attested by the birth of such holistic methods as composition criticism, canonical criticism, and narrative criticism. Although a comparable age of the reader is hardly at hand, there is evidence of a mounting interest in readers, reminiscent of the situation in literary criticism of about a decade ago. One can tentatively schematize *literary* studies in terms of three successive "ages" of criticism (author, text, reader), but to schematize *biblical* studies thus would simply mislead. In gospel criticism, for instance, appreciably more than in non-biblical literary criticism, each new stage has tended less to displace the previous one than simply to be superimposed on it: reader-response criticism in gospel studies is largely an extension of narrative criticism, and both remain close to author-oriented redaction criticism. New Testament critics who have grappled with the issue of reading have tended to stay close to shore.

From "Why Did the Markan Author?" to "How Might a Markan Reader?"

In "The Disciples in Mark: The Function of a Narrative Role" (1977), Robert Tannehill inaugurated the appropriation of reader-response criticism for New Testament exegesis.[5] Significantly, "Disciples in Mark" was also a seminal study in narrative criticism. A preoccupation with the unfolding plot of a gospel marks a substantial overlap between reader-response and narrative criticism in the New Testament context. Narrative criticism frequently shades over into reader-response criticism. Indeed, reader-oriented gospel studies generally seem specialized extensions of narrative criticism.[6]

4. For a full exposition of "the circle of possible critical emphases," see Brooke Rose, "Diagram." (Felperin, *Beyond*, 202, comments: "Within the logic of the secular protestantism of which pluralism is the product, the interpretive authority once ascribed to the hieratic author has devolved upon the individual reader.")

5. In the same year Wittig's "Multiple Meanings" appeared, a semiotic analysis of textual polysemy with special reference to the parables, which, like Tannehill's "Disciples," drew on Iser's reception theory. We begin with Tannehill simply because his exegetical article better approximates the form reader-oriented work on the Gospels subsequently took than Wittig's theoretical article.

6. Keegan gets it the wrong way around when he defines narrative criticism as "a form of reader-response criticism used in the study of narratives, e.g., the Gospels and Acts" (*Interpreting*, 169; cf. 73–75, 92).

Tannehill investigates the narrative role of the disciples—how it is plotted and how the disciples are characterized—as it bears on the experience of reading Mark. To read Mark is to be acted on, and to be activated, by its narrative rhetoric. Rhetoric in Tannehill's sense denotes the author's standpoint on the characters and events of the story. "The rhetoric of the story also reflects, by anticipation, a dialogue between author and reader." That is, "the author has a view of his readers and anticipates how they will respond to his story. Therefore, not only the standpoint of the author but also the standpoint of the reader (in the view of the author) may find indirect expression in the story" (389–90). The reader is activated to different kinds of involvement with the story. As the plot develops expectations are aroused and are fulfilled or remain unfulfilled by what ensues. Other elements of the narrative can puzzle (Jesus' commands to silence, perhaps), eliciting further involvement in the hope of enlightenment. In addition "the reader may anticipate several clear but mutually exclusive outcomes," or the reader can be fairly certain of the outcome "but still . . . emotionally involved . . . as he anticipates the outcome for important persons in the narrative" (390–91)—the disciples in particular.

The surest guide to the author's evaluation of the disciples, for Tannehill, "is to follow the shifting relationship between Jesus and the disciples, noting where they are in concord and where they are not" (391). This in turn provides the key to the reader's evaluation of the disciples, as Mark anticipates it. "Assuming that the majority of the first readers of the Gospel were Christians, they would relate most easily and immediately to characters in the story who respond positively to Jesus" (392). The disciples are first presented positively in the gospel, strengthening the reader's natural tendency to identify with them. Then, gradually, the inadequacy of the disciples' response to Jesus is made apparent. They are presented in conflict with Jesus on important issues, and finally as disastrous failures. The tendency to identify is thus "countered by the necessity of negative evaluation. A tension develops between these two attitudes, with the reader caught in the middle" (394–95). Something of the initial identification remains, however, for there are similarities between the problems of the disciples and problems the first readers faced. The more clearly the reader sees his/her own situation in that of the disciples, "the more clearly the necessary rejection of the disciples' behaviour becomes a negation of one's past self " (395), a realignment of one's existing values and assumptions. In contrast to Theodore Weeden, Werner Kelber, and others who probed the Markan disciples' negative portrayal, Tannehill argues that there are indications in the text (the testimony of authoritative speakers in Mark 14:27–28 and 16:7) that the severed relationship between Jesus and the disciples can be restored.[7] But for Tannehill, the story does not end even there. It continues into the reader's own time. Mark 13 links the fate of the disciples to the situation of the reader in the continuing story. The time between the resurrection and the parousia will be one of trial and testimony, of endurance or apostasy. And so failure is a continuing possibility, for the reader no less than the disciples.[8]

My synopsis of "Disciples in Mark" has homed in on its reader-response side—its preoccupation with the role of reading that Mark elicits. However, it has a narrative critical side that is just as prominent—a preoccupation with the Markan disciples' story. Narrative criticism's fascination with story, as against theology or *Sitz im Leben,* tends to open a distance between it and redaction criticism. However, contrary to what one might expect, the additional preoccupation with the reader evident in "Disciples in Mark" (the appropriation of reading theory in addition to narratology) has the effect not of widening the distance even further, but of diminishing it instead.

Why should this be? One reason suggests itself in a surprising feature of historical-critical style: a fondness for throwaway remarks on the reader. While researching for *Loaves and Fishes* (1981), Robert Fowler was intrigued to find, scattered throughout the literature on Mark, a profusion of "random, fortuitous, and, for the most part, accurate observations on how the reader of the gospel experiences the text. In other words, countless interpreters with no special interest in the reader's experience of the literary work have casually made numerous perceptive and astute observations along these lines" (*Loaves,* 149). Selecting a work on Mark with no explicit investment in a literary approach—Howard Clark Kee's *Community of the New Age*—Fowler scanned it for references to Mark's reader and emerged with the following catena:

> This literary technique . . . serves here to occupy the attention of the reader . . . already disclosed to the reader. . . . Mark recalls for the

7. The intense interest in the Markan disciples during the 1970s, especially in the United States, catalyzed by Weeden, *Mark,* in which the disciples become stand-ins for opponents against whom the gospel is directed, is the context of Tannehill's article. For Tannehill, Mark's purpose is a more indirect one, demanding close, literary attention to the development of the disciples within the plot ("Disciples," 394).

8. The relationship between the Markan reader and the disciples is further traced, sporadically or peripherally, in Fowler, "Rhetoric," *Loaves,* and *Reader;* Kelber, *Mark's Story;* Magness, *Sense;* Petersen, "Reader"; Rhoads and Michie, *Mark;* Tannehill, "Narrative Christology"; van Iersel, *Reading Mark;* and Williams, *Gospel,* and it is traced persistently in Dewey, "Disciples," and Malbon, "Disciples/Crowds."

reader . . . Mark is addressing (or portrays Jesus as addressing) his
readers . . . only the "reader" who "understands" will perceive . . .
gives only tantalizing hints to his reader of the real meaning . . . he
puts the responsibility on the reader to provide the answer . . . using
the device of a rhetorical question, or one that only the discerning
reader is prepared to answer accurately . . . Mark intends the reader
to discern the hidden meaning of the incident behind the outward
phenomenon . . . the reader of Mark has already been alerted . . .
there is for the reader no surprise, therefore, when the plot to have
Jesus killed is actually put into action . . . Mark gives the reader the
impression . . . the rhetorical questions place the responsibility on the
reader to decide . . . the reader can see in them the signs of the gospel.
(150)

Kee is by no means untypical. Appeal to a hypothetical reader's experience
has long been a standard feature of exegetical style. This is hardly surprising when one considers that the biblical exegete himself or herself has
traditionally been engaged in reenacting a role of reading. In gospel studies, once the idea took hold that the evangelists were authors as well as
collectors, the scholar's task became more than ever one of reenacting the
roles scripted for original audiences, of assuming the roles of intended
readers (or hearers), attuned even to subtle nuances of the author's purpose. Clearly redaction criticism is not quite reader-response criticism (redaction critics are not simply reader-response critics who have yet to come
out of the closet). There are marked differences, but there are also strong
points of contact.

The conflation of redaction criticism and literary criticism is remarkably smooth in Tannehill's essay. Indeed, his study of the reader seems a
logical extension of Markan redaction criticism that builds on certain of
its premises. These premises are only of the most widely agreed sort; for
example, that the gospel was written for a largely Christian audience, and
that Mark 13 reliably indicates that this audience was suffering some sort
of persecution. Tannehill's strategy is to invert the type of question traditionally asked about the situation in which the gospel was produced,
readdressing it instead to the situation of reception. Implicitly, he replaces
the question about writing (What in the situation in which Mark wrote
might explain his handling of the disciples?) with a hitherto neglected
question about reading (How might a member of Mark's target audience,
reading the gospel for the first time, relate to the role of the disciples?).[9]

9. But can one meaningfully speak of the original readers of a gospel? Tannehill begs

What the two questions have in common—and this is the point of contact I wish to examine—is that both are historical. The question about the reader, as Tannehill implicitly poses it, is a question about the probable responses of a historical audience, an audience whose life situation, so far as it is reconstructible, is strongly determinative of its response to the aspect of the story being investigated (the role of the disciples in relation to Jesus). If this is a fair summation of Tannehill's strategy,[10] then the reader is the crucial grounding factor that keeps his study from becoming an "overly intrinsic" one—a study of the interaction of characters within the story-world, which might seem to bracket historical concerns. By consistently asking how the reader might have related to these interacting characters, Tannehill paradoxically manages to keep the link with author-oriented redaction criticism unbroken. The reader responds in the way that he or she does, in Tannehill's implicit view, because the author has structured the plot so as to elicit, or at least to encourage, just such a response. In ceding a manipulative role to the author, Tannehill tacitly assents to the primacy of the author's intention as an exegetical control. But to do so is also to automatically enter into dialogue with redaction criticism, for the question of what the author actually meant is also central for redaction criticism. In contrast to biblical structuralism, in its ascent at the time in which Tannehill was writing, with its bracketing of the historical author, Tannehill retains the umbilical link with traditional exegesis.

But if Tannehill's goal (to read Mark as its author intended) is essentially the same as a redaction critic's, why is his essay so clearly not a work of redaction criticism? Part of the answer is immediately apparent: instead of a preoccupation with the evangelist's theology here, we find a preoccupation with story instead (the interaction of Jesus and the disciples). But the added preoccupation, that of enacting the role of Mark's intended reader, while it does face Tannehill in the same general direction as redaction criticism, impels him at the same time along a very different meth-

---

the question by using the term *reader* throughout (as opposed to *hearer*). This same question might be put to reader-oriented exegesis of the Gospels generally.

10. It is based on statements such as: "a reader will identify most easily and immediately with characters who seem to share the reader's situation. Assuming that the majority of the first readers of the Gospel were Christians, they would relate most easily and immediately to characters in the story who respond positively to Jesus" ("Disciples," 392); "Identification [of the reader with the disciples] is encouraged later in the Gospel by the similarity between the problems faced by the disciples and the problems faced by the Gospel's first readers (and, perhaps, by later Christian readers also)" (395). Preoccupation with the original audience runs deeper here than in most of the other studies reviewed in this chapter.

odological path from any a redaction critic might take. The difference is
that whereas redaction critics commonly invoke the experiences of a hypothetical reader in passing (as in the examples from Kee above), reader-
oriented exegetes give us sustained *stories of reading*.

Virginal Gospel Readers and Jaded Gospel Critics

Story and reader, in that order, are the foci of "Disciples in Mark." But
the reader with whose responses Tannehill is preoccupied is never directly
described. As the article progresses, however, it becomes clear that this is
a reader who has little or no previous knowledge of the story:

> A story may arouse expectation of an event and then report the re-
> alization or nonrealization of our expectations. This not only em-
> phasizes through repetition (our attention is drawn to the event
> before it happens and again as it happens) but also involves the reader
> through his interest in the outcome of events. The reader may be
> involved in several different ways. There may be elements of the nar-
> rative which are puzzling, causing the reader to look forward to fur-
> ther enlightenment. The reason for Jesus' commands to silence may
> constitute such a puzzle in the first half of Mark. Or the reader may
> anticipate several clear but mutually exclusive outcomes. Or the reader
> may be fairly certain as to how the story will turn out but still be
> emotionally involved through fear or hope as he anticipates the out-
> come for important persons in the narrative. Jesus' announcements
> of his passion and his prediction of the disciples' behavior in 14:27–
> 31 leave little uncertainty, but they can awaken fearful anticipation.
> (390–91)

This "virginal" reader, however, who is exposed to the text for the first
time, is very different from the experienced reader with whom the redaction critic identifies. Gospel critics of most persuasions might feel a good
deal closer to the later Tannehill, no longer so enamored by the reader,
when he says of his 1986 book on Luke that it "represents part of what
might be said after reading a second, third, or fourth time. It is not
confined to what is happening when reading for the first time, with much
of the text still unknown" (*Narrative Unity*, 6). Traditionally, critical reading of the Bible has been built on a process of repetition—an exponential
process of refinement, potentially without end, to which the sequential,
cumulative impact of a first reading is largely irrelevant. In a first reading,
a verse or passage receives its meaning principally from everything that

has gone before (its anterior context). But in exegesis in the mode of redaction criticism, and more especially in the mode of composition criticism or of the narrative criticism represented by Tannehill's *Narrative Unity,* the exegete's overview of the total message of the biblical work becomes the primary control in interpreting any portion of it. The anterior context is secondary. To give a simple example, Luke 9:27, which reads, "But I tell you truly, there are some standing here who will not taste of death before they see the kingdom of God," is regularly "deeschatologized" by Lukan scholars, especially in light of the more overtly eschatological Markan parallel: "before they see the kingdom of God *come with power*" (Mark 9:1). But would not a first-time reader or hearer of Luke, especially one innocent of Mark, be more likely to interpret the phrase "kingdom of God" in Luke 9:27 as something initiated by the coming of the Son of Man, situated as it is immediately after "For whoever is ashamed of me and of my words, of him will the Son of man be ashamed *when he comes in his glory* and the glory of the Father and of the holy angels" (9:26)—and take the *lego de humin* that introduces 9:27 to be "*And* I tell you" rather than the more usual "*But* I tell you"? The deeschatologized reading generally wins out, however (some softened, "realized" eschatology is proposed)[11] because the evangelist's probable overall intention—hazarded from close attention to Acts too, with its low-profile eschatology—is regarded as the ultimate arbiter of local ambiguities. (The *validity* of a second, third, or fourth reading is not at issue here; the issue, rather, is that reader-response critics of the gospels claim an equal, complementary validity for their reconstructed "first readings." Witness James Resseguie: "Whereas most traditional holistic interpretations of texts neglect the sequential interpretations and effects upon the reader in favor of the final holistic interpretation, reader-response critics believe that the series of interpretations and effects which lead up to the final synthesis are also important and have value" ["Reader-Response," 317].)[12]

The role of reading that traditional commentators find written into the gospel text and that they attempt to reenact is one implying supreme familiarity with every detail of the text in advance. Contrast the typical practice of the narrative critic when he or she turns his or her attention to the role of reading implied, or anticipated, by the text. Richard Ed-

11. E.g., Conzelmann, *Theology,* 56; Ellis, "Eschatology," 32ff.; Schneider, *Lukas,* 1:213; and Marshall, *Luke,* 378. Also Tannehill, *Narrative Unity,* 223.

12. Fowler makes the same point at greater length in *Loaves,* 145–46. Cf. Staley, *First Kiss,* 33ff. (Fowler, Staley and Resseguie list between them six literary critical discussions of the issue of first vs. second readings.)

wards, for example, whose method in *Matthew's Story of Jesus* is substantially similar to that of Tannehill in "Disciples in Mark," is quite explicit: "I intend to examine the narrative from the point of view of a reader who begins at the beginning. . . . Since reading is a cumulative process that extends over a period of time, the sequence of information and its relation to earlier portions of the story will be my primary concern" (9).[13] As is the norm in biblical commentary, particularly of the popular kind, Edwards narrates his reading in a blow-by-blow present tense, the absence of the usual historical and theological digressions heightening the flow and suspense of the Matthean narrative. Edwards's narration slides repeatedly from a paraphrase of the action of the story, to a paraphrase of the narrator's action of telling it, to a paraphrase of the reader's action of receiving it. For example: "The Spirit, who has just alighted on Jesus, now leads him 'into the wilderness'—the place where John the Baptist preached (3:1). . . . The privileged position of the narrator is now quite obvious; he or she knows what takes place between Jesus and the devil. We are not told, however, what Jesus' attitude is or what his thoughts are, rather, the narrator only reports the dialogue. Thus the reader must judge the significance of the confrontation on the basis of the information already supplied by the narrator" (18). The heuristic construct of a first-time reader is strictly adhered to throughout. To give a further example, a few pages earlier we read: "The second phase in establishing the framework [of the story of Jesus] begins with a very vague time reference ('in those days') to introduce John the Baptist's preaching and baptizing (3:1). The reader will assume that it is the same time as that of the previous episode, and it is not until Matt. 3:13 that we realize that Jesus is now an adult" (15). More often than not, reader-response criticism in the New Testament context amounts to a reader-oriented narrative criticism. Edwards's method neatly illustrates this. Upon the usual paraphrase of the story characteristic of narrative criticism, a second story is superimposed. This is a story of reading,[14] in which the interpreter, approaching the evangelist's story as

13. Compare Staley's reader construct, which has knowledge only "of what has been read up to the given moment. It is thus encoded in the unidirectional, forward movement of the text, and as such, does not know what word comes next" (*First Kiss,* 35), and Magness, who keeps the following question foregrounded in his study of Mark's abrupt ending: "How would a first-time reader . . . have understood these closing verses?" (*Sense,* 123). Cf. Burnett, "Prolegomenon," 91–92; Fowler, "Who Is?," 19–20; and Resseguie, "Reader-Response," 317: "A primary critical move of reader-oriented critics and the strategy which distinguishes this method from traditional forms of biblical criticism is the *description of successive reading activities.*"

14. This expression is borrowed from Culler, who may have borrowed it in turn from de Man. See Culler, *On Deconstruction,* 64–83, and de Man, *Blindness,* 286–87.

if for the first time, narrates a tale of anticipations and reversals, of puzzles, enigmas, and the struggles to solve them, of beliefs and presuppositions challenged and overthrown. The reader is the hero or heroine of this story of reading and functions as a fictional character within it. His or her fresh, virginal responses to the text distinguish him or her from the jaded or voyeuristic critic who records them. Redaction criticism has no sustained, fleshed-out story of reading of this sort. There is no unfolding, suspenseful, moment-by-moment side to the redaction critic's reading, as we saw. His or her assumed role in regard to the text is one of intimate familiarity—that of a lifelong spouse rather than a virgin groom or bride.

The Exegete as Hero or Heroine in a Story of Reading

[Q]uite simply, this reading will be filmed in slow motion.
—Roland Barthes, "Textual Analysis of a Tale"

Do redaction critics, and others for whom the reconstructed first-century context is the primary exegetical one, need to sit up and take notice of these critical first readings? Before tackling this question it would help to have a clearer idea of the workings and potential findings of such a reading. Jouette Bassler's "Parable of the Loaves" (1986) provides an elegant example.[15] The strict successive approach enables Bassler to tell a great story of reading. The text with which Mark's implied reader must wrestle, especially from chapter 6 on, is replete with entangling impediments to coherence. For one thing, the comment about the loaves in 6:52 ("they did not understand about the loaves, but their hearts were hardened") seems to have little connection with the sea-walking episode that precedes it. "Its presence is jarring, the flow of the narrative is blocked, and the reader is provoked into considering possible modes of connection yet is unable to resolve the problem with the information provided by the text." However, the "importance of establishing this connection is emphasized in chapter 8 [vv. 14–21], where the disciples (again at sea) are again chastised for their lack of understanding about the loaves and for their hardened hearts" (163). Examining the substance of Jesus' rebuke, Bassler decides that the reader is now more than ever in the dark—but this is integral to the gospel's intended effect on the reader. "Not enough information has been supplied in the narrative up to this point to clarify the

---

15. This article is untypical of Bassler's general output. Indeed, with the exception of Fowler, none of the New Testament critics discussed here have had a long or sustained involvement with reader-response criticism.

confusion and the reader is led, at a crucial point in the narrative, to *the same internal disposition that the disciples possess in the narrative: misunderstanding and confusion*" (165). Earlier in the gospel the disciples' positive response to Jesus encouraged the reader to identify with them. "Now the reader would like to dissociate from the disciples, but the gaps in the text at this point render this impossible. Thus the identification with the disciples initially undertaken quite willingly by the reader, continues—but now unwillingly—insofar as the reader shares their condemning lack of understanding" (165–66). Then comes the key section, 8:22–10:52, in which Jesus interprets his commission in terms of his passion and defines discipleship in the same light. It is not a "disinterested reader" who moves into this section, "but one whose attention to and involvement in the text have been heightened by the narrative gaps" (167). But here, even as the disciples' lack of understanding intensifies, each repetition of Jesus' passion prediction being followed by a clear indication of the disciples' inability to comprehend, light finally begins to dawn for the reader. Acquiring the understanding so elusive to the disciples, he or she finally begins to draw away from them.

> Thus when, at the end of this section, blind Bartimaeus receives his sight (10:46–52), the reader has a new figure with whom to identify. It has always been puzzling that this unit would close with a miracle clearly symbolizing the achievement of insight, since the disciples appear as blind as ever. Yet if the text has "worked," the disciples and the reader are no longer one. The disciples continue their blind way through the narrative, but the newly enlightened reader can now identify with the newly sighted Bartimaeus and has, like him, the potential of following Jesus. (167)

And what of the loaves? Though the reader has achieved a degree of separation from the still-befuddled disciples, the significance of the loaves remains an enigma. But this also is strategic and keeps the reader attuned to the text until chapter 14, "where the final piece of the puzzle falls into place." With

> the blessing, breaking, and distributing of the eucharistic bread, which is Jesus' body, the reader's quest for consistency is finally rewarded. For these words recall the language of the feeding miracles where the loaves were also blessed, broken, and distributed. Thus the reader can now recognize what was opaque at that point in the narrative: that on some inchoate level the loaves referred to Jesus' broken

body on the cross. But this insight is clear only in retrospect. And on further retrospection it also becomes clear that the discussion of the passion in chapters 8–10 *did* address the question of the loaves, and the understanding that the reader reached in those chapters was not only understanding of the significance of Jesus' suffering but also, ultimately, insight into the enigma of these loaves. (168)

The more traditional, eucharistic reading of the feeding miracles tacitly posits a reader able to recognize overtones that put her or him in an immediate position of superiority to the disciples. Such a reading, for Bassler, fails to honor "the time flow of the reading process and the direction of the narrative." The implied reader, however, shares the disciples lack of understanding initially, gradually achieves understanding, and only in chapter 14 "with the 'aha!' of discovery" can make the final connection. "The gradual release of information thus keeps the reader involved over an extended portion of the narrative, and the impact of the final connection is heightened by the prolongation of the tension under which the reader has awaited some resolution" (169).

In a work of narrative commentary, such as Tannehill's *Narrative Unity of Luke-Acts,* the critic's own text takes on strong narrative characteristics as he or she paraphrases and augments the gospel story, emphasizing the forward movement and interconnectedness of the plot, and amplifying these qualities where they seem in short supply. (This style of commentary we dubbed postcritical targum.) The protagonist of the gospel, Jesus, naturally retains the leading role in the narrative commentator's retelling. It remains preeminently a story of Jesus. In the stories of reading, however, told by reader-oriented gospel critics, the reader emerges as the hero or heroine whose actions and progress are central. Jesus generally plays the supporting role, as the one whose enigmatic words and deeds provide the complicating factors that fuel the plot of the story of reading. As a perusal of studies such as Bassler's suggests,[16] reader-oriented readings of gospel texts tend to result in critical texts that bear the same striking degree of *story-likeness* as narrative commentaries. Like the latter, the reader-oriented critical texts are fully plotted texts, stocked with interacting characters (Jesus, the reader, the disciples, etc.). These texts mime the narrativity of the works being analyzed. The reader-oriented text thus evokes the ancient genre of targum, just as did the narrative commentary:

---

16. More intricate than Bassler's by far, though less amenable to summary, is the remarkable story of reading told by Staley, *First Kiss,* 96–116. Fowler, *Reader* (forthcoming), promises to be equally elaborate.

the gospel is similarly rendered by means of narrative paraphrase and augmentation. But in this case, the narrative that augments the gospel text is that of a hypothetical reader reading. Every obscurity in the gospel story with which an exegete has ever had to wrestle, every enigma or lacuna, can become a plot-engendering complication in a story of reading. The exegete's workaday attempts to make sense of a difficult text become the subject matter for a script in which a hypothetical reader, fresh to the text and capable of being surprised by it (unlike the jaded critic), is let loose in an adventure of reading. The exegete's workaday frustrations are narrativized in this script in the form of suspenseful setbacks and befuddlements encountered by the reader on her or his journey. And the exegete's arrival at a satisfactory solution to the set of problems is allegorized as the happy ending to the story in which the reader finds enlightenment at last.

But What if the "Readers" Were Listening?

The swerve to the reader has broken new paths for exegesis. Classicist George Kennedy has argued in a different context that the rhetorical qualities evident in our New Testament texts "were originally intended to have an impact on first hearing" (*Rhetorical Criticism*, 6). Given passages are thus best situated "in contrast to what has gone before, especially what has immediately gone before" (5). The readings of Bassler, Tannehill, and Edwards that we discussed are acutely attuned to the cumulative rhetorical thrust of gospel narrative.

The reader-response approach is not without its problems. "[W]hen I speak about the reader," writes Edwards, "I am not attempting to describe a real person (of the first, third, tenth, or twentieth century) but the person posited *by the text* as the reader" (*Matthew's Story*, 10).[17] But is the person posited by a gospel text really a reader? In speaking thus do we not transfer the psychocultural assumptions of a typographic (i.e., print-centered) culture back into the ancient oral and scribal context? New Testament scholars attuned to recent advances in the study of orality-literacy contrasts in various fields of the humanities and social sciences[18] fault historical criticism and reader-response criticism alike for such anomalies:

Contemporary biblical scholarship has consistently assumed that the

17. Others echo this assertion, e.g., Bassler, "Parable," 172; Fowler, *Loaves*, 140–41; Rhoads and Michie, *Mark*, 137; and cf. Petersen, "Reader," 40ff.
18. See Foley, *Oral*, for a multidisciplinary bibliography.

relationship of the original audience of the biblical literature was a relationship of readers to texts. Discussions about "the reader" and "the text" abound in 20th century historical critical exegesis. While there are often some qualifications of this paradigm with phrases such as "readers or hearers" and "audience," the general assumption is that biblical books such as the Gospel of Mark were read as documents by a single reader who read the document in silence. Thus, literary criticism of biblical texts has uncritically appropriated the paradigms of works such as Wolfgang Iser's *The Implied Reader* with the apparent assumption that a modern and an ancient reader's relationship to the text is the same. The question is then: what did Mark assume about the manner in which his written Gospel would be experienced? Did Mark write a text that he assumed would be read in public or in private, aloud or in silence? (Boomershine, "Peter's Denial," 51–52)[19]

"Public and aloud" seems the correct reply. With the help of Moses Hadas's *Ancilla to Classical Reading*, Boomershine is able to line up convincing evidence that throughout ancient history, most readings were public readings. Even in private, reading was normally done aloud, and there are no signs of anything that could be construed as silent reading in the biblical tradition. "Therefore, the answer to the question of Mark's intended medium is that Mark would have assumed that his Gospel would be read aloud, either from a manuscript or from memory, probably in a public reading" ("Peter's Denial," 53–54).[20]

This announcement would raise few eyebrows within the New Testament guild. Where the guild has missed out, however, in the view of the orality-literacy specialists, is in failing to realize that the aural appropriation of a text (in a public reading, for example) fosters a markedly different way of conceptualizing it than the predominantly visual appropriation of a private, silent reading.[21] The utter regularity, completedness, and compactness of the modern printed text, its portability and perfect reduplicability, all encourage its conceptualization as object, artifact, static

19. Cf. Kelber, "Hermeneutics," 98–99, and "Narrative," 124, and Ong, *Orality,* 171.
20. Cf. Kelber, *Written Gospel,* 90, 127, 217–18, and Beavis, "Trial," 593.
21. Kelber, *The Oral and the Written Gospel,* led the way in the full-scale appropriation of orality-literary studies for New Testament work (Güttgemanns, *Candid Questions,* 193–215, and Ong had already broken the path). Silberman, ed., "Orality," sifts and extends Kelber's project. In addition there have been assessments of gospel, and general biblical, scholarship by secular orality-literacy specialists, e.g., Graham, *Written Word,* 45–66, 117–54; Lord, "Gospels"; and Ong, "Gospel," *"Maranatha," Presence,* 179–91, 273–77, "Psychodynamics," and "Mark." For a more challenging assessment, see Boomershine, "Megatrends."

spatial form (cf. Ong, *Orality,* 122, 125–27). This is yet more true of the biblical text with its numbered chapters and verses. These late-appended numbers achieved their apotheosis in the print culture; enveloping the text-object in a handy reference grid, they foster the precision, quantification, and descriptivism of a scientific scholarly method. With the synopsis, the concordance, the textual apparatus, and the lexicon they become the indispensable "tools" of the exegete (a tool being something one uses on an object). A rigorous comparative method like redaction criticism would be inconceivable without this equally rigorous reification of the text. Narrative criticism, which tends to conceive of the text in terms of wholeness, the integration of parts, well-formedness (all object-related terms and spatial metaphors), is no less the unwitting purveyor of print-derived habits of thought.

Precise comparative and analytic methods, redaction criticism in particular, require that the words of the text be present all at once. But what if these texts were originally read aloud? Spoken words "are events, not things: they are never present all at once but occur seriatim, syllable-after-syllable" (Ong, "Mark," 22; cf. Ong, *Orality,* 31–32). Clearly, in attempting to play out the roles of the audiences envisioned by the evangelists, exegetes have failed to give due weight to the fact that these audiences were listeners first and foremost. At first blush, reader-response critics of the Gospels would seem to emerge with more egg on their faces than anyone else. After all, to call the evangelist's intended listening audience "the reader" and then produce minute analyses of a reading that in all probability never occurred (at least not in the modern sense) would seem the ultimate waste of time.

Paradoxically, the situation may be the reverse. It may well be that the reader-response exegetes inadvertently do justice to the oral-aural factor in a way that redaction critics and narrative critics do not. We noted earlier how Tannehill distances himself in the *Narrative Unity of Luke-Acts* from reader-response criticism's attempts (and implicitly his own earlier attempts) "to record the reading process with its myriad temporary interpretations, anticipations, and adjustments." He steps back from the text instead with "a second, third, or fourth" reading in order to bring into focus those features that make it a "well-formed narrative." The word *form* applied to a text is a spatial metaphor; biblical scholars, nurtured in a hypervisual print-culture, tend to conceive of the text in spatial terms. Spoken words are events, however, not things. They exist not in space but in time, not all at once but in sequence, and resist consolidation as objects. "Sound exists only when it is going out of existence. It is not simply perishable but essentially evanescent. . . . When I pronounce the word 'permanence,' by the time I get to the '-nence,' the 'perma-' is gone, and has to be gone" (Ong, *Orality,* 32; cf. Kelber, "Hermeneutics," 99). If the Gospels were originally designed to be read aloud and in public (if they are products of a culture with a heavy oral residue), historical exegetes may need to find a way to reduce their print-based proclivity to reify texts maximally (to overcome their hypervisual bias) in order to better approximate this originary oral-aural experience. Reader-oriented critics of the Gospels inadvertently discovered a way to do just that when they began to harness the reception theory of Wolfgang Iser.[22] It is with the reader (the private, silent variety) that Iser is preoccupied, and not with the hearer, but a reader whose experience of the text is a radically temporal one. Bassler sums up Iser's method, preparatory to using it on Mark:

> Iser works with the concept of the "implied reader," the reader implied by the text itself with its network of response-inviting structures, who embodies all the presuppositions laid down by the text, but only these presuppositions, and who is cognizant of all the information supplied by the text, but only this information and only in the sequence laid down by the text. *Thus Iser's implied reader is bound to the time flow of the narrative.* At any given point in the narrative this reader can certainly look back and review past developments, but future developments can only be *anticipated,* and this anticipation may be confirmed or disconfirmed by the subsequent narrative. Through this "reader," admittedly an artificial construct, Iser seeks to uncover what one could call the natural force of the text. ("Parable," 160, emphasis added)[23]

The left-to-right reception of the verbal string, which figures so prominently in Iser's phenomenology of reading, however, has clear affinities with the syllable-by-syllable experience of hearing a text read, an experience

22. Gospel readings that take their lead in significant ways from Iser include: Anderson, "Sermon" and "Triple Stories"; Bassler, "Parable"; Edwards, "Matthew's Portrait" and *Matthew's Story*; Keegan, *Interpreting,* 115–27; Kotzé, "John"; Petersen, "When Is?"; Plunkett, "Samaritan"; Resseguie, "Reader-Response"; Scott, "Accounting," "Mismanage," "Praise," and *Word,* 45–56; Tannehill, "Disciples"; and cf. Wittig, "Multiple Meanings."

23. Fowler's exegeses (e.g., *Loaves, Reader,* "Rhetoric"), while they range well beyond Iser, nevertheless employ the same time-bound reading method. So too, e.g., Burnett, "Prolegomenon," and Staley, *First Kiss.* Iser's principal works are *The Implied Reader* and *The Act of Reading.* Further on the time axis in his theory, see *Act,* 148–50. For the best short introduction to his overall approach, see his "Interaction," an abridged version of *Act.* The early work of Fish (e.g., *Surprised*; *Text,* 21–67) also deals with the temporality of reading and has also had an impact on audience-oriented gospel work.

that makes all the difference for one's conceptualization of the text. The literary phenomenologists' pronouncements on reading would be most of all true for the experience of hearing a text read in an oral or residually oral culture, lacking the concepts or presuppositions that depend on a printed text: "The 'form' of the text is a belated and recollective construction; it does not exist. Readers do not encounter form. The flow of words, the temporal being of the text, requires from the reader active involvement and interested exploration. Thus *the text is an event*."[24] Compare the following statement by Werner Kelber: "We treat words primarily as records in need of interpretation, neglecting all too often a rather different hermeneutic, deeply rooted in biblical language that proclaims words as an act inviting participation" (*Written Gospel*, xvi). In reconceptualizing the gospel text as event rather than as object, reader-oriented exegetes have latched onto something crucial. Even as they move away from traditional historical criticism, they take a significant if inadvertent step on behalf of the historical exegesis of the Gospels. They show us a time-bound exegetical method that is more adequate to the oral-aural situations that would have formed the original noetic and hermeneutic horizon of the Gospels.[25]

The Reader at the Last Supper

Reader-oriented critics of the Gospels, by and large, have yet to connect explicitly with orality-literacy concerns. Robert Fowler has been virtually unique in this regard:

> In arguing for a temporal model of reading, rather than a spatial one, we are actually returning to an understanding of language that has affinities with the language of oral culture. The written word is spatial; it constitutes a literate/visual mode of consciousness. The spoken word, however, is temporal; it constitutes an oral/aural mode of consciousness. Since the world of orality lingers and is still so prominent

24. Leitch, *Deconstructive Criticism*, 69–80, paraphrasing the Heideggerian phenomenology of Spanos (see, most recently, Spanos, *Repetitions*). Cf. de Man's observations on form, likewise indebted to Heidegger, noted in chapter 5.

25. Despite the advent of the written gospel, the noetic economy of early Christianity would have remained essentially oral—so Kelber, *Written Gospel*, 17, echoing the widespread agreement among orality-literacy specialists that hearing-dominance continued to prevail even in literate cultures in the manuscript or codex stages. It took print to finally replace "the lingering hearing-dominance in the world of thought and expression with the sight-dominance which had its beginnings with writing but could not flourish with the support of writing alone" (Ong, *Orality*, 121).

in the biblical texts . . . the temporal model of reading employed by reader-response critics is well-suited to the study of biblical narrative. ("Who Is?," 20–21)

Fowler was one of the first New Testament scholars to become attuned to the orality-literacy debate as well as to the debate on the reader, hence his apperception of the link-up.[26] In general, however, reader-oriented gospel studies have yet to exploit this connection. Iser and the other theoreticians from whom they draw have had nothing to say on oral-aural matters, and New Testament scholars who do take orality-literacy contrasts seriously (a very small clan indeed) tend to entertain a limited perception of reader-response criticism as being merely another child of modern reading habits.[27]

One would expect an interpretation of a gospel attuned to the temporality of reading to diverge occasionally, if not frequently, from scholarly consensuses derived by making the entire work (all the words "present together") the dominant context for interpreting any part of it. An inductive successive approach encourages an eschatological reading of Luke 9:27 in place of the usual deeschatologized one. Bassler's provocative rereading of the Markan miracles of the loaves provides a much more intricate example of such divergence. A third instance of a revisionary reader-oriented interpretation, which interestingly parallels Bassler's reading, is provided by Robert Fowler.

In his 1978 dissertation, *Loaves and Fishes*, Fowler attempted to swim "against the prevailing current of interpretation regarding the relationship of the feeding stories [Mark 6:30–44; 8:1–10] and the Last Supper narrative. It is widely accepted that the feeding stories are to be read in the light of the Last Supper narrative and the familiar Christian practice of the Eucharist" (138). However, it seemed to Fowler that

> this attitude is shaped more by the intense scholarly interest in the origin of the Christian Eucharist than by a careful, unprejudiced examination of all the meals in Mark. . . . [T]he Last Supper is in fact

26. But for the bare statement just quoted, this perception barely figures in "Who Is?" It figures more prominently, however, in Fowler, *Reader*. Audience and orality factors also combine to an extent in Dewey, "Tapestry," and "Oral Methods."

27. Staley is a case in point. His reader-oriented *First Kiss* deals insightfully with the relevance of orality-literacy studies for biblical studies (1–5, 119–21), but overlooks the connection between reader-response criticism's time-centeredness and the temporality of the spoken word. For him (as for Boomershine) reader-response criticism is one other "critical approach that arose from our internalization of writing and print mediums" (*First Kiss,* 120, 4).

one of many meals in the gospel. The earlier meals prepare for and lead up to this one last meal, making it crucial not to overlook or minimalize the significance of these earlier meals. Often the verbal similarities between 6:41, 8:6, and 14:22 are noted and used to justify the discovery of "eucharistic" overtones in the two feeding stories. Regrettably, to argue in this fashion is to stand the gospel on its head. *As the author has structured his work, Jesus' last meal with his disciples in Mark 14 presupposes the earlier feeding stories and not vice versa.* Here we are making a conscious decision to adhere to the internal chronology of the author's story, according to which the last meal is preceded by, and read in the light of, the previous meals in Mark. (134–35)

And the consequences of this decision? Having already noted how prominent direct conflict between Jesus and the disciples is in the feeding stories and in related material (e.g., 8:13–21), Fowler argues that by the time we arrive at the Passover meal in Mark 14 in a strictly consecutive reading,

the issue foremost in our minds will be the ongoing dinner table conflict between Jesus and the Twelve and not the traditional scholarly questions of the historical origin of the story, the *ipsissima vox* of Jesus, and the variance of traditions in Mark 14:22–25, Luke 22:15–20, and I Cor. 11:23–26. These may be legitimate scholarly concerns, but they are not Mark's concerns. When we take care to read the account of the last meal of Jesus and his disciples in light of the previous meals in Mark, we are struck by the recurrence of the dominant theme of discipleship failure in this account. To be sure, we are by now accustomed to portrayals of the disciples' ineptness and misunderstanding at the dinner table, but here [14:18, 20, 27–31] their failure assumes shocking proportions. (135)

Arguing that Mark's presentation of the Last Supper is dominated by the theme of discipleship failure, and that this theme must be given its due weight in the plot, Fowler is skeptical that the Last Supper in Mark is intended to represent "the institution of the Christian eucharist" (147). (By comparison, Bassler's reading of the Last Supper was decidedly more "eucharistic" ["Parable," 168, quoted above]. The divergence of Fowler and Bassler on Mark's Last Supper, not only from traditional interpretations but from each other, suggests—if one could have had any doubts— that the reader-oriented approach is no more apt to produce interpretive agreement than the traditional one.)

What the Reader Knew

Loaves and Fishes antedates Fowler's interest in the orality-literacy issue. He does not claim to be attempting a critical approximation of the preprint psychodynamics of hearing Mark read in sequence, and perhaps in its entirety, though such a claim might not be altogether unwarranted. His reading, however, does draw our attention to a problem in the consecutive, retrospective-prospective method. Given the traditional nature of much of the gospel material, and the widespread scholarly agreement that the authors of Mark and Luke-Acts, and probably those of John and Matthew, would have envisioned mainly Christian audiences, the construct of a first-time hearer/reader unfamiliar with the unfolding story, on which the consecutive method depends, might seem somewhat inept.[28] Reader-oriented gospel critics, by and large, have been slow to face up to this problem. Fowler, confronted head-on with the unmistakably traditional Last Supper material, can hardly evade it. His solution is instructive:

> We share with the advocates of the eucharistic interpretation [of the feeding stories of Mark 6 and 8] their enthusiasm for considering how a reader perceives the feeding stories in Mark, but whereas their "reader" is distinguished by knowledge extrinsic to the text—knowledge of eucharistic traditions—we prefer to examine how a reader operating with the intrinsic knowledge provided by the text itself would read the feeding stories. Far greater authority must be accorded the text itself to inform, control and mold its reader. We prefer to allow the text to educate and guide its own reader, rather than insisting on inventing a hypothetical reader characterized primarily by knowledge and experience external to the text. To see how the text molds its own reader involves seeking out those features of the text that shape the reading experience of *every* perceptive reader, ancient or modern. This approach restores to the text its rightful measure of autonomy. The fundamental datum imposed on us by the text of Mark with regard to the feeding stories and the Last Supper is, we repeat, the priority of the feeding stories over the Last Supper. (*Loaves*, 140–41)

28. Beavis, "Trial," 595, poses the problem differently. Proper attention to the Greco-Roman context "would tend to invalidate the idea that a Gospel should be interpreted in a 'first reading,' because no first-century lector would have read a Gospel only once before reading it publicly: he or she would have prepared and even memorized the copy." The question which Beavis does not address, however, is whether the gospel lector's audience might have had a detailed foreknowledge of the story.

The formalist critic in Fowler thus triumphs over the historical critic in him. To allow the text "its rightful measure of autonomy" means attending to the unfolding plot first and foremost, making that the primary control on interpretation, and giving extrinsic factors (e.g., "knowledge of eucharistic traditions") a decidedly secondary place. Bassler, forced to come to grips with same problem, opts independently for a similar solution: "Only the informed reader has the background to recognize the eucharistic language [in the feeding miracles of Mark 6 and 8], for it has not yet been presented as such in the gospel (see 14:22–23). Only the informed or ideal reader has the information required to penetrate the allegorical details that enhance this interpretation. And only the historical reader would be caught up in the particular set of circumstances that could allow the polemics of the christological debate to be understood" ("Parable," 162). The implied reader, however, "who embodies all the presuppositions laid down by the text, but only these presuppositions, and who is cognizant of all the information supplied by the text, but only this information and only in the sequence laid down by the text" (160), will strive to make sense of the feeding miracles by contextualizing them in relation to the developing plot. These remarks, like those of Fowler, bespeak that bias for intrinsic analysis that sets the reader-response critic with the narrative critic against the historical critic and that makes the historical critic squirm.[29]

These comments of Fowler and Bassler also serve to highlight another paradoxical feature of the time-bound approach. The strict sequential reading has an unrecognized illustrative value for historical exegesis. This radically temporal appraisal of the unfolding story is the best analogue available to the modern exegete of the psychodynamics of the oral-aural encounter that would have constituted the original noetic horizon in which the Gospels were written and received. The paradox is that to be

---

29. Eslinger, "Wooing," 181 n. 16, feels less compelled to cleanly distinguish the intratextual reader of the Fourth Gospel from the historical reader, and he discovers a historical critic who might squirm less than most at his "experiment of following . . . a [first-time] reader through the Gospel": "If one might allow . . . that the gospel of John was not written with a specifically Christian audience in mind, [the] first-time reader would not be such an implausible intended audience. . . . Nevertheless, it is possible for even a jaded Christian reader . . . to follow the logic of such a reading and to receive a similar impress from it. . . . Moreover, Wayne A. Meeks has gone so far as to suggest that even educated readers of the Johannine community might be taken in by the ambiguities, ironies, and other occasions for reader response. '*The reader cannot understand any part of the Fourth Gospel until he understands the whole.* Thus the reader has an experience rather like that of the dialogue partners of Jesus.' [E.'s emphasis] . . . Regardless of the reader's background, says Meeks, it is designed to involve the reader in sharing some of the same confusions and misunderstandings as the characters within it" (citing Meeks, "Heaven," 161–62).

rigorously temporal and aural, and hence most illuminative of the original reception processes, the consecutive reading should be fully intrinsic also; that is, it should bracket the extrinsic historical question of what the encoded listener would be likely to know besides the information consecutively provided by the text. The retrospective-prospective approach would be at its best, from a historian's standpoint, in suggesting what it might have been like to experience a gospel as *heard event* rather than as printed object. And the event-character of a gospel is best approximated when the text is given full leeway to build its reader dynamically in the time-flow of the reading process, the reader's interaction with the characters at any given moment being defined principally in terms of what has gone before in the story and what he or she anticipates may follow. The heuristic potential of the consecutive reading for historical exegesis depends on the extent to which it can successfully simulate this backward-hearkening/ forward-hearkening process. Which is not to say that the temporal model can exhaust the experience of gospel reception which the original audiences might have had, or which the Gospels' authors might have anticipated. Another aspect of this reception would have entailed a competence brought to the hearing (a knowledge of eucharistic traditions and much more), and a preacquaintance with the broad lines of the story and its ending. This aspect is no doubt better accounted for by traditional exegetical methods, in which strict sequentiality plays little part.

Reader-response exegesis is not invariably linear. Alan Culpepper has used a nonconsecutive style of reader-oriented criticism in an attempt to clarify the competence assumed of the Johannine reader. In the final chapter of *Anatomy of the Fourth Gospel,* Culpepper revisits the problem of the gospel's intended audience with the *narratee,* the narrator's addressee specifically as defined by the text. For Culpepper the vital question is, What does the narratee know or not know? In contrast to the strict sequential approach, Culpepper's approach is topical and analytic. He analyzes the narratee's knowledge in five areas, persons, places, languages, Judaism, and events, finding that "a remarkably coherent and consistent picture of the intended reader emerges from the narrator's comments," one familiar with all the major characters in the story, with the exception of the Beloved Disciple, but unfamiliar with most of its specific locations. Correspondingly, the readers know Greek but not Hebrew or Aramaic, use the Roman rather than the Jewish system for reckoning the hours of the day, have some familiarity with the Old Testament, but little with the practices of Jewish ritual purity, and so on. "In sum, it appears that the intended readers are not Jewish, but their prior knowledge of many parts of the gospel story shows that the intended audience is either Christian or at least is familiar with the gospel story" (224).

But Culpepper's findings are more nuanced than this. Earlier he noted that the discourses uttered by Jesus in the context of Jewish festivals can be grasped in their full significance only by readers who are themselves familiar with the festivals, while the narrator's introductions to the festivals (e.g., 2:13; 6:4; 7:2; 11:55) presume little or no such knowledge. In a fully intrinsic analysis of the kind proposed by Gerald Prince, the narratologist from whom Culpepper is drawing,[30] the narratee would begin to come apart as a coherent construct. What of the Johannine narratee? It is, of course, a group narratee (see 20:31) (cf. Prince, *Narratology*, 23–24). But is it one group or several? The inconsistency regarding the festivals is the main one encountered by Culpepper, and its significance need not be overplayed. Nevertheless, it illustrates the type of difficulty, occasioned by the complex redactional history of the material, that one might expect to run into in an intrinsic analysis of a gospel's audience. And when that happens, one can exercise one of two options: (1) stick with the intrinsic analysis and conclude that the audience-in-the-text is so rift with contradictions as to render the concept unusable,[31] or (2) appeal to a source hypothesis to decide which indicators of the audience should count as evidence in the analysis and which indicators should not. In contrast to Fowler in *Loaves and Fishes*, the historical critic in Culpepper triumphs over the formalist critic in this moment of crisis, and he opts for the source hypothesis. He deals with the inconsistency regarding the festivals by speculating that "by the time the composition of the Fourth Gospel was completed a broader readership was envisioned than was originally intended. The later readership included gentile Christians who knew little about Judaism" (225).

Culpepper marches to a slightly different drum in this study than to that generally animating recent reader-attuned work on the Gospels. He is not simply more directly preoccupied with the original audience's historical situation.[32] Rather, relative to most of the other examples listed earlier, he is a good deal less preoccupied with the reader's consecutive responses to the plot, that is, with fashioning a sustained story of reading. (Staley maintains, "Because Culpepper concentrates so much upon the

30. See Prince, "Introduction," and cf. Piwowarcyzk, "Narratee," and Prince, "Narratee Revisited."

31. This is my inclination; see my "Homiletics," 80–90.

32. As is, e.g., Beavis, "Trial," or (to a lesser degree) Tannehill, "Disciples," and Petersen, "Reader," 45ff.

'anatomy' of the Fourth Gospel, one rarely sees the 'physiology' of the narrative—that is, its temporal aspect—and how that forms and transforms the implied reader" [*First Kiss,* 15]). In assessing whether reader-response criticism has any relevance for the historical investigation of the Gospels (in posing some of the questions a more traditional critic might have posed), the more usual, sequential style of reader-exegesis has been kept to the fore. From a historian's standpoint, the temporalized model characteristic of reader-exegesis must be regarded an insufficient and distorting one. The tradition-attuned hearers/readers that the gospel texts presuppose surely know more than the reader-oriented exegetes (Culpepper and Staley being the main exceptions)[33] give them credit for. If so, then the virgin reader is an anachronistic construct for gospel research. But the situation is actually a more unhappy one. Gospel historians risk worse anachronisms if they fail to assimilate the lessons of orality-literacy research, thriving in disciplines with less at stake in the distinctions it poses than theirs. Typographic exegetical models seem to sabotage historical exegesis. That we occupy a different world from that of first-century Christianity is a truism. But the orality-literacy factor persuades us that this is not the whole truth: we occupy not just a different world, but a different galaxy as well—"the Gutenberg galaxy," to recycle McLuhan's phrase. Scholarly approximation of the original audiences' reception of the biblical texts thus assumes an aspect of hitherto unsuspected crudity. Since Gutenberg we have exchanged a primal sea for dry land, as it were, and now our water-breathing is confined to mime. Thus contextualized, the consecutive mode of exegesis, which seeks to immerse itself in the time-flow of the text, offers at least some corrective to our print-shaped, sight-dominant conception the biblical texts—that is, as quiescent, immobile objects to be dismantled or quantified.

The Unfeeling Reader

Although it has helped obliquely to draw our attention to a concealed pocket of modernity within the historical exegetical methods, the reader-oriented style of exegesis itself conceals a predisposition that is characteristically modern. Gospel reader-critics need to attend to certain objections that have been leveled against reader-response criticism in the nonbiblical sphere. For the rhetoricians of antiquity and the Renaissance—precursors

33. Staley follows Culpepper in noting that the Johannine narratee has a degree of prior knowledge concerning certain events in the life of Jesus and certain characters in the story (*First Kiss,* 44–45).

of reader-response theory—a literary work is designed to affect its readers, to move and sway them. Thus, classical commentators—for example, Plato, Aristotle, Horace, and Longinus—"all discuss literature in terms of its effects upon an audience" (Tompkins, "History," 202). However, there is a crucial difference in approach between the classical and contemporary critics of response. The experiences that modern audience-oriented critics ascribe to their hypothetical readers are, in contrast to their ancient or Renaissance counterparts, "generally *cognitive* rather than *affective*: not feeling shivers along the spine, weeping in sympathy, or being transported with awe, but having one's expectations proved false, struggling with an irresolvable ambiguity, or questioning the assumptions upon which one had relied."[34] The reader constructs that reader-response critics of the Gospels employ differ from each other in various ways. None of them shivers or weeps, however. Their experience of the text is an ineluctably cerebral one. Identification with story participants, potentially the most affective sphere of reader involvement, is typically framed in epistemic terms. Here are some examples:

> Although the implied reader [of the fourth gospel] has been encoded with a higher degree of knowledge than any character in the story, save Jesus, the implied author at various times deflates the implied reader's ego by forcing him to erroneous conclusions regarding the story. Yet the implied reader is learning from his hasty judgements, for from the various groups of people in whose company he is placed, it is obvious that he is moving onward and upward. He has moved from the level of making the same errors as the Pharisees, to a level where he makes the same errors as "the brothers of Jesus." From there he has progressed to the level of making the same errors as the disciples. (Staley, *First Kiss,* 107)

> The reader of [Matthew's] eschatological discourse does not have everything revealed to him or her. Although he or she has occupied a superior place throughout the narrative by knowing more than the characters, in this reading instant the reader knows no more about the [time of the] End than do the characters (including Jesus). (Burnett, "Prolegomenon," 101)

---

34. Culler, *On Deconstruction,* 39, emphasis added, extending Tompkins' argument. Cf. Jauss, "Hero," 284: "Prevailing aesthetic theory . . . tends, as far as possible, to remove all the emotional identification from aesthetic pleasure in order to reduce the latter to aesthetic reflection, sensitized perception, and emancipatory consciousness."

In Mark all the characters except Jesus and the unclean spirits wrongly view Jesus in terms of the things of men, and the readers know this because the narrator has both told them so and also allowed them to view Jesus in terms of the things of God (cf. 8:33). We readers possess a level of knowledge that is superior to the actors' knowledge because the narrator lets us see, hear, and understand things they do not. (Petersen, "Reader," 47)

Keegan's reader is still more cerebral, let loose on an epistemic adventure: "The women of the [Matthean] genealogy [1:3, 5, 6] are precisely the kind of thing that reader-response criticism focuses on, things that strike one as unusual, things that one has to stop and deal with. It is in places like this that the reader is being pulled into the text and forced to think. 'What does this mean? Why is this here? How am I to reconstruct the world where all of this fits together and makes sense?'" (*Interpreting*, 116). Edwards concludes a similar account of the Matthean reader's recollections, anticipations, hesitations and uncertainties, thwarted expectations, considered judgements, filling of narrative gaps—of the cognitive side of the reading experience—with the comment that as our understanding of Matthew's story grows, we can anticipate a "growing appreciation of the narrator's intent" (*Matthew's Story*, 95). But if it is a wholly cognitive role of reading that has been charted, can it be said (other aspects of the intentionality problem aside) to have adequately connected with this ancient narrator's intent?

Dispassionate objectivity and psychological distance are, of course, the sine qua non of modern scholarship: hence the emotionally retarded reader of reader-response exegesis. The rules, however are occasionally bent. Bassler's implied reader is, in places, more affectively active than most:

it is with some surprise and consternation that the reader suddenly finds the [Markan] disciples the object of stern criticism in chapters 6 and 8. . . . Now the reader would like to dissociate from the disciples, but the gaps in the text at this point render this impossible. Thus the identification with the disciples initially undertaken quite willingly by the reader, continues—but now unwittingly. . . . By 8:21 the position of the disciples has become quite desperate, but this desperation is shared by the reader. . . . The primary emotion the implied reader experiences at this point is confusion. ("Parable," 165–66)

These conjectures, which smack strongly of subjectivism by conventional critical standards, shows at what peril the reader-oriented exegete ventures into the realm of affections. "Damned if you do and damned if you don't" neatly sums up the predicament.

However, there is a third axis of reader-response, besides the cognitive and affective axes. This third axis (crucial for the rhetorico-didactic genre of gospel) is best exemplified, among recent studies of the gospel reader, by Gary Phillips's "History and Text: The Reader in Context in Matthew's Parables Discourse" (1985). Consider the following catena from that study:

> The case that we will argue is that the reader of Matthew 13 is manipulated by the narrator into acquiring a cognitive *and pragmatic* ability to hear and to speak Jesus' parables and to engage in a praxis that produces both word and deed. . . . Thus parable hearing is more than a cognitive operation. . . . It means producing a harvest of action. . . . If the reader says "yes" along with the disciples [to Jesus' question "Have you understood?"] then the reader's own transformation itself becomes an interpretant to the narrative, a lived transformation not only of speaking parables/speaking about parables but also of becoming a righteous one equipped for teaching and preaching that is yet to come. . . . Matthew 13 is a manual for scribal and interpretive self-development, a working template of how to be a competent scribe oneself; it is a text that leads to the production of the reader. (121, 126–27, 132, 136, emphasis added)

Though Phillips shares the general, perhaps inevitable, critical inability to take adequate account of reading's affective side, his pragmatic focus does counterbalance his strong cerebral emphasis.[35]

Critics in Readers' Clothing

> 'The birth of the reader' has proven to signify not 'the death of the Author' . . . but its resurrection.
> —Samual Weber, *Institution and Interpretation*

A second problem facing reader-oriented criticism of the Gospels concerns the status of the reader of which it speaks. The so-called "reader in the

35. Cf. Phillips, "Hard Saying." The cognitive and praxical dimensions of reader-response are also forcefully (though very differently) combined in Croatto, *Hermeneutics,* and Scott, *The Word,* 45ff. Other reader-oriented commentators sound an occasional praxical note, e.g., Rhoads and Michie, *Mark,* 139–40; Stock, *Discipleship,* 207; and Tannehill, "Disciples," 393, 395, 404–45.

text" (the reader strictly as defined by the text) is something that stands in a certain relationship to the actual audience. But is the actual audience primarily conceived as an ancient one, a contemporary one, or both? In general, reader-oriented critics of the Gospels have tended to bracket the ancient audience.[36] Culpepper states, for example, that "a characterization of the narratee [the audience as textually defined] could be used in the debate over the actual, historical audience only on the assumption that the narratee accurately represents the intended audience and that the author's judgements about his actual audience were also accurate" (*Anatomy*, 212). This is a commonsense view of biblical audience, antedating reader-response criticism. In an essay on the Lukan prologues, written when he still subscribed to historical criticism, Schuyler Brown argued that "more important than the insoluble question of the *personal identity* of Theophilus [Luke 1:3; Acts 1:1] is the question of *whom he represents*." Brown went on to quote Günther Klein: "Luke does not compose his work with a view to convincing an historical individual. . . . In Luke's mind, the intended effect on Theophilus represents the effect of the work on each reader" (Brown, "Prologues," 107, quoting Klein, "Lukas," 213).[37] The adequacy of the critic's rendering of the intended reader is still measurable against what is known of the ancient milieu. But is the contemporary gospel audience a more vital reality than the ancient one for the reader-oriented critic?

There seem to be at least two answers to this question. On the one hand, some reader-oriented exegetes suggest that the reader defined in and by a gospel is an unchanging property of the text, in which case all flesh-and-blood audiences are bracketed equally—or included equally, depending on how you look at it. Here are some examples:

> [W]hen I speak about the reader I am not attempting to describe a real person (of the first, third, tenth, or twentieth century) but the person posited *by the text* as the reader. (Edwards, *Matthew's Story*, 10)

> [T]he "reader" we [refer] to is not an actual reader since it is not possible to predict the responses of an actual reader. Rather our reader is a hypothetical "implied reader," an imaginary reader with the ideal responses implied or suggested by the narrative. . . . The

---

36. A notable exception is Schuyler Brown, for whom "the response to the text by *contemporary* readers is paramount" ("Resistant Reader," 1).

37. Parallel statements occur in Fitzmyer, *Luke (I–IX)*, 300; Maddox, *Purpose*, 12; and Minear, "Dear Theo," 132.

implied reader is properly an extension of the narrative, a reader that the author creates (by implication) in telling the story. (Rhoads and Michie, *Mark*, 137)

We prefer to allow the text to educate and guide its own reader, rather than insisting on inventing a hypothetical reader characterized primarily by knowledge and experience external to the text. To see how the text molds its own reader involves seeking out those features of the text that shape the reading experience of *every* perceptive reader, ancient or modern. (Fowler, *Loaves*, 140–41)

Original readers, informed readers, and contemporary readers will bring more to the text than the implied reader and thus will extract more from it. But the perspective of the implied reader allows us to focus on the text as an encounter and thus to uncover its innate potential, whether fully realized or not, for leading *any* reader to the desired response. (Bassler, "Parable," 172)

But that is only one approach. On the other hand, there is an attempt to give the individual contemporary reader a role in addition to the trans-historical "reader in the text." The redoubtable difficulties that beset this attempt are illustrated by James Resseguie's "Reader-Response Criticism and the Synoptic Gospels" (1984).[38] The question of whether reader-oriented criticism can take adequate account of the probable experience of the original gospel hearer leads to the question of whether reader-oriented criticism can adequately include the personal experience of the contemporary gospel reader. Having measured the method with a historical yardstick, I will attempt to measure it with a hermeneutical one.

Wolfgang Iser's implied reader is a cerebral, modern construct. What would transpire were such a reader, a child of the novel, set loose to roam free in a gospel? Resseguie's "Reader-Response Criticism," an Iserian reading of selected gospel passages, is the most thoroughgoing exegetical appropriation of Iser available. The general plausibility of these readings is surprising, given that Iser himself has had little time for ancient narrative.[39]

---

38. We might equally have discussed Phillips, "History," which so clearly would have Matthew speak to the contemporary reader, or Brown, "True Light," a companion piece to his "Resistant Reader" ("Reader" prescribes an exegetical approach, which "Light," though it is the earlier essay, demonstrates).

39. Epic and allegory do not provide the indeterminacies or "gaps" that Iser tends to prize in narrative (see Iser, *Implied Reader*, 28, 103, and cf. Scholes, "Cognition," 14). Didactic works too "set an obvious problem for Iser's theory" since they do not privilege the creativity of the reader (Brinker, "Phenomenologies," 209).

Repeated statements to the effect that the reader is encouraged, through the "rhetoric of negation" embodied in Jesus, to sift and reassess the norms of opponents, disciples, and others, and ultimately his or her own norms, seem not at all amiss, given that much of Jesus' activity in relation to his fellow characters in the synoptic Gospels can plausibly be described in such terms. Custom-built in part for absorbing the dissolution of personal and social norms, Iser's implied reader seems at home in much of the gospel text.

The problem with Resseguie's study lies rather in the status of its reader-construct, which in full accord with Iser's, differs sharply in theory and in practice. A salient feature of Iser's reader, as posited theoretically, is that it is neither wholly actual nor wholly ideal. Whereas an ideal reader would be entirely manipulated by a text, as its complete property or reflection, Iser's implied reader would bring a sociocultural and personal history to the text. A reader's dealings with a text, according to Iser, will invariably be colored by his or her "own characteristic selection process. For it is not given by the text itself; it arises from the meeting between the written text and the individual mind of the reader with its own particular history of experience, its own consciousness, its own outlook" (*Implied Reader*, 284; cf. *Act*, 27–38). Iser's implied reader is in part a creation of the text and in part a real individual.

Iser's reception theory is heavily indebted to the Polish phenomenologist Roman Ingarden, who was the first to posit a notion of the literary work as a partial or unfinished object whose gaps of indeterminacy (e.g., informational gaps) require completion by an act of consciousness.[40] For Ingarden, however, both true and false realizations of literary works are possible, a classical notion to which Iser is opposed (*Implied Reader*, 14). Iser would affirm a spectrum of acceptable completions for any given text, for "the potential text is infinitely richer than any of its individual realizations" (280). Although the realization of text as literary work is grounded in immanent textual features, "it is by no means independent of the individual disposition of the reader" (274–75). His oft-cited analogy is of two people gazing at the night sky "who may both be looking at the same collection of stars, but one will see the image of a plough, and the other will make out a dipper. . . . The 'stars' in a literary text are fixed; the lines that join them are variable" (282).

This aspect of Iser's theory dovetails with the "responsible pluralism

---

40. See Ingarden, *Literary Work* and *Cognition*. Detweiler ("Sacred Text," 224–25) has some interesting insights on the type of gap with which the religious reader must deal.

of readings" championed by certain theologians.[41] Therefore, it is highly instructive to see how it is applied in the practical realm— or not applied. For as a striking number of commentators have observed, Iser grants freedom to his reader in theory only to take it away again in practice. In theory Iser affirms the pertinence of individual reader-response, yet in his readings of specific works all such individuality is bracketed: "Although Iser wants to present reading as a process which balances text and reader, he always presents the reader in the firm grip of the text" (Berg, "Psychologies," 259). "His concept of the reader is not different from Ingarden's in that both are essentially normative" (Barnouw, "Critics," 222). Other critics go further, arguing that Iser's reader is even less free than Ingarden's. All Ingarden's reader is asked to do is to be faithful to the basic aesthetic value-structures specific to a given work, whereas Iser's must identify the specific communicative intentions of the work and realize them under its control (Brinker, "Phenomenologies," 210). Iser's theoretical description of the reading process thus "allows for a great deal more latitude in individual realization than does his actual critical practice" (Suleiman, "Varieties," 24),[42] and the reasons are not hard to fathom. Iser the phenomenological theorist can safely endorse the individual creativity of the reader (as can Tracy and other theological pluralists), but Iser the practical critic must answer to his peers in the literary critical guild, recently and aptly defined as "a cultural institution for presenting *model responses* to literary texts" (de Beaugrande, "Syncretism," 85).

Of course the biblical critical guild is still more in the business of producing model readings. By and large, reader-oriented critics of the Gospels have seized on the undifferentiated, prescriptive side of Iser's implied reader—its textually defined, manipulated side—and relegated its individualistic, actual-reader side to the margins.[43] That is why the opening

41. Notably Tracy (see *Imagination* and *Plurality*). The expression "a responsible pluralism of readings" is his.

42. Identical conclusions are reached by Holub, *Reception Theory*, 85ff.; Ray, *Literary Meaning*, 50ff.; and Weber, "Caught," 199. Weber notes that Iser's *Act of Reading*, "which begins precisely by questioning the traditional conception of literature as a repository of univocal meaning, nevertheless gravitates toward the very position it sets out to criticize."

43. The implied reader's historicity is either mentioned in passing (e.g., Bassler, "Parable," 160; Tannehill, "Disciples," 395), or not mentioned at all, as is more often the case. Even when mentioned, it seems to be utterly without consequence for the actual reading enacted. Keegan, in contrast, explicitly lays the contingency factor aside: "the implied reader involves both the role presupposed by the text and the specific realization of that role by a given real reader. [Here], however, the main focus will be on indications within the Gospel of Matthew that specify the role to be assumed by the implied reader of that text" (*Interpreting*, 110). In effect, Petersen adopts the same measure in "Reader," 44ff., as does Staley in *First Kiss*, 32–37.

of Resseguie's "Reader-Response Criticism and the Synoptic Gospels" is striking. Foregrounded there is the notion that the implied reader is not an ideal reader, but "an individual who comes to the text" and fills in its gaps in his or her own way (308). The prospect of an ensuing proliferation of idiosyncratic readings does not bother Resseguie, for "[a]lthough there may be several realizations, even infinite realizations, of a given text, they are always implied and circumscribed by the text" (322).[44] The competent reading is guided by the text, but the implication from the outset is that it will not be overdetermined by it. Resseguie's initial gesture is to distinguish his Iser-inspired "dialectical form of reader-response criticism" from alternative versions, including the one that focuses exclusively on the reader "inscribed or encoded in the text" (307).

Not only does Resseguie follow Iser the theoretician; he also follows Iser the critic into deep contradiction. In sharp distinction to his theoretical introduction, Resseguie's actual readings of selected gospel passages are classically normative and "correct." The following examples convey the general tenor. If sympathy for the rich man of Mark 10:17ff., who seeks eternal life, were not encouraged by the strongly positive description of him, "his failure would not seem tragic, and reader involvement in the narrative would have been kept to a minimum. However, as the narrative stands the rich man's failure in his quest encourages the reader to reconsider a norm that may not have been previously considered a blocking factor for entrance into the kingdom, namely, one's wealth. The reader's involvement with the character encourages him to resolve the tension between a desire for material security and the fact that possessions act as a blocking factor for entrance into the kingdom" (313). Such is the effect of the positive portrayal of this character. But distance can also

> be reduced between a character and the reader by the type of question or request posed to Jesus. At times a request not only seems reasonable, but it even appears unreasonable to the (implied) reader for Jesus to refuse the request. For example, the request of a potential disciple to bury his father in Luke 9:61, or the request of a potential disciple to say farewell to one's family in Luke 9:62, appears reasonable, and refusal of the requests by Jesus comes as a surprise to the reader, forcing him to find the motives underlying the rejection. Similarly, in the story about the choice of guests at a banquet (Luke 14:12-

44. Cf. 308: "the realization of the text is [not] a subjective fabrication of the reader, for the text itself guides the reader in its realization; the written portions place limits on the reader's production of textual meaning."

14), it is natural for a host to invite friends, brothers, relatives, or rich neighbors. It is almost certainly a surprise to the (implied) reader that Jesus summons the host to invite the poor, the maimed, the lame, and the blind to the banquet. In both examples the element of surprise negates the familiar, causing the reader to reexamine underlying norms that were previously held, but perhaps never before examined. (Ibid.)

What sense is there here of an individual reader "who fills in the gaps in his or her own way"? In what sense is Resseguie's implied reader *not* an "ideal" reader? (He defines the ideal reader as one "so manipulated by the text" that he or she "can perfectly interpret [its] meaning" [308].) Throughout the article we find Resseguie's implied reader being drawn into the Gospels' spheres of norms and values in carefully specified ways, being impelled to draw premature conclusions that are then overthrown, being sympathetic or distant from characters as appropriate, examining previously unexamined personal convictions, and so forth. What we miss is any intimation that these detailed responses should be regarded as simply one response-set out of a wide spectrum of potential, no less valid response-sets. The "several . . . even infinite realizations" of the given text, affirmed in the theoretical sections, swiftly reduce to the definitive realization (what its author might have intended) in actual practice.

It is difficult to imagine how Resseguie might have remained true to his theoretical tenets while remaining within the pale of scholarly respectability. Phillips' "History and Text," ostensibly a much more radical piece than Resseguie's (he brings Derrida and Foucault to bear on Matthew), is faced with the same problems. The contemporary reader and the textually prescribed reader elbow for room in Phillips' article, but the contest swiftly goes to the latter. Despite his or her desire for contemporaneity, Phillips' reader remains an idealized construct. Contrast Temma Berg's "Reading in/to Mark" (forthcoming), which, like Phillips' piece, contains a poststructuralist reading of a gospel—but by a literary critic unacquainted with New Testament scholarship. The many faux pas that ensue bespeak the gulf separating even radical biblical critics such as Phillips from nonspecialist Bible readers such as Berg. Susan Wittig's "A Theory of Multiple Meanings" (1977) stresses the variability of reader response, like Resseguie's "Reader-Response Criticism," but without any resulting contradictions. Wittig's article was written for the "Theory" section of the *Semeia* issue on "Polyvalent Narration" in which it appears, as opposed to its "Practice" section. And what of those "practical" examples (by Mary

Ann Tolbert, Dan O. Via, Jr., and Bernard B. Scott), each structuralist and/or psychoanalytic in orientation? Wittig's verdict is telling: "According to each of these theories (at least as they have been practiced here), there is and can be only one meaning of the text: that one produced by the model that is used to explain it" ("Multiple Meanings," 83).

The factors inducing us to remain author-oriented critics in reader's clothing are powerful ones. The biblical guild, like all guilds, enforces strict rules of accreditation. Biblical scholars might recognize themselves in the following description:

> By dint of long work and faithful tenancy, "recognized authorities" establish a claim to their particular bailiwick. Accumulated scholarly property, in the form of notes, references, bibliography, and the like, assures them of the respect of newcomers—and provides them an inheritance to pass along to their chosen heirs. Those heirs in turn will become the wardens of the domain, once they have cultivated it sufficiently. At that point they will have the right to determine what the authors under their jurisdiction mean, and the discipline will respect their opinions. (Ray, *Meaning*, 208)

Switching from feudal to socialist metaphors, we can say that collectively held reading methods, in limited variety, are the bulwark of the biblical profession. Thereby are the subjective proclivities of member readers kept within manageable bounds, critical consensuses and orderly disagreements made possible, and a business-as-usual regularity maintained. Symptomatically, projects in secular literary criticism vigorously affirm the rights of the reader have run counter to the organizing principles of the discipline and been duly relegated to the margins. A notable example is the empirical studies of the psychoanalytic critics Holland and Bleich into how it is that real readers read, and their forthright endorsement (more emphatic in Bleich) of the subjectivism of reader-response.[45] For Holland, it is the analysis of what readers actually say about how they read that differentiates reader-response critics like himself and Bleich from others, such as Iser, who work with reader constructs (Holland, "Unity," 822 n. 81).[46] But the secret of Iser's success in America has been precisely that of giving the

45. See Holland, *Dynamics, Five Readers, The I*, and *Poems*, and Bleich, *Readings* and *Subjective Criticism*.
46. Not that Holland and Bleich thereby elude the traps that are laid out for all reader-response critics. Critiques can be found in Culler, *On Deconstruction*; Freund, *Return*; Mailloux, *Interpretive Conventions*; Ray, *Literary Meaning*; and Suleiman, "Varieties."

American literary critic—and the biblical critic—*"just enough of the reader but not too much"* (Mailloux, *Conventions,* 56, emphasis added).

The Repressed Reader

For biblical studies the moral is plain: criticism is an institution to which real readers need not apply. A reader-oriented approach to the Gospels that would seek to ground itself in traditional gospel scholarship—as current literary criticism of the Gospels generally does—is severely limited in the kinds of readings it can propose. As the foregoing discussions suggested, such readings will be stunted versions of regular reading that disallow the personal associations that reading invariably sparks, that disallow the affective aspects of reading as opposed to its cognitive aspects, and that can admit the dynamic, retrospective-prospective side of reading only by setting arbitrary limits on the degree of foreknowledge that the reader brings to the text. Remarkably subjective readings result, seemingly, in spite of all this pruning. Hearing how the implied reader of the Gospels forms expectations here only to revise them there, is distant from some character at this point and drawn closer at some other, is frustrated, thwarted, discomfited, startled, challenged, puzzled, or enlightened, I am compelled to ask: Why do I experience none of these things when I read the text? Why is there so little evidence that the Church, historically, experienced them? And does the reader-critic who pulls the reader's strings actually experience them either? One suspects that the general answer to the latter question is no, for the reader seems less an extension of the critic (whose jaded responses, after all, would hardly make a good story of reading), than an idealized alter ego. Which is simply to say that the reader-oriented exegete is a *homo institutionis,* just as the more conventional exegete is. Like the conventional exegete (the redaction critic, for example), the reader-oriented exegete feels an understandable need to excise incoherent, trivial, oversubjective, or otherwise inappropriate elements from his or her responses so as to assume a readerly alter ego that meets the profession's standards of accreditation. On this view, the readings that reader-oriented gospel critics produce are not qualitatively different from those of other critics. Indeed, one of their valuable features, other than the primary one of being able to present the gospel as dynamic event rather than as static object, is precisely that of making the implicit features of our critical reading explicit by narrativizing our standard moves and reflecting them back to us as in a mirror (cf. Freund, *Return,* 6).

Finally, reader-oriented exegesis is subject to the same epistemological vicissitudes as conventional exegesis. It proves no easier to say what is in the reader's experience than to say what is in the text (cf. Culler, *On Deconstruction*, 82). Elaborate stories of reading result, which attempt to orient and organize themselves in relation to semantic properties in the text. But because there are so many semantic properties, and because they never all stay still but are always shifting and reforming in the tide of critical discourse, always being dislodged and refixed, they require endless stories of reading to account for them, whether the covert stories of reading told by traditional critics, or the overt stories of reading told by reader-response critics. And there is a strong familial resemblance between the overt and the covert stories of reading. Reader-response criticism of the Gospels, because it is an enterprise that tends to feel accountable to conventional gospel scholarship, has worked with reader constructs that are sensitively attuned to what may pass as permissible critical reading. That is why reader-oriented exegeses can often read disappointingly like the familiar critical renditions of the given biblical passage, lightly reclothed in a reader vocabulary. The reader of audience-oriented gospel criticism is a repressed reader. Its parents are mainstream gospel exegesis on the biblical side, and reader-in-the-text formalism on the nonbiblical side. Its sibling, of course, is narrative criticism, which has the same exegetical-formalist ancestry. Audience-oriented gospel criticism also has black-sheep relatives that it has excluded or disowned, whether deliberately or innocently. Reader theory in literary studies is a Pandora's box into which we, infant literary critics of the Bible, have barely begun to peer. Opened more fully it might release some unsettling, but possibly timely, ways of reconceiving biblical interpretation.

7

Stories of Reading That Have No Ending: An Introduction to the Postmodern Bible

Tracking the reader-in-the-text is what reader-oriented literary study has amounted to in New Testament studies. In literary studies, however, critics of reading have taken a theoretical path, straying into philosophy and other adjoining fields and reemerging with new ways of conceiving text and reader. Less than ever is there a distinct critical school to which reader-response criticism might refer. Rather, it is best thought of as a single, waning manifestation of a more general, still undiminished phenomenon. This phenomenon is that literary theory generally over the past two decades has evinced a strong interest in reading and interpretation, the status of texts in relation to readers, of theory in relation to praxis, of interpretation in relation to institutional controls, and so on.[1] Over that time span, literary theory became, almost more than anything else, a "problematics of reading, for to examine the process of reading is to raise a host of difficult, though fascinating questions" (Berg, "Psychologies," 248). And the principal question that arises is: Where should we arrive were we to

1. Suleiman, "Varieties" (1980), distinguishes six brands of audience-oriented criticism: rhetorical, semiotic and structuralist, phenomenological, subjective and psychoanalytic, sociological and historical, and hermeneutic. The approaches to the Gospels surveyed in chapter 6 roughly span the phenomenological (e.g., Iser), semiotic-structuralist (e.g., Prince), and rhetorical (e.g., Booth) axes. Suleiman's hermeneutic axis, however, best represented by deconstruction, must be regarded the wild card in the pack, though easily the most influential, whose dissimilarities to reader-response criticism (generally associated with early Fish, Iser, Holland, Bleich et al.) outweigh its similarities.

redirect our gaze from the reader in the text to the reader and the text in the context of interpretation? (A hint can be found in the term *context*, originally from *contexere* [Lat.], "to weave." Consigning text and reader to the weave of interpretation, can we ever pull them asunder again?)

Outside the Shrine of the Single Sense

Frank Kermode's *Genesis of Secrecy* (1979) "is about interpretation, an interpretation of interpretation." (2). What fascinates Kermode is the great cloud of conflicting readings that a single text can provoke. Whence this astonishing fecundity? It is, to an extent, the result of an institutional fiat: "Once the institution licenses a text for full-scale exegetical exploitation there is no limit" (10).[2] Given the degree of institutional endorsement the Gospels have enjoyed and the centuries of unremitting interpretation they have provoked, it is not surprising that Kermode should see them as offering "peculiar opportunities" for his inquiry. He is struck with Mark in particular. "Mark is a strong witness to the enigmatic and exclusive character of narrative, to its property of banishing interpreters from its secret places" (33–34). Indeed, Mark becomes emblematic in *Genesis of Secrecy* not only of the recalcitrant narrative text but also of the interpreter's own situation relative to that text. Like the hapless disciples in Mark, the professional exegete occupies the peculiar position of an insider who is really an outsider. Those officially outside the guild of professional readers "indeed see but [do] not perceive, and . . . indeed hear but [do] not understand" (see Mark 4:11–12). Theirs is the manifest or carnal sense—the simple primary sense or surface story. Latent or spiritual senses, however, are the special province of those inside, within the guild, who divine the non-manifest senses of the narrative text, its hidden meanings. They read the Gospels as allegories, for instance (as seen in chapter 2), in which disciples, opponents and other characters stand in for historical groups. The illumination that divination brings, however, is momentary. The text lights up partially but quickly relapses into opacity again. "One divination spawns another. If I say the fishes [in the first feeding story in Mark] are one thing, that does not prevent your saying they are another, just as plausibly . . . though there will be a family or institutional resemblance between our interpretations" (37). Interpretations are hopelessly plural, so that interpretation is endlessly disappointing. And so the situation of the

2. Cf. Hartman, *Criticism*, 202: "The more pressure we put on a text . . . the more indeterminacy appears." Barthes too writes of literary analysis "advancing not into the text . . . but into its own labor" (*Essays*, 89).

professional interpreter is fraught with paradox: "being an insider is only a more elaborate way of being kept outside" (27).

In the chapter entitled "The Man in the Macintosh, the Boy in the Shirt," Kermode sets his sights on the kinds of aporias that pop up when a text—*Ulysses,* for example, or Mark—"is scrutinized with an intensity normally thought appropriate only after institutional endorsement" (49). Gaping aporias in Mark include the youth who flees naked from the scene of the arrest (14:51–52), and the concluding words of the gospel, "for they were afraid" (16:8). Kermode reflects dryly on the long history of unsuccessful, occasionally desperate attempts to shut these aporias, finishing with the general observation that if

> there is one belief (however the facts resist it) that unites us all, from the evangelists to those who argue away convenient portions of their texts, and those who spin large plots to accommodate the discrepancies and dissonances into some larger scheme, it is [the] conviction that somehow, in some occult fashion, if we could only detect it, everything will be found to hang together. . . . We are all fulfillment men, *pleromatists*; we all seek the center that will allow the senses to rest, at any rate for one interpreter, at any rate for one moment. [72]

But Mark and *Ulysses* and their interpreters, after all, are barn-sized targets for Kermode's arrows. It is difficult to build general arguments about the interminable failure of interpretation ever to halt the movement of potential senses in a text from the interpretive histories of these crux-ridden works. However, in the preceding chapter, "Why Are Narratives Obscure?" Kermode had turned his attention to a far simpler story, the parable of the Good Samaritan (Luke 10:25–37), as a way of showing the susceptibility of stories in general to multiple interpretations. "Here is a narrative that seems to be a simple exemplary tale. The detail that could be called redundant to its merely exemplary purpose may be explained away as a gesture toward realism, a way of adding the interest of verisimilitude, or even of topicality, to the folktalish triple design of the story." He goes on to enact a plausible, Sunday-sermonlike interpretation of the parable—the manifest, ethical interpretation—interspersing suitable bits of background on the dangers of the Jericho road, the value of two denarii, and so forth. However, "This simple view of the story is very far from having gained universal acceptance. And in understanding why this is so we happen upon an important, if obvious, reason for the interminability of interpretation. My way of reading the detail of the parable of the Good Samaritan seems to me natural; but that is only my way of authenticating, or claiming as universal, a habit of thought that is cultural and arbitrary. My reading would certainly not have seemed 'natural' to the church Fathers, for instance" (35). Sample allegorical readings follow, culled from Irenaeus, Augustine, and others. Certain modern exegetes, Kermode notes, have likewise divined latent senses in the parable, reading it as a legitimation of a mission to Samaria, for example. The point is "that a story need not be manifestly obscure to be thought to possess that which only interpretation may disclose" (41). Outsiders read but do not perceive. Insiders read and divine but their divinations are hopelessly plural. "No one, however special his point of vantage, can get . . . into the shrine of the single sense" (123). Insiders remain outside.

Certainly my brief rendering of Kermode subjects him "to that benign distortion which usually or always accompanies interpretation" (5). Perhaps I have made the *Genesis of Secrecy* sound like a dense Derridean meditation rather than the leisurely, sometimes rambling, discussion that it in fact is. There is, however, little doubt but that the urbane Cambridge don has absorbed a heady dose of French poststructuralism somewhere.[3] Precisely because he bridges two very different styles of critical discourse—a heavily theoretical, self-reflexive, continental style, and a more practical, and more familiar, Anglo-American style—Kermode has been well positioned to issue us a clear and telling challenge in biblical studies to stand back for a moment from our disciplinary task of adding interpretation to interpretation, to ask what it is that we expect our interpretations to achieve, and whether we can reasonably entertain such expectations.

Behind the Wall of Wavy Glass

"Since you cannot interpret absolutely, you can interpret forever," writes John Dominic Crossan (*Cliffs*, 102). Kermode would undoubtedly agree. We can halt the movement of potential senses in the text momentarily, but then the institutional machine rolls on, new interpretations churn out at an alarming rate, and any attempts to proclaim the definitive sense get left in the dust. There is a general sense of knowledge accumulating, of

3. As he himself readily concedes in *Telling*, 3–5. Essentially, Kermode is a moderate who attempts to assimilate the new without abandoning the old (8) but who also recognizes that "[t]here is a war on, and he who ventures into no-man's-land brandishing cigarettes and singing carols must expect to be shot at" (7). He would hardly have been startled, then, by, inter alia, Greenwood, "Biblical Studies," an entertainingly polemical but wildly inaccurate attempt to situate *Secrecy*, which collapses all the substantial distinctions between Kermode and those way to the left of him. Curiously, none of Kermode's biblical work since *Secrecy* has evinced anything like the same radicality.

consensuses forming. Small-scale problems do get solved, one at a time. But eventually the pendulum will swing, the reigning paradigm will be unsettled on its foundations or will crumble altogether, and many of the old problems will be swept away as pseudoproblems as a new agenda is ushered in by a Wellhausen or a Gunkel, a Schweitzer or a Bultmann. (The semishift from diachronic to synchronic methods is the most recent example of such change in biblical studies.) Kermode implies that few of us can face these hard realities head-on. All too quickly "we slip back into the old comfortable fictions of transparency [i.e., that our texts are transparent on historical reality], the single sense, the truth" (*Secrecy*, 123). Is the text too a "comfortable fiction"? To put it crudely, if the spectacle is of an interminable succession of interpretations, each producing a slightly different version of the text, might not the skeptical, empirically minded observer be tempted to interject: "But where is *the* text of which you speak?" and conclude that the emperor has no clothes and that the text does not exist? Kermode does not take such a counterintuitive view. For him the text is an extraordinarily slippery item, but it is there nonetheless, somewhere. He speaks in one place of "structures of explanation which come between us and the text . . . like some wall of wavy glass" (125). Structures of explanation are one thing, it is implied, the text another. When he wheels in the big guns of philosophy and poststructuralism, as he does in the "What Precisely Are the Facts?" chapter, it is to line them up against the tenacious notion of a noninterpreted bedrock of historical fact underlying the gospel passion narratives. It is interpretation all the way down, he concludes, no matter how many layers we peel away. What would we find were we to line up the same artillery against the notion of a bedrock text, somehow intact beneath all the layers of interpretation, behind the "wall of wavy glass"? The *Genesis of Secrecy* does not say.

How are traditional assumptions about texts affected when literary criticism opens the door to contemporary philosophy? Stanley Fish has built an interesting career on this question. Fish, in the early part of his career, was one of the seminal reader-response critics, a pioneer of the moment-by-moment method of critical reading, which is the method preferred by New Testament critics of reading. The shift in Fish from a method of reading in which the reader is constrained by objective features in the text to a theory of reading in which the reader is constrained only by his or her situation in a community with shared interpretive premises focuses nicely two alternative ways of talking about readers and reading, which we can then bring into dialogue with biblical criticism.

The Vanishing Text

"The answer this book gives to its title question," writes Fish in the preface to *Is There a Text in This Class?: The Authority of Interpretive Communities* (1980), is "there is and there isn't." There isn't a text in this or any other class if one means by text what traditional interpreters have generally meant, a fixed and stable entity that remains the same from one moment to the next. But there is "a text in this and every class if one means by text the structure of meanings that is obvious and inescapable from the perspective of whatever interpretive assumptions happen to be in force. The point is finally a simple one," concedes Fish, "but it has taken me more than ten years to see it" (vii).[4] Fish's mature theory is the product of an intellectual conversion. His 1970 manifesto, "Literature in the Reader: Affective Stylistics," sprang from his experience of writing *Surprised by Sin: The Reader in Paradise Lost* (1967), which had argued the strategy of the poem to be one of a skillful deployment of Satanic rhetoric that induces "little moments of forgetfulness" in the reader that mimic and repeat those of the beguiled Adam and Eve. Thus "*Paradise Lost* is a poem about how its readers came to be the way they are" (*Text*, 21). The method of *Surprised by Sin* received explicit formulation and added development in "Literature in the Reader" as one "simple in concept, but complex (or at least complicated) in execution. The concept is simply the rigorous and disinterested asking of the question, what does this word, phrase, sentence, paragraph, chapter, novel, play, poem, *do*? And the execution involves an analysis of the developing responses of the reader in relation to the words as they succeed one another in time" (26–27). Fish's close reading comprises a slowing down of the reading experience so that "events of reading" that ordinarily go unnoticed "but which do occur, are brought before our analytical attention. It is as if a slow-motion camera with an automatic stop-action effect were recording our linguistic experiences and presenting them to us for viewing" (28). This time-bound critical method has been the one most commonly adopted to date by New Testament reader-critics. Their impetus has come less from Fish than from Wolfgang Iser. This is surprising, given Fish's accessibility relative to Iser, but early Fish's phenomenological criticism does bear a strong, independent resemblance to that of Iser.

Where Fish deviates from Iser and other reader-critics is in his firmer

4. This volume collects Fish's major essays of 1970–80, framing them with a general introduction, a series of lengthy headnotes, and four previously unpublished essays.

grasp of the consequences of a reader-oriented position for one's manner of conceiving the text. One sees this already in "Literature in the Reader." Meaning is not something embedded in a text to be extracted "like a nut from its shell" but is rather "an experience one has in the course of reading." Literature in consequence "is not regarded as a fixed object of attention but as a sequence of events that unfold within the reader's mind."[5] However, to thus redefine literature is also to obliterate the traditional separation between reader and text. Once the locus of signification is firmly fixed in the reading consciousness rather than in the printed page or between the covers of the book, literature yields up its traditional image of stable artifact and becomes an activity that readers perform, a "kinetic art" (*Text,* 43). Although Fish would thus shift the focus of criticism from the text to the process of reading, the text nonetheless retains, in his early theory, its manipulative role relative to the reader by virtue of rules of competence (linguistic, generic, etc.) shared by author and reader, and objectified in the text as regulative restraints on response (44ff.). One suspects that most of the New Testament reader-critics critiqued in the preceding chapter would assume their readings too to be triggered by, or to be responsive to, objective features in the text.

A 1976 piece, "Interpreting the *Variorum,* " has reader and text jostling once more for power. In the second part of the essay the autonomous text collapses and "disappears" as Fish moves into the position that he has since occupied. Fish's argument in this pivotal essay is too tightly structured for adequate summarization, but its gist can be rendered as follows. He establishes a plausible interpretation of some lines from Milton, and then dismantles it to show how easily one surrenders to the metaphorics of critical language and begins to talk as if poems, not interpreters, did things. Words like *encourage* and *disallow* (as in "the poem is continually encouraging and then disallowing") imply agency. Conventionally we assign such agency, first to an author's intentions, and then to the forms that embody them. What really happens, thinks Fish, is something altogether different: "rather than intention and its formal realization producing interpretation (the 'normal' picture), interpretation creates intention and its formal realization by creating the conditions in which it becomes possible to pick them out. In other words, in the analysis of these lines from *Lycidas* I did what critics always do: I 'saw' what my interpretive

5. Tompkins, "Introduction," xvi–xvii, paraphrasing "Literature." To Tompkins' metaphor of the nut, compare Croatto, *Hermeneutics,* 66: "One does not 'emerge' from a text . . . with a pure meaning, gathered from within, as a diver might swim to the surface with a piece of coral in hand, or as one might take something out of a bag or trunk."

principles permitted or directed me to see, and then I turned around and attributed what I had 'seen' to a text and an intention" (163). The demarcations and patterns that his interpretive framework yielded became "by a sleight of hand" demarcations "in" the text, which then became available for the designation "formal features." And as formal features they were "(illegitimately) assigned the responsibility of producing the interpretation which in fact produced them" (ibid.).

These ideas might be utterly counterintuitive to some. Is not the material text a given? And is not what it says, to a degree, plain? Fish anticipates these demurrals. These things can be hard to see, he admits, when interpretive strategies have become so habitual that the forms they yield "seem part of the world" (166). But nothing in the text is innocent of interpretation, not even the facts of grammar. The critic who confidently rests his analysis on the bedrock of syntax is unwittingly resting on an interpretation (167). The interpretive apparatus creates the data and "produces the work . . . from the ground up."[6] Indeed, Fish would want to descend even lower "in the direction of atoms" to argue that any "bedrock level" to which a critic might appeal (be it only black inked markings on processed wood pulp) has "palpability and shape only because of the assumption of some or other system of intelligibility" and is "therefore just as available to a deconstructive dissolution" as any other level of the text (331). Richard Rorty, Fish's counterpart in the field of philosophy, is rather better than Fish when it comes to countering the argument that the datum itself must be utterly real quite apart from the interpretation it receives. "The pragmatist meets this objection," writes Rorty (who, along with Fish and others, is often labeled *neopragmatist*)

> by differentiating himself from the idealist. He agrees that there is such a thing as brute physical resistance—the pressure of light waves on Galileo's eyeball, or of the stone on Dr. Johnson's boot. But he sees no way of transferring this nonlinguistic brutality to *facts,* to the truth of sentences. . . . [A]s many *facts* are brought into the world as there are languages for describing . . . causal transaction. As Donald Davidson says, causation is not under a description, but explanation is. . . . To say that we must have respect for facts is just to say that we must, if we are to play a certain language game, play by the rules. To say that we must have respect for unmediated causal forces is pointless. ("Lumps," 4)

6. Tompkins, "Introduction," xxii, paraphrasing *"Variorum."*

Thus, Fish's position is not "that 'there's nothing out there, its all in your head,' but rather that what we perceive is always given its shape and meaning by interpretive acts" (Rendall, "Fish," 51). If Fish can be assigned a specific philosophical location, it is firmly against naive empiricism, or hermeneutic realism. Naive empiricism is the position that the reader's mind is a mirror reflection of, or neutral report on, some objective state of affairs, "a position that has stubbornly held on in traditionalist theory by the telling claim that it is common sense and therefore need not be stated, much less discussed" (Lentricchia, *After,* 146). In recent philosophical history, naive empiricism has had no serious proponents. And relative in particular to certain recent strains of Anglo-American philosophy (Quine, Kuhn, Davidson, Putnam, Rorty et al.) there is nothing startling in Fish.

But the question arises nonetheless, which Fish addresses to himself, If there is no independent text to constrain our manner of interpreting it, why should two or more readers ever agree? "What is the explanation on the one hand of the stability of interpretation (at least among certain groups at certain times) and on the other of the orderly variety of interpretation if it is not the stability and variety of texts?" (*Text,* 171). In answer Fish advances the notion of *interpretive communities,* which has been the cornerstone of his work since the mid-1970s. Interpretive communities are "made up of those who share interpretive strategies not for reading (in the conventional sense) but for writing texts, for constituting their properties." This is why there are interpretive agreements and why disagreements can be debated in a principled way:

> not because of a stability in texts, but because of a stability in the makeup of interpretive communities. . . . Of course this stability is always temporary (unlike the longed for and timeless stability of the text). Interpretive communities grow larger and decline, and individuals move from one to another; thus, while the alignments are not permanent, they are always there, providing just enough stability for the interpretive battles to go on, and just enough shift and slippage to assure that they will never be settled. The notion of interpretive communities thus stands between an impossible ideal and the fear which leads so many to maintain it. The ideal is of perfect agreement and it would require texts to have a status independent of interpretation. The fear is of interpretive anarchy, but it would only be realized if interpretation (text making) were completely random. It is the fragile but real consolidation of interpretive communities that allows

us to talk to one another, but with no hope or fear of ever being able to stop. (*Text*, 171–72)

Here we are perhaps closer to an adequate explanation for the interminability of interpretation than we were with the *Genesis of Secrecy*. Kermode located the cause squarely in the text: the narrative text is dark, obscure and alien, despite intermittent radiances; it excludes interpreters from its inner precincts. Fish is less lyrical, more literal-minded. The text of which he writes is less an opaque quantity than an insubstantial one, which can have no status whatsoever independent of interpretive acts.[7]

Do Critics Make or Do They Find?

Assaults on Fishian interpretation theory, or qualified endorsements of it, have run from the dozens to the hundreds in recent years.[8] In reaction Fish digs in deeper, skillfully modulating his interpretive communities theory to absorb new objections.[9] For late Fish, the business of criticism ceases to be one of demonstration, becoming one of persuasion instead. Criticism's business is not the determining of a correct way of reading, since every determination will be made and remade as interpretive contexts successively displace one another. Critical activity becomes "an attempt on the part of one party to alter the beliefs of another so that the evidence cited by the first will be seen *as* evidence by the second" (*Text*, 365). In the new Fishian dispensation, the rationalist mandate of modern criticism (serving truth and objective knowledge) gives way to a postmodern political mandate (serving the critic and his or her community) (cf. de Beaugrande, "Syncretism," 116).

This last, Foucault-like turn of the screw verges on a cynicism that

7. Wittig, "Multiple Meanings," also addresses the question "of how a text . . . can have multiple, often apparently contradictory meanings," a question that "assumes an even more urgent importance in the study of scriptural texts" (76). But her way of posing the question—"How does [the] phenomenon [of plurisignificance] occur? What are the conditions of its occurrence? *What features does the text possess* which make it polyvalent?" (84, emphasis added)—takes as given certain ground (text, textual features) that Fish and others would call into question.

8. A number of books have chapters on Fish, e.g., Cain, *Crisis*; Culler, *Pursuit*; Freund, *Return*; Goodheart, *Skeptic*; Ray, *Meaning*; Scholes, *Textual Power*; Weber, *Institution*; and cf. Norris, *Contest* and *Paul de Man*. Similar material is available in back issues of such journals as *Critical Inquiry, Diacritics,* and *New Literary History*.

9. A more considered version of the theory must wait for Fish's forthcoming *Change*, but one that is just as uncompromising on the issue of the objective text. The concluding chapter of *Change* has already been published as "Consequences." For a résumé of Fish's development since "*Variorum*," see Ray, *Meaning*, 162ff.

traditional critics have found particularly unpalatable, and they have not been slow to respond. Preferring familiar or even colloquial language to the imposing continental idiolect that keeps such critics at arm's length from the deconstructors, Fish looks a deceptively easy mark (cf. Rendall, "Fish," 49). Yet he has a powerful undergirding. What he has done in effect has been to take, through direct and indirect influence, the theme of language as world construction that has pervaded continental and Anglo-American philosophy and other fields of the humanities and social sciences for generations, and to lay it squarely on the doorstep of an indignant literary critical institution.

But the question persists uncomfortably: What happens to practical criticism once the ontological tablecloth is whipped away? Does it fly off in disarray? Fish would entirely subsume the pragmatic dualistic model of subject and object, interpreter and thing to be interpreted, in a radical monism, which would entirely undercut traditional criticism's subject-object distinction (Culler, *On Deconstruction*, 74; cf. Fish, *Text*, 335–36). And yet that distinction has a kind of indestructible resilience, as Culler notes, that any amount of epistemological dismantling cannot affect. Fish might cause the text to "disappear" momentarily, "yet it reappears as soon as one attempts to talk about interpretation" (*On Deconstruction*, 74). Interpretive practice can proceed only from the dualistic model of a reader and something to read. Culler finds an instructive analogue to the problematic engendered by monistic interpretation theory in the kinds of questions asked by philosophers of science: "Are there properties *in* nature that scientists discover, or do their conceptual frameworks *produce* [them]. . . . Does science *make* or does it *find*" (77)? He invokes Richard Rorty in reply, for whom "nothing deep" turns on the choice between the two phrases—between the imagery of making and of finding. Rorty would, however, opt for the classic notion of "better describing what was already there" for physics, "not because of deep epistemological or metaphysical considerations, but simply because, when we tell our Whiggish stories about how our ancestors gradually crawled up the mountain on whose (possibly false) summit we stand, we need to keep some things constant throughout the story." Atoms and natural forces are good choices for this role. Yet

> it is not as if we had some deep insight into the nature of reality which told us everything save atoms and the void was "by convention" (or "spiritual" or "made up"). Democritus's insight was that a story about the smallest bits of things forms a background for stories about

changes among things made of these bits. The acceptance of this genre of world-story (fleshed out successively by Lucretius, Newton, and Bohr) may be definatory of the West, but it is not a choice which could obtain, or which requires, epistemological or metaphysical guarantees. (Rorty, *Mirror,* 344–45, quoted in Culler, *On Deconstruction,* 77–78)

In much the same way, argues Culler, "the notion of a given text with unchanging, discoverable properties provides an excellent background for arguments about interpretation and accounts of changing interpretations" (78).[10]

Thus, an ontological text-theory becomes a pragmatic text-theory. Although the ontological tablecloth is whipped away, interpretive practice remains in place. Fish releases in Anglo-American literary study a timely and merciless challenge to the naive-empiricist assumption of the reified literary text, but it can no more inhibit interpretive practice than skeptical philosophies of science inhibit, say, the manufacture of consumer goods (a fact of which Fish himself is well aware). This is not to say that Fish's theory is inconsequential on all levels; far from it.

The Bible as a Sea Seventy Thousand Fathoms Deep

> I have found that people who say, "Of course interpretation is a part of every human activity," don't know what it means to say that, or what kinds of notions have to be given up.
> —Stanley Fish, "Theory and Consequences: An Interview"

Fish's brand of skepticism is not without analogies in theology. In *God-Talk* (1967), for example, John Macquarrie reechoes the call for a philosophical theology to replace the old natural theology, one which would not "set out to prove the existence of God or the immortality of the soul or anything of that sort," but would instead "show the basic structure of religious faith, what kind of situation gives rise to our talk about God, how this talk is meaningful in the context of that situation, and what kind of validity can be claimed for it" (121). Like the "negative hermeneuticians" on the literary text (Paul Ricoeur's term) and the philosophers of science on the material universe, Macquarrie too argues the necessity of laboring without epistemological or ontological guarantees: "Frankly, I do not sup-

10. For further discussion of these analogies, see Cohen, ed., "Philosophy," which contains contributions by Rorty, Fish, Hilary Putnam, E. D. Hirsch, Jr., Mary Hesse, and others.

pose there is any way in which one could prove that the assertions of faith and theology do refer to a Reality (God) that is independent and prior to the experiences which we call 'experiences of God'" (244; cf. 102–22).

If we can assimilate with comparative ease the theologian's application of the principles of analytic philosophy to our theological thinking, it is ultimately because these principles reinforce what we in any case assume, namely, Reality (God) is a matter of faith. When related principles are brought to bear on our hermeneutical thinking, however, we balk, precisely because it throws into question general assumptions about our texts, whether sacred or secular. But what precisely is it with respect to the biblical text that a Fish-like theory would throw into question? How would our understanding of its status change?[11]

First, even a moderate reading theory, of the sort advocated or assumed by the generality of the New Testament reader-response critics, can undercut the traditional authority of the Bible by suggesting its radical incompleteness. Without the engagement of a creative reading subject to take its cues and fill in its many "blanks" (Iser's *Leerstellen*), the Bible remains a partial or unfinished object. This view of the biblical text is not unrelated to certain ecclesiastical views; for example, the Roman Catholic insistence that the Bible needs to be supplemented by tradition. Rather, it is a question of degree. The more the temporality of the reading experience is stressed—its cumulative, successive side—the more the Bible sheds its familiar image as meaning-full object. This image achieved an unprecedented heightening with the advent and interiorization of print. In the hyperspatial object model, one which has been deeply interiorized for centuries across the span of Judeo-Christian faiths, the Bible is conceived (speaking with sweeping generality) as having all its meanings assembled and accounted for within its covers, rather like toy soldiers in a box. But even in a moderate phenomenology of reading, the text's meanings are reconceived as being momentarily available only, before they recede and disappear in the inexorable flow of the reading process that recontextualizes, supersedes, and constantly alters meaning. (Indeed, the object model is undermined every time the Bible is read liturgically.) In a temporal model the spatially conceived text-object is robbed of its "solidity" (see chapter 6) and is reassigned a new status as an event or temporal experience. Its locus of meaning is resettled from between the covers of

---

11. Two further Fishian siftings of biblical interpretation with a New Testament emphasis are forthcoming: Adam, "Sign," and Burnett, "Postmodern" (the latter deals with Fish only to resolutely "pass beyond" him). For a theologian's critique of Fish, see Jeanrond, *Interpretation*, 110–13.

the book or between the margins of the page to the consciousness of the one who reads (or the community that hears). To press the point, given that no two readers share exactly the same consciousness, and that consciousness itself seems best conceived as process rather than as stasis, it follows, by a kind of Heraclitean logic, that the biblical text can never be the same for any two readers, or even for the same reader twice. This already raises problems for any notion of the biblical text as an entity that remains the same from one moment to the next, a fixed and stable repository of meanings. This notion of the Bible has been as fundamental to the critical as to the noncritical reader. With little exaggeration it can be said that the modus operandi of the biblical guild has generally consisted of an *adequatio intellectus et rei,* the aim of interpretation being one of correspondence to the essential semantic properties of the biblical texts, properties contained within the texts, awaiting discovery. Realist assumptions of this sort continue unabated in biblical studies. (If in doubt, try scanning the introductions to exegetical articles in back issues of the professional journals, especially those with "Once Again," "The Meaning of," "A Reconsideration," "Another Look at," or some similar phrase in the title.)[12] But such assumptions need reexamining even in light of a moderate phenomenology of reading, as represented by early Fish, for example, or by Wolfgang Iser, that defines interpretation as a two-way, dynamic process. Criticism is an ineluctably creative activity. Prior to the interpretive act, there is nothing definitive in the text to be discovered.

To say these things is merely to reiterate in an updated register what Barth, Bultmann, and the New Hermeneutic said, in their different ways, decades ago.[13] But what might be the implications for the Bible of a postmodernist (for example, a neopragmatic) theory of reading in which the prior, ontological text collapses like a dead star—less Kermode's emitter of "momentary radiances" than a kind of black hole swallowing galactic quantities of interpretation but without ever giving back so much as a glimmer of its inner essence in return? Kermode's "wall of wavy glass" becomes infinitely thick and opaque. Of course, the wall shatters, or seems to, once we begin to interpret again; meaning rushes in to fill the vacuum that theory served to create. Yet all is not as before. Take the biblical text

12. Cf. Noll's incisive reflections on American biblical scholarship ("Review," 500–9). His first conclusion is that "the history of American Bible scholarship is not fully informed by the realization that scholarship fits within dogmatic boundaries, that normal science proceeds within paradigms, that presuppositions shape conclusions" (506).

13. The classic statement is Bultmann, "Presuppositions." For updates other than my own, see, inter alia, Brown, "Reader Response," and Schüssler Fiorenza, "Ethics."

as a traditional locus of revelation, inspiration, or authority, for example. Rather than the biblical text generating an intricate network of convictions and practices, do convictions and practices themselves not generate the text?[14] More pointedly, if the text is rigorously reconceived as the product of a matrix of interpretive premises, must not the locus of authority, inspiration, or of any other quality then be reconceived in turn as residing—where? The biblical text ceases to be conceived as a secure, extrainterpretive Archimedean point—one that might partake in the immutability of its transcendent Referent. Text and believer alike are abandoned to the mutability of history, and faith is abandoned to utter insecurity, as, perhaps, it must be. The succession of infinitely different interpretations generated by the same biblical text are reconceived as the succession of infinitely different biblical texts that interpretations generate through history.

The situation is parallel for biblical scholarship. It "may be hard to see," as Fish would say, but the methodological fields of biblical scholarship generate the text and its meanings, in sufficient variety to enable principled discussion and disagreement "with no hope or fear of ever being able to stop." Historical discussion, for example, generates versions of individual biblical books that, subtly or markedly, are endlessly different. Like a mirror, the book assumes different aspects when held up against different historical contexts. Kermode, in the "What Precisely Are the Facts?" chapter of the *Genesis of Secrecy,* mounts a kind of neo-Bultmannian attack on the notion that the Gospels might, even in some minimal sense, be transparent on a bedrock of fact. He invokes the philosophical and poststructuralist discourse on history and historiography to argue that facts, whether behind the Gospels or in general, appear as such (are intelligible) only within the framework of some discourse that plots them, interrelationally and teleologically, in a manner akin to fiction writing. We

---

14. The commonsense retort is, of course, "both/and." One might argue that beliefs, etc., do shape the text in part, but that the text in turn shapes belief. This corresponds to the moderate reader-response position outlined above. This commonsense retort (inadequate, as we will see) has a seeming ally in deconstruction, whose response to the question would also be "both/and." The empty text that theory yields and the full text that reading yields would be seen as the products of two irreconcilable, mutually undermining perspectives: "for the reader everything is to be done and everything is already done. For the reader the work is not partially created but, on the one hand, already complete and inexhaustible—one can read and reread without ever grasping completely what has already been made—and on the other hand, still to be created in the process of reading, without which it is only black marks on paper. The attempt to produce compromise formulations fails to capture this essential, divided quality of reading" (Culler, *On Deconstruction,* 76; the first sentence is from Sartre, *Literature,* 32). Freund, *Return,* 85–89, 153ff., extends Culler's observations.

think relationally, metaphorically, and narratively. In consequence, there is no nude, unplotted, uninterpreted bedrock of fact. It is interpretation all the way down, as Kermode might say. What we see in the text is decided less by what is present behind it than by its specular propensity to reflect our own presuppositional structures. Fish too is at pains to deny the opposition between discourse that is true to some extrainstitutional reality and discourse that is not. This is not to deny "that a standard of truth exists and that by invoking it we can distinguish between different kinds of discourse: it is just that the standard is not brute, but institutional, not natural, but made" (*Text,* 243). The multidisciplinary debate in the humanities over the status of historical discourse invites us to redefine rigorously our aims, claims, and functions as biblical historians.[15]

Kermode would argue that since the transparency model is so easily shattered we should pay more heed to "what is written" in the Gospels than to "what is written about." One purpose of the *Genesis of Secrecy* is precisely "to reverse that priority," assumedly by helping to promote a "genuine literary criticism" of the Gospels (118–19; cf. 136–37). Here he echoes a leitmotif of much recent gospel work, exposing his flank at the same time to Fish and the other neopragmatists. In a strong, Fish-like interpretation theory, the intrinsically oriented literary model shatters just as easily as the extrinsically oriented historical one does. This is an important point, which can be spelled out with an illustration. Introducing the *Lukan Voice,* James Dawsey has explicit recourse to a premise that grounds much contemporary literary criticism of the Gospels:

> There is something of a wonderful mystery in the way that the gospels mean what they mean for each new age. Readers bring much that is individual and subjective to their understanding. The concerns of the church play an important part in exegesis. There are many ways to listen to a text, and it is a fascinating as well as humbling experience to trace the diverse interpretations of a work such as Luke from Marcion to Irenaeus and Augustine, down through the age of the established Church, into the reformation and its many denominational branches.
>
> Nevertheless, at some point—behind the individual reader and

15. A topic much in need of book-length treatment. In addition to *Secrecy,* 101–23, the following discussions are recommended: Canary and Kozicki, eds., *History*; Ricoeur, *Time,* 1:91–231; and White, *Tropics.* For a glimpse of the kinds of issues that recur in these discussions, see Martin, *Recent Theories,* 71–75, or White, "Question." Certain New Testament scholars have also addressed these issues: Güttgemanns, "Normativität"; Via, *Ethics,* 209–25; and cf. Phillips, ed., "Text, Context," and Seeley, "Poststructuralist."

behind Church tradition, homiletics, theology, ethics, and meditation—*lies a text that strains to be understood in its own categories.* (1–2,
emphasis added)

To turn back the great horde of concealing if edifying interpretations, and
release the essential, pristine text, is the task that Dawsey sets himself
(compare our comments above on the introductions to exegetical articles).
For many other critics too of a narrative, structuralist, compositional, or
canonical stamp, it is the extrinsic tradition of biblical scholarship, preoccupied with source and history, that has neglected and obscured the essential text. Does Kermode think in similar terms when he speaks of
"structures of explanation which come between us and the text . . . like
some wall of wavy glass"? Perhaps I have made too much of a single phrase.
But perusing the *Genesis of Secrecy* one does get the impression that there
is something hard and essential for him behind the wall of glass. Any
definitive grasping of that something, however, would be doomed to failure from the start. For Kermode, it is the recalcitrant nature of narrative
texts not to yield up their secrets, not even to initiates of the guild. Further
still along the scale from guarded optimism to unbridled skepticism come
the literary pragmatists: Fish, Walter Michaels, Steven Mailloux, and others.[16] In these latitudes, the notion that the critic might somehow "get
back to the text" would be viewed as a thoroughly mystified one, as would
the corollary notion that the critic might let the text "speak for itself " in
its "own" categories, and not bring extrinsic concerns to bear on it. The
fallacy, for the pragmatists, would lie in thinking that one can downplay
or otherwise relativize the role of interpretation to allow the real text to
appear. This is an impossibility, because in order to present the text in its
own categories one must at the very least describe it, and description can
proceed only from within some comprehensive context or situation (socio-
economic, cultural, gender-specific, institutional, etc.), that yields up the
object of description in all its "essential" detail. To interpret at all is to
interpret absolutely but to interpret absolutely is to produce absolutely.

16. The approach has variously been called interpretationism, institutionalism, profes-
sionalism, constitutive hermeneutics, and New Pragmatism. Representative works, in addition to those of Fish, include: Fowl, "Ethics"; Knapp and Michaels, "Against Theory";
Mailloux, *Conventions* and "Hermeneutics"; Michaels, "Formalism" and "Saving"; Rorty,
"Lumps"; and Stout, "Meaning." Related, though less identifiably pragmatic, are Culler,
Poetics and "Prolegomena"; Ellis, *Theory*; Horton, *Interpreting*; and Kermode, *Telling*, 156–
84. Finally (or first of all) see Mitchell, ed., *Against Theory*, a series of positions and responses
including Knapp and Michaels's manifesto, Fish's "Consequences," and contributions by
Rorty, Mailloux, E. D. Hirsch, Jr., et al.

The distinction between intrinsic and extrinsic criticism, which many exegetes adduce or presuppose (including myself at times in preceding chapters), is, in this view, a dubious or misconceived one, since there is nothing
proper to the text, nothing it owns prior to description, that an intrinsic
criticism might uncover.

Essentialist views of the biblical text are rife in biblical scholarship.
The following example is selected from the work of a distinguished New
Testament hermeneutician: "we must ask how to determine whether that
which molds the life of a given Christian community is actually the Bible
or simply a particular interpretation of the Bible mediated through selec-
tive and privileged ways of understanding and using the text" (Thiselton,
"Reader-Response," 81). The phrase "actually the Bible," as used in this
sentence, is problematic for precisely the same reason that Dawsey's "a
text that strains to be understood in its own categories" was. What the
Bible actually is, is so completely a function of interpretive context that
the actually must always be an "actually." Any view of what the Bible
actually is, however conscientious and considered, will always be a "selec-
tive and privileged way of understanding" it from the standpoint of some
other person or group: women, gays and lesbians, Jews, blacks, AIDS
victims, and many others, have, at different times and in different ways,
been given the short end of the stick (generally across their shoulders) by
appeal to what the Bible actually says, or is. But by enabling the "actually"
always to be put in quotation marks, neopragmatic and other radical interpretation theories might be appropriated by critical theologies of liberation to put the various discourses of oppression in question.[17]

One corollary of the foregoing considerations is that our interpretive
decisions do have consequences of a sort not adequately taken into account
by Fish—and not only when we take a stand on loaded ethical issues.
Take the seemingly innocuous example of a methodological shift in biblical

17. Though radical interpretation theories would put most of the current discourses
of liberation out of action just as swiftly, e.g., Belo, *Reading*; Collins, ed., *Perspectives*; Clévenot, *Approaches*; Russell, ed., *Interpretation*; Schottroff and Stegemann, eds., *God*; Schüssler-
Fiorenza, *In Memory* and *Bread*; and van Tilborg, *Sermon*. We lack biblical scholars who
combine the ethical commitment of a Belo or a Schüssler Fiorenza with the epistemic
perspicacity of a Foucault, a Said, or even a Fish—though certain of the articles in Fisher
and Jobling, eds., "Ethics," and Phillips, ed., "Text, Context," come close. That philosophical
skepticisms at least of the order of Foucault's need not be incommensurate with theologies
of liberation is at any rate evident from such works as Welch, *Communities,* and West,
Prophesy. While biblical theologians of liberation have been shielded to date from the epistemic challenges of nonfoundationalist critical theory, many of their Marxist and feminist
counterparts in neighboring disciplines have had to confront such challenge and adapt to it;
see, inter alia, Ryan, *Marxism*; Spivak, *Other Worlds*; and Weeden, *Practice*.

scholarship. Having reflected on what it cannot mean, epistemically speaking, to choose an intrinsic method of biblical criticism over an extrinsic one, let us now reflect on what it might mean, politically speaking. Biblical criticism seems to run on the assumption that the solid bottom of all critical activity is a biblical text densely packed with describable properties. So long as this assumption holds good, the claim that one's critical method is more true to the text's intrinsic properties (its properties as a narrative, for example) than somebody else's (historical or theological) method will be seen as a persuasive one that, given time and converts, might resettle the loci of influence and authority within the guild. (I doubt the narrativist position is that persuasive, but let it suffice as an example.) Interpretations do have consequences that pertain to economic survival (i.e., employment), publishability, tenure, promotion, and prestige within the academy, and to relations with the churches, the seminary, the university, and society in general—Küng, Schillebeeckx, Curran et al. are sobering reminders of this. What Fish fails to take sufficient account of is "that interpretive communities are bound to be communities on other grounds as well, bound to have common interests besides the production of interpretations, bound to correspond to other social differentiations" (Pratt, "Strategies," 228). Though he does recognize, some of the time,

> that consensus is never peaceful, that interpretations are always jostling for space, thumping on each other's walls . . . he seems unwilling to pursue the full consequence of this fact, namely that there is always doubt, conflict, disagreement, because interpretations are always there in multiplicity denying each other the illusion of self-containment and truth, the full confidence of belief that each would like to maintain. People and groups are constituted not by single unified belief systems, but by competing self-contradictory ones. Knowledge is interested, and interest implies conflict; to advance an interpretation is to insert it into a network of power relations. (Ibid.)[18]

That is why the shift from an ontological to a pragmatic text-theory does not engender a relativism in which "anything goes" or in which all interpretations are now equal(ly wrong)—"silly relativism," as Rorty carica-

18. Pratt's reservations regarding Fish are widely echoed; see, inter alia, Burnett, "Postmodern"; Freund, *Return*, 110–11; Norris, *de Man*, 125–48 passim; Shepherd, "Authority," 139–42; Ray, *Literary Meaning*, 165–69; Weber, *Institution*, 34ff.; and cf. Said, "Opponents." Further on the politics of biblical interpretation, see (in addition to Burnett), Noll, "Review," 506–9, and Schüssler Fiorenza, "Ethics." Kermode too is very much better on the politics of interpretation than Fish; see "Control," an incisive account of biblical and literary interpretation.

tures it ("Lumps," 12).[19] What constrains and prevents interpretive anarchy in the academy? Is it the presence of objective, invariant, primary texts? Or is it the shape of the rest of social and material life—the network of interests and forces whose complex intersection determines the meanings of the texts, meanings on which real issues hinge, obstructing or foreclosing their subjective determination?

Returning to our revaluation of exegetical options, we can say that the moderate reader-response method that predominates in reader-oriented New Testament work fares no better epistemologically in a strong interpretation theory than do historical or narrativist methods. Moderate reader-response theory, which stresses the textual engagement of a creative reading subject, does unsettle the traditional image of the replete biblical text, as we saw above, by suggesting its radical incompleteness. This moderate interpretationism, however, is itself unsettled in turn by a neopragmatic theory of reading. Earlier I cited Wolfgang Iser's analogy of the roles of readers to two people gazing at the night sky at the same collection of stars; one may see the image of a plough, the other that of a dipper. "The 'stars' in a literary text are fixed," writes Iser, "the lines that join them are variable." Iser's residual realism, however, his insistence that texts do have some properties that are fixed and innate, leaves his flank open to attack from the pragmatist camp: "Gaps are not built into the text," replies Fish, "but appear (or do not appear) as a consequence of particular interpretive strategies. . . . There is no distinction between what the text gives and what the reader supplies; he supplies *everything*; the stars in a literary text are not fixed; they are just as variable as the lines that join them" ("Afraid," 7).[20]

Right around the methodological board, then—historical, narrativist, reader-centered—a Fish-like theory would unsettle and resettle claims and stakes. I should stress that Fish's theory, which commended itself for use

19. Cf. Rorty, *Consequences,* 166–67: "Except for the occasional cooperative freshman, one cannot find anybody who says that two incompatible opinions on an important topic are equally good. The philosophers who get *called* relativists are those who say that the ground for choosing between opinions is less algorithmic than had been thought. . . . So the real issue is not between people who think one view is as good as another and people who do not. It is between those who think our culture, or purposes, or intuitions, cannot be supported except conversationally, and people who still hope for other sorts of support." (To Rorty's pragmatic "conversationally," we should add a Foucauldian clause: "or by the operations of power, whether covert or overt.")

20. For Iser's reply to Fish, see "Whales." Iser's postulate of constraining textual "givens" is similarly challenged by Culler, *On Deconstruction,* 75–76, and Mailloux, *Conventions,* 197–99. For a differently nuanced argument challenging both Iser and Fish, see Freund, *Return,* 148–51.

in this chapter by reason of its rigor and clarity, is merely one drop in a large pond. As one commentator puts it, there are three "very large claims" that have converged in continental and Anglo-American critical theory in recent years. These are "(i) the rejection of what (under various labels) may be termed *foundationalism* . . . (ii) the advocacy of *historicism*; and (iii) the admission of *praxical* constraints on the powers and scope of human cognition" (Margolis, "Threads," 96; cf. Dean, "Challenge," 266ff.). The ensuing prospect must be an epistemologically discomfiting one for biblical critics. The prospect is of biblical interpretation that can never hit bottom. In this perspective, a vertiginous one for scholarship as for faith, the biblical text loses its status as an objective and stable entity: one which might guarantee belief (for it is itself a product of belief and other ways of sense making), and one which might validate or overrule interpretations (it cannot if it is itself a product of interpretation). In this perspective, biblical criticism itself takes on the aspect of faith, of belief in a prior and independent text that is the origin and end of all interpretation. It is Bultmannian skepticism about the recovery of an historical foundation for faith turned, not just on the concept of a recoverable historical sub-stratum in the gospel text, but on the concept of the text itself in addition. And it is Bultmannian insistence on the impossibility of a purely scientific presuppositionless understanding turned up to the topmost notch. This time it is the scholar, and not just the believer, who must leap into the epistemological abyss.

(It should be remembered that this chapter is a debunking exercise designed to exorcise whatever vestiges of naive realism cling to our collective exegetical psyche. Epistemologically the text is an abyss but praxi-cally it spills over with properties, as noted earlier. Such debunking does, however, have undeniable implications for religious faith.)

Without becoming unduly apocalyptic, it seems to me that the first faint tinges of a philosophical biblical criticism, or something very like it, are now perceptible on the horizon—a criticism twinned to philosophical theology and content to labor (as philosophical theology sometimes is) without epistemological or ontological guarantees. The challenge is to move on from a hermeneutics of innocence. We know we must interpret, must drink the sea (Kierkegaard's sea "seventy thousand fathoms deep"). We chase down meanings for a living, but leaden-limbed we cannot keep up with them. The biblical text never stays still. The movement of its potential senses is perpetual; it never slows or stops. Should that not give us pause for thought? Might our bloated critical practice not need lancing with a metacritical acuity? Today, it is biblical criticism itself that cries out for demythologizing.

In *Beyond Deconstruction* (1985), Howard Felperin urges a "theoretical practice" on his fellow literary critics, one "that is philosophically informed, reflective, and critical, but purged of all epistemological or quasi-scientific claims or pretensions" (40 n. 19). What might be the practical consequences of a philosophical swerve in biblical criticism? This is a difficult question to address. On the more trivial level, we might expect a lessening off of the sort of claim in which one brings out long-buried meanings from the biblical text, put in there long ago, which have lain dormant and undisturbed like the Qumran caves or the library at Nag Hammadi, in favor of a more lively awareness that criticism is an inescapably creative activity. Chastened by this humdrum, weak interpretationism, business would go on much as before except claims would now be formulated more circumspectly. Indeed, a widespread change of this sort would be no real change at all, merely a license for us to proceed exactly as we always did, but with "a gold star for being honest and call[ing] an interpretation an interpretation instead of a fact" (Pratt, "Strategies," 228). However, I doubt that we are doomed to such blandness. Consider the following remark of Ernst Troeltsch, made when historical criticism was still young: "Once the historical method is applied to biblical science . . . it is a leaven that alters everything, and, finally, bursts apart the entire structure of theological methods employed until the present" (*Schriften,* II: 730, quoted in Poland, *Literary Criticism,* 23). What precisely today's leaven is, and what transformations it will wreak, is much harder to say. All that can be said is that the modernist certainty that animated Troelsch—the certainty that the world represents "a fixed object of analysis quite separable from the forms of discourse by which men speak of it" (Reiss, *Modernism,* 44)—is breaking down across the humanities, the social sciences, and even the hard sciences today. The world that is being reconceived is no longer the modern world; rather, it is a "modern-becoming-postmodern world" (Cox, *Religion,* 176). We are straddling two epistemic paradigms at present, the newer of which is still inchoate. I confess that the "postmodern Bible" is one calculated to give little comfort—"Some of the consequences of what I am saying dismay even me" (Bloom, *Kabbalah,* 125)—but then the modernist (historical critical) Bible was daunting too at first, not to say shocking, and indeed it still is for many. And as the challenge was once to come to terms with the modernist Bible, so now the challenge is to come to terms with its postmodern successor. There are two paradigm shifts impinging on biblical studies at present. The first is a methodological shift, a shift from diachronic to synchronic methods, one trajectory of which is a shift from history to story. But reports abound of seismic activity in neighboring fields. This latter upheaval is more than a methodological shift; it is rather an epistemic shift that portends to change the way we think, across a span of disciplines, about texts, about method, even about the human and material world.[21] In biblical studies today the epistemic shift is considerably less obtrusive than the methodological shift, but we can expect it to move steadily to the fore in coming decades.

21. This is, of course, a greatly simplified sketch of the modern-postmodern shift. My usage of the term modern, like that of Habermas ("Modernity") and Reiss (*Modernism*), suspends the privilege usually accorded to the aesthetic axis of modernity in the debate on postmodernism versus modernism. Messmer, "Making Sense," offers a useful entrée to that debate, whose important statements include: Lyotard, *Condition*; Huyssen, *Great Divide*; Foster, ed., *Anti-Aesthetic*; Hassan, *Turn*; and Hutcheon, *Postmodernism*. Specficially on the biblical trajectory, see Burnett, "Postmodern"; Fowler, "Biblical Criticism"; Martin, "Paradigm"; and Phillips, *Biblical Exegesis*, "Different Voices," and "Praxis"; and cf. Breech, *Jesus*, and McKnight, *Postmodern Use*.

8

Stories of Reading That Come Undone: Misadventures in Postcriticism

[T]he disputes among literary theorists more and more appear to be like quarrels among theologians.
—Paul de Man, *The Resistance to Theory*

The process of . . . reading . . . is similar to the classical dialectic of sin and grace: one must be cleared of the illusions of self-sufficiency (of mastery over the text) before one can attend to the word of grace (to the mystery present within the text).
—David Fisher, "The Phenomenology of Displacement"

[I]n the experience of mortality you understand that . . . we are caught up in [an] extraordinarily complex texture . . . which we cannot unravel. [T]he experience of being unable to dominate a text, to get control of everything that is happening in it, is part of being "mortal" in this sense.
—John Caputo, *Radical Hermeneutics*

Works like Kermode's *Genesis of Secrecy* and Fish's *Is There a Text?* throw whatever essentialist or naive-realist tendencies we harbor as biblical exegetes to the wolves. It was to indicate something of the ferocity of the beast that I switched from Kermode to Fish, whose merciless rigor on the topic of the text's status relative to the interpreter distinguishes him from Kermode and almost every other critic-theoretician.

But with Fish, who takes his lead principally from strains of Anglo-American philosophy, we have not yet arrived at deconstruction. Fish is an excellent entrée to postmodernist ways of thinking about texts, but ultimately he leaves us at the threshold. However, my intention in the present chapter is not to have some other thinker (Derrida, for example) take the baton from Fish and press relentlessly on to the "finishing line," in the way that we had Fish take over from Kermode. My intention is far less ambitious. Given that Fish's later ideas, despite their interest and importance, are ill-equipped for reading individual texts (unless it be the reading of their interpretation), and that deconstruction's domain and forte is precisely that of reading texts, I wish to illustrate its potential in the sphere of gospel studies, using the recent work of Werner Kelber on the Fourth Gospel as an example and attempting to extend that work with a reading of my own. Before that, I assess John Dominic Crossan's post-structuralist reflections on the parables of Jesus, which culminated in his

Cliffs of Fall. Still outlining my agenda in reverse order, I preface these three items with a brief introduction to deconstruction.

A Brawler in the House of Being

One way of grasping deconstruction (which extends a greasy palm to the grasper) is as a means of thinking language through that hones to a razor-sharp edge certain strains of continental philosophy that wend their way circuitously from Hegel down through Heidegger. Crucial to the honing in question is a strategic drawing on linguistics. Ferdinand de Saussure, father of modern linguistics, had argued that the linguistic sign is arbitrary and conventional: for example, different languages have entirely different words for the same thing. In consequence, the linguistic sign is defined not by *innate properties*—its "proper" (acoustic, graphic) qualities are arbitrary, after all—but by the *differences* that distinguish it from other signs; in a linguistic system, says Saussure, "there are only differences" (*Course,* 118). For example, *pig* can function the way it does, not because of what it is, acoustically speaking, but because of what it is not, that is, *jig, fig, big,* and so forth. The linguistic sign had two constituents for Saussure: the *signifier,* which is the sensible (acoustic or graphic) constituent, and the *signified,* which is the concept communicated by the signifier.

Derridean deconstruction can be understood in part as an emphatic affirmation of Saussure's dictum that language is a network of differences, joined to a still more emphatic rejection of Saussure's order of signifieds. The signified, for Derrida, can neither orient nor stabilize the sign. The signified is itself perpetually caught up in the play of signifiers; like the signifier, it can be grasped differentially and relationally only, by its difference from other signifieds, other concepts. The very distinction between signifier and signified is thus an arbitrary and conventional one; "the signified always already functions as a signifier" (*Grammatology,* 7). The history of Western thought, for Derrida, amounts to the "powerful, systematic, and irrepressible desire" for a "transcendental" signified—an order of meaning that would be originary, self-identical, and self-evident and that would "place a reassuring end to the reference from sign to sign" (49). But this would require a signified capable of being grasped in itself, nondifferentially. What recognition of the irreducible relationality of the signified denies such concepts is presence. The play of differences

> prevents there from being at any moment or in any way a simple element that is present in and of itself and refers only to itself.

Whether in written or in spoken discourse, no element can function
as a sign without relating to another element which itself is not simply
present. This linkage means that each "element"—phoneme or gra-
pheme—is constituted with reference to the trace in it of the other
elements of the sequence or system. . . . Nothing . . . is anywhere
simply present or absent. There are only, everywhere, differences and
traces of traces. (*Positions*, 26)

What is rocked on its (for Derrida, illusory) foundations by such thinking
is metaphysics, preeminently a framework of ultimate oppositions (tran-
scendent/immanent, intelligible/sensible, necessary/contingent, nature/cul-
ture, object/representation, speech/writing, etc.) in which one term belongs to presence and the other denotes a fall from presence. Derrida's
general claim is "that all the names related to fundamentals, to principles,
or to the center have always designated an invariable presence—*eidos, arche,
telos, energeia, ousia* (essence, existence, substance, subject), *aletheia,* tran-
scendentality, consciousness, or conscience, God, man, and so forth"
(*Writing,* 279–80). His project is directed against that Western nostalgia
for full presence that bespeaks a dread of insecurity—that *ontotheological*
yearning, which has petrified philosophical thought from the overt metaphysics of Plato down to the covert metaphysics of Heidegger.[1]

What has all this got to do with texts? Still speaking very generally,
we can say that in deconstruction, as in neopragmatism in the style of
Fish, the text is denied a substantial presence. The Platonic notion of an
ideal text untouched and uncontaminated in its inner, essential structure
by the incessant wash of interpretations goes overboard in both kinds of
thinking. But deconstruction's dissolution of the essential text is of a piece
with its dissolution of the sign:

[T]exts are necessarily intertextual. . . . Since each text becomes itself
in relation to other texts, no text is self-contained. . . . There can no

1. Listed roughly in order of adequacy and difficulty, the following are authoritative
introductions to Derrida and deconstruction: Norris, *Deconstruction*; Harland, *Superstructuralism,* 125–54; Culler, *On Deconstruction*; Norris, *Derrida*; Descombes, *French Philosophy,*
136–52; Leitch, *Deconstructive Criticism*; Gasché, *Tain*; and Ulmer, *Grammatology.* The following assess deconstruction's implications for biblical studies: Atkins, *Reading,* 41–48;
Blank, "Babel"; Detweiler, ed., "Derrida" (see Schneidau, "The Word," esp.); Hunter, "Deconstruction"; LaFargue, "Determinate"; Mackey, "Bethlehem" (the best in my opinion,
along with Schneidau); McKnight, *The Reader,* 84–94; Seeley, "Criticism"; and cf. Aichele,
Limits; Faur, *Doves*; Handelman, "Derrida" and *Slayers*; Hartman, "Struggle"; Jacobson,
"Absence"; Schneidau, *Discontent,* 248–306; Via, *Ethics,* 210–13; and Phillips, ed., "Text,
Context." Derrida himself has also written on (or round about) biblical interpretation, e.g.,
"Apocalyptic Tone," "Des Tours," and *Writing,* 64–78, 294–300.

more be a text-in-itself than there can be independent signifiers. Texts, like the signs which comprise them, ceaselessly cross and criss-cross in a perpetual process of interweaving. As a result of this oscillating interplay, texts are neither stable nor static, but are transitory. The meaning of a text, therefore, is never fully present; it is always in the process of forming, deforming, and reforming. (Taylor, "Deconstruction," 400)[2]

Fish and Derrida inhabit different mental continents, assuredly, but they breathe the same thin antisubstantialist air. And though Fish is not himself a card-carrying deconstructor,[3] he does effect something like a deconstruction of the primary text (the Bible, for example) as traditional criticism has conceived it. His brutal handling of that solid-seeming text corresponds, for example, to a deconstructive critique as Barbara Johnson has defined it: "The critique reads backwards from what seems natural, obvious, self-evident, or universal, in order to show that . . . the starting point is not a (natural) given but a (cultural) construct. . . . Every theory starts somewhere, every critique exposes what that starting point conceals, and thereby displaces all the ideas that follow from it" ("Introduction," xv). And indeed, right around the methodological board, as we saw—historical, story-centered, reader-oriented—Fish's theory unsettled and re-settled foundations and claims.

But Deconstruction (the capital-D, Derridean or Demanian kind) would undoubtedly cast an unsettling glance in turn on Fish's aspirations for discursive transcendence—his endeavor to offer a definitive interpretation of interpretation by way of a text (his own), which, by sheer fiat and sleight of hand, would seek to make itself immune from the necessity of unending redefinition, which, on Fish's diagnosis, is the incurable condition of every other text. For Derrida and de Man, in contrast, there are no uninfected physicians (this will be developed below, particularly with reference to Derrida).[4]

2. Cf. Taylor, *Erring*, 178–80; Phillips, "Intertextuality"; and Derrida, "Living On," 83–84: "a 'text' . . . is henceforth no longer a finished corpus of writing, some content enclosed in a book or its margins, but a differential network, a fabric of traces referring endlessly to something other than itself, to other differential traces."

3. In "Consequences," 457 n. 12, Fish describes himself as being situated "in the practice and convention-centered tradition that includes Ludwig Wittgenstein, W. V. Quine, Hilary Putnam, Richard Rorty, and Donald Davidson, in addition to Jacques Derrida, Michel Foucault, and other continental thinkers."

4. Pertinent also to the contrast between Fish and Derrida (and between Anglo-American theory and French) is the status of the self in each. Fish, while willing to appropriate text-dissolving strains of French thought, leaves virtually untouched corresponding

Unquestionably, this poses a challenge to our preceding chapter, which depended heavily on Fish. But that challenge is situated within an even broader one: deconstruction would question all the binary oppositions in which all our preceding chapters traded—the text/reader opposition, and also the story/theology, story/discourse, intrinsic/extrinsic, form/content, orality/literacy, and immediacy/mediacy oppositions. This is not to argue that everything finally reduces to an undifferentiated primal soup but to argue that even as we elevate one term over another in our critical discourse (*content,* or *text*), the systematically repressed term (*form,* or *reader*) can be unobtrusively establishing the foregrounded term, presiding over its production. But deconstruction tends to insist that there is always a vice versa to this process. From another angle, the text (to take our chapter 7 example) will be governing the reading experience, presiding over its production. Thus, deconstruction's rejoinder to Fish would be that "[t]here is neither interpretation without text nor text without interpretation. Text and interpretation form a symbiotic relationship in which each simultaneously feeds on and nourishes the other" (Taylor, "Deconstruction," 401; cf. Taylor, *Erring,* 180). Our ability to oscillate back and forth between these two conflicting perspectives is enabled by "an economy of presence and absence . . . a shifting ground of perceptions . . . a figure/ground relationship which does not allow for total visibility of both at the same time" (Harvey, "Wellsprings," 140). Although we can best apprehend this operation by reflecting on one opposition in isolation (e.g., text/reader), to engage in even the simplest act of interpretation is to juggle a multiplicity of oppositions all at once: "in a way which has been felicitously described by Gestaltists and phenomenologists, we organize, interpret, read, alter, and configure patterns in amazingly swift, adroit, and complex ways. We do not pass through a series of ordered steps, we do not run through all the combinatorial possibilities. We are not presence/ absence machines, electronic switchboards with one switch on and one switch off, but rather some kind of fluid movement which is all too messy for [artificial intelligence] research to master" (Caputo, *Hermeneutics,* 226–27). Interpretation cuts into the flux of combinatorial possibilities to hazard certain configurational resolutions—not haphazardly, certainly (interpretation is irreducibly transpersonal, as Fish and others have persuasively shown), nor consciously for the most part (we "always already" inhabit

---

theories of the subject in which the subject ceases, like the text, to have any transcendent status prior or extrinsic to language. This counterhumanism has long been a driving force in French theory, variously impelling Althusser, Barthes, Deleuze, Derrida, Foucault, Lacan, Lévi-Strauss et al. (see further Berman, *Reception*; Smith, *Subject*).

some interpretive context, so that the flux assumes shape independently of our conscious efforts). But "[b]eneath, behind, around, to the side of all grounding and founding, in the ground's cracks and crevices and interstices, is the play" (225). We can oscillate between two conflicting perspectives and settle on one of them. But the repressed perspective generally returns to unsettle our attempted repose. And when we pass from the case of a hypothetical single opposition to the multioppositional juggling act of interpretation, that latent instability is multiplied exponentially. Our configurational resolutions are erected on seething flux—not that we have any other choice. Certain pragmatic constraints do lend a temporary stability to our constructions. And since they make our lives livable—or cast long dark shadows over them, as the case may be—our constructions can not be taken lightly. But we do need occasional reminding of the "coefficient of uncertainty" attaching to our constructions. We need to have our "level of vigilance about their constituted, contingent nature" raised "lest we become so habituated to them as to . . . begin treating as 'self-evident' what are no more than . . . temporary stabilizations of the flow" (145). Hence my tactical insistence that *text* and *content*—ostensibly the primary, stable, given terms in two of our nodal oppositions (text/reader and content/form)—were contingent, constructed, secondary terms.

But let us elucidate the differences between neopragmatism and deconstruction a little further. For the empirically minded Fish, the things that bring a solid-seeming text into view (contexts, premises, practices) are precisely the things to watch. In Fish-style pragmatism, language plays a very minor role; it is a relatively innocuous and stable element. For the metaphysically fixated deconstructors it is language itself, always dragging the whole of metaphysics in its wake, that begs to be demystified. In "The Ends of Man" (1972) Derrida distinguishes two possible strategies for dealing with the metaphysical alluvium in language. The first, Heidegger's destruction (*Destruktion, Abbau,* hence "deconstruction") of the history of ontology labored "without changing terrain . . . by using against the edifice the instruments or stones available in the house." The second, Derrida's deconstruction of that same history (which now includes Heidegger) attempts instead "to change terrain, in a discontinuous and irruptive fashion, by brutally placing oneself outside, and by affirming an absolute break and difference" (*Margins,* 135). The first, over-gentle style of deconstruction can be called the "soft" style—though Heidegger is a poor example of deconstructive docility; infinitely better examples abound in the work of his and Derrida's many epheboi. The second, utterly pitiless, no-holds-barred style of deconstruction can be called the "hard" style, which has not been applied to the Gospels to date, while the softer style has been. (The soft style typically submits the apparent self-consistency of literary texts to stringent interrogation—uses "against the edifice the instruments or the stones available in the house"—which can result in a tottering or collapse of their internal logic.)[5] I introduce Werner Kelber's recent Johannine work as an unusually ambitious example of the soft style, and I supplement it with a marginally firmer deconstruction of my own. En route we tarry by Derrida's adamantine deconstruction, in the manner of a tour group confronted with some cultural enigma. But first, to better illustrate the intellectual climate of poststructuralism and the respiratory difficulties it can induce—especially in an environment as inimical to it as biblical studies—let us turn to John Dominic Crossan's innovative work on the parables of the late 1970s.

The Joyous Affirmation of the Play of the World

Here, in one of the most frequently quoted passages of his earlier work, is how Derrida contrasts classical interpretation with (post)modernist: "There are . . . two interpretations of interpretation. . . . The one seeks to decipher, dreams of deciphering, a truth or an origin which escapes play and the order of the sign, and which lives the necessity of interpretation as an exile. The other, which is no longer turned toward the origin, affirms play" (*Writing,* 292).[6] Derrida characterizes the living of the necessity of interpretation "as an exile," as "the saddened, *negative,* nostalgic, guilty, Rousseauistic side of the thinking of play" (ibid.). Kermode's ruminations

5. "Soft" deconstruction is an American product, whose corporate headquarters might be said to have been at Yale University until Paul de Man's death in 1983. Deconstruction's image in current biblical studies (the very latest fad, something one has heard about, something entirely peripheral) corresponds to its image in American literary criticism in the early 1970s. Interestingly, therefore, if deconstruction seemed to threaten the literary critical institution in the 1970s, by the close of the 1980s it has been incorporated into it (cf. Arac, ed., *Yale Critics,* 3–40, and the now steady trickle of titles in the *After Derrida* and *Beyond Deconstruction* mode). The merger might be said to have been officially sealed by the 1986 election of J. Hillis Miller (an unrepentant arch-Derridean) to the presidency of the Modern Language Association. At the same time, "Yale deconstruction" has been succeeded by a more heterogeneous and more political "poststructuralist criticism" (Machin and Norris, eds., *Readings* is a typical example), which may hold sway for quite some time (I have in mind the longevity of the New Criticism after it had taken hold in the 1930s and 1940s after much initial resistance).

6. The essay is "Structure, Sign, and Play in the Discourse of the Human Sciences." Originally delivered at a 1966 Johns Hopkins conference designed to welcome structuralism to America, this paper later came to be seen as indicating the arrival, neck and neck with structuralism, of a mutinous or stowaway poststructuralism.

in the *Genesis of Secrecy* on the necessity of interpreting ad infinitum uncannily confirm these declarations of Derrida. Kermode writes: "The plea-
sures of interpretation are henceforth linked to loss and disappointment"
(123). And again:

> World and book, it may be, are hopelessly plural, endlessly disap-
> pointing; we stand alone before them, aware of their arbitrariness and
> impenetrability, knowing that they may be narratives only because of
> our impudent intervention, and susceptible of interpretation only by
> our hermetic tricks. Hot for secrets, our only conversations may be
> with guardians who know less and see less than we can; and our sole
> hope and pleasure is in the perception of a momentary radiance,
> before the door of disappointment is finally shut on us." (145)

Perpetually outside, the interpreter lives the necessity of interpretation as
an exile. Or as Derrida puts it: "The necessity of commentary . . . is the
very form of exiled speech. In the beginning is hermeneutics" (*Writing*,
67).

To the "saddened, *negative,* nostalgic, guilty, Rousseauistic" way of
thinking, Derrida opposes a Nietzschean way that is the "joyous affirmation of the play of the world and of the innocence of becoming, the
affirmation of a world of signs without fault, without truth, and without
origin which is offered to an active interpretation. *This affirmation then
determines the noncenter otherwise than as loss of the center.* And it plays
without security" (*Writing*, 292).[7]

Nietzschean affirmation found expression in New Testament studies
in a book that appeared around the same time as the *Genesis of Secrecy* and
that accorded a similarly privileged role to Jesus' parable of the Sower:
John Dominic Crossan's *Cliffs of Fall: Paradox and Polyvalence in the Parables of Jesus* (1980). Here, Crossan completes a series of reflections initiated
in *In Parables* (1973) and developed through *The Dark Interval* (1975), *Raid
on the Articulate* (1976), and *Finding Is the First Act* (1979). Crossan's
parables oeuvre has two aspects. It is an interpretation of Jesus and his
parables. It is also an intellectual pilgrimage (analogous to that of Stanley
Fish), which takes Crossan all the way from the New Critics and the New
Quest to Derrida and "negative atheology." I locate Crossan at the end
(or thereabouts) of his intellectual adventure, centering principally on his
Cliffs of Fall. Crossan's contribution to parables scholarship is not my direct

---

7. But as Derrida goes on to intimate, one can not simply exit the first way of thinking
to pass cavalierly to the second. Elsewhere he uses other figures to allegorize the two ways:
Husserl vs. Joyce (*Geometry,* 102–3); the rabbi vs. the poet (*Writing,* 67ff.).

concern; that has been handled by others.[8] Neither am I presenting *Cliffs of Fall* as paradigmatic of the deconstructive reading of the Gospels. *Cliffs of Fall* is less an instance of deconstructive criticism (it lacks the rigorous, nose-to-the-text attitude that so frequently characterizes the latter, at least in the United States), than a forerunner of deconstructive theology. But what *Cliffs of Fall* does supply for us here is an entry to the universe (or multiverse) of poststructuralist thought.[9]

Cliffs of Fall is a collection of three related essays. The first, "Paradox and Metaphor," takes as its point of departure Paul Ricoeur's description of parable as "the conjunction of a narrative form and a metaphorical process" (*Cliffs,* 1, quoting Ricoeur, "Hermeneutics," 30). To these two defining characteristics, Crossan adds a third: brevity. Then, still following Ricoeur—Ricoeur of *The Rule of Metaphor,* whom Crossan believes is but a heartbeat away from Derrida[10]—Crossan argues that the constitutive principle of language in general is metaphor. There is no literal or proper language that is nonmetaphorical, nonfigurative, or nonrhetorical.[11] Furthermore, since a narrative form can be joined to a metaphorical process as in a parable, might this not "mean that narrativity might be just as humanly ubiquitous and ineluctable as metaphoricity itself?" (*Cliffs,* 12). Does narrative not "refer to a world and a reality that it itself has created and which without it is humanly incomprehensible and unintelligible, is just the humming buzz of meaningless sense impressions?" If so, the real issue lies "not in setting existence against language or world against metaphor or reality against narrative, but in facing the ultimate implications of a radically linguistic existence, a radically metaphorical world, and a radically narrative existence" (13).

Crossan reads Jesus as one who did just that, or something very like

8. Though appraisal of Crossan's parables scholarship is almost always interlinked with appraisal of his narrative theology. See, *inter alia,* Brown and Malbon, "Parabling"; Hoffman, *Law,* 15–38; Kee, "Polyvalence"; Thiselton, "Reader-Response," 101ff.; Poland, *Literary Criticism,* 108–20; and Tolbert, "Polyvalence."

9. Though he admits the decisive impact of Derrida on his thinking on metaphor (*Cliffs,* 9), Crossan in the period with which we are concerned does not style himself a deconstructor or a poststructuralist. He does espouse a liminal structuralism, however (e.g., *Cliffs,* 71–72), which would be termed poststructuralism today.

10. Erroneously, as Brown and Malbon point out ("Parabling," 534, n. 2). Crossan's key quotation from Ricoeur is actually Ricoeur's rendering of Derrida's position, which Ricoeur goes on to contest.

11. "[N]one of this denies that in certain cases and situations we may wish to render a given speech as univalent and literal as possible. But language is intrinsically not on our side in such perfectly legitimate endeavors" (Crossan, *Cliffs,* 8). Clearly, this matter could be debated at some length.

it. In addition to metaphor, narrativity and brevity, Jesus' parables were characterized by paradox. In later parables ascribed to Tannaitic scribes and rabbis (ca. 220 C.E.), contextualization leaves little doubt as to the intended meaning of the parable. Jesus' strategy was just the opposite, according to Crossan, resulting in a deliberate and extravagant paradoxicality, which Crossan, echoing a theme of *Raid on the Articulate* and *Finding Is the First Act,* reads as a late expression of Israel's *aniconic monotheism.* "Such a monotheism can only generate single paradoxical images, or double contradictory images, or multiple and polyvalent images of its God" (*Cliffs,* 58). And in Jesus, Israel's monotheistic tradition forced "the aniconicity of God onto the surface of language itself and, with inevitable paradox, announced that God could no more be trapped in the forms and genres of linguistic art than in the shapes and figures of plastic art" (20).

Crossan's Jesus is thus a precursor of the *via negativa,* a parabler-poet at the limits of language and possibility, who evokes for us "the other side of silence" (*Raid,* 49–50). And Jesus' parables, which adapt chameleon-like to the postmodernism that colors Crossan's thinking in ever more vivid hues from *In Parables* through *Cliffs of Fall,* cease, in the latter stages, to reveal anything of the character of divinity whatsoever, but only of the unknowability of the divine. Crossan himself in *Raid on the Articulate* and *Cliffs of Fall,* by the same token, is intermittently engaged in a retrieval of negative theology, one that has passed through the detour of postmodernism, that articulates itself by a "philosophy of absence," and that is cognizant of its own impossibility.

Cliffs of Fall's second essay, "Sower and Seed," begins somewhat more conventionally. Crossan attempts to reconstruct the parable of the Sower as told by the historical Jesus, in its *ipsissima structura* if not in its *ipsissima verba.* He breaks the parable down into five basic units (The Sowing, The Path, The Rocks, The Thorns, The Good Soil), and compares each unit in its Markan, Matthean, Lukan, and Thomasian versions. The analysis is lengthy and need not be summarized. Suffice it to say that he finds the two best texts to be those of Thomas and an antepenultimate Mark (disclosed by stripping back pre-Markan and Markan alterations), which agree substantially and which bespeak a "common ancestral text." (Compare the lengthier but equally positivistic reconstruction of the Treasure parable that preoccupies him in *Finding.*) An exuberant interpretation of the reconstructed parable then follows, which can be summarized only in snatches. The parable is not just a teaching about the Kingdom, it is "also a teaching about teaching the Kingdom. It is not just a parable of the Kingdom . . . but rather as metaparable, it is a parable about parables of the Kingdom" (*Cliffs*, 49). Like Kermode, though independently of him, Crossan reads the Sower parable as an allegory for interpretation as such. The parable is not about the sower, Crossan thinks (its traditional title is a misnomer), but about the seed and the yield. And the yield is a plurality of possible realizations, not only for the parabled Kingdom and its mode of arrival, but for the parable's interpretation as well: "When . . . the tradition changed [the] parable internally in the transmission, or when Thomas omitted any explicit explanation and the pre-Synoptic tradition added a canonical interpretation . . . or when exegetes, ancient and modern, deliberate intention and multiply meaning, all that happens is that the polyvalence asserted for the yield is repeatedly verified" (51). The parable thus prefigures its own (mis)reading. Crossan does not adduce this deconstructionist adage explicitly (whose variants include: "Literature stages the modes of its own misreading"/"[T]he text . . . tells the story, the allegory of its misunderstanding"/"Through its very reading, the text . . . acts itself out")[12]—and Kermode might not care to—but this is the claim that each implicitly makes. For Kermode, the Markan framing material—Jesus' explanation to the disciples with its contrast of outsiders who do not see with insiders who do (Mark 4:11–12), but who subsequently prove to be outsiders too—is suggestive of the interpreter's situation. For Crossan, however, the explanatory frame is itself a first fruit of the plural readings prefigured in the parable by the multiple yield of the sowing: "The parable remains always a metaphor for its own hermeneutical task" (53–54; cf. 102). For Kermode the impossibility of a definitive or final reading seems to be a matter for regret, but for Crossan it is a matter for bliss. Here he takes his lead from Roland Barthes, who distinguishes the text of pleasure (*plaisir*) "that contents, fills, grants euphoria . . . comes from culture and does not break with it, is linked to a *comfortable* practice of reading," from the text of bliss (*jouissance*) "that imposes a state of loss . . . that discomforts (perhaps to the point of a certain boredom), unsettles the reader's historical, cultural, psychological assumptions, the consistency of his tastes, values, memories, brings to a crisis his relation with language" (*Cliffs*, 62, quoting Barthes, *Pleasure*, 14). The text of bliss shocks, disorients, induces a loss of footing. And Jesus' parable of the Sower is just such a text, in Crossan's mind, and much else besides (he mines the parable further with the aid of Fish and Derrida).

12. Respectively, Johnson, *Difference*, xii; de Man, *Blindness*, 136 (cf. de Man, *Allegories*, 76, 205); and Felman, "Screw," 101. Cf. Miller, "Thread," 162: "Any terminology of analysis or explication is already inextricably folded into the text the critic is attempting to see from without." (All are, or were, "Yale critics," and this was their distinctive claim.)

Such an interpretation would likely induce profound dubiety in almost any historical exegete, smacking as it does of the transposition of contemporary sensibilities back into the ancient milieu. But Crossan's construal of the Sower parable begs a poststructuralist dismantling also, as we shall see.

The final essay, "Polyvalence and Play," asks "How and why is it possible to have such different exegeses of the Sower as are evidenced from the very transmission of its text as well as from the tradition of its interpretation?" (65). Is there a model, asks Crossan, or a metaphor, to describe this fecundity of interpretations? What is the model of interpretive models? What is the metaphor of metaphors? At one time, says Crossan, this question might have seemed a misguided one. "One might easily have responded that over against the metaphorical stood the literal and that there was no such thing as a metaphor for metaphor since reality [or literal language] firmly limited metaphor and stopped immediately this dangerous and vertiginous possibility of a *regressus ad infinitum*" (67). But Crossan's working assumption is that that security—the security of being able to distinguish comfortably between the literal and the metaphorical, objective reality and our ways of framing it—is lost to him and to many others forever. "This means we can no longer imagine ourselves at play with models and metaphors within some clearing in the forest of reality whose solid trees and firm branches establish both our security and our limitation" (46). Indeed, it is our incessant play with these models and metaphors that gives the "solid trees and firm branches" their shape in the first place. *Play*—Crossan's metaphor of metaphors, a nonserious activity, but a rule-bound and intensely absorbing one—does not occur against the backdrop of a fixed reality. Instead, "all reality is caught up in the play of the concepts which designate it" (*Cliffs*, 76, quoting Ehrmann, "Homo Ludens," 56). The way in which concepts (or linguistic signifiers: following Derrida, Crossan refuses to distinguish between the two) play, in the absence of firm ground or of the possibility of the game ever ending, is the topic of the dense tissue of philosophical quotations and Crossanian aphorisms that fill the remainder of the essay and resist summarization.[13]

13. Further on polyvalence and parables, see Tolbert, *Perspectives,* and Crossan, ed., "Polyvalent."

To Kill a Minotaur

[T]here is much of the ancient in what I have said. Everything perhaps. It is to Heraclitus that I refer myself in the last analysis.
—Jacques Derrida, "The Original Discussion"

For Crossan, echoing a recurring (post)modernist theme, the ubiquity of language means that we live in a labyrinth without exits or foundations. It "has no center . . . it is infinitely expansible . . . we create it as play and for play, and . . . one can no more consider leaving it than one can envisage shedding one's skin" (*Cliffs*, 72). How might the Bible appear were we to open it up within such a labyrinth? Crossan does not say exactly. His focus is more general and diffuse, like the philosophers and poets on whom he draws. However, readers who come to *Cliffs of Fall* with the assumption that language can accurately reflect a reality that is extralinguistic are unlikely to leave it thinking otherwise. The contrary assumption, that language is coextensive with knowledge, is what animates this essay collection from start to finish, though it is never the object of close, reasoned argumentation.[14] Unless one shares Crossan's assumption from the outset, much of his book will seem counterintuitive. Here, for instance, is what Howard Clark Kee has to say concerning Crossan's labyrinth: "The labyrinth in which play occurs is created by us, has no center, yet we cannot escape it. Where is it? In A. A. Milne's familiar lines, 'It isn't really anywhere; it's somewhere else instead,' this unconvinced reader might respond" ("Polyvalence," 58). What Crossan needed to make a dent on unbelieving positivists like Kee were some good old-fashioned arguments as opposed to apodictic declarations. Rigorous argumentation is not the forte of the Crossan of *Cliffs of Fall, Raid on the Articulate,* nor even *The Dark Interval.* In these books he is a wordsmith first and foremost, who finds it "radiantly silly to think about language without having read a lot of poetry or to write about language without indicating what such reading has taught one" (*Cliffs*, 66). One thing it seems to have taught him is a mischievous disregard for the proprieties of scholarly discourse. Who among biblical scholars but Crossan would dare end an essay thus: "to end as I began, with *Finnegans Wake,* one could say that this Galilean

14. For a more extended presentation of his philosophical position, Crossan does refer us in *Cliffs*, 67, to *The Dark Interval*, 13–46. But *Cliffs*, whose final essay "tests the edge of language" more severely than did *Interval*, would necessitate (should we insist on a *summa philosophica*) a restatement of that position. That a *summa* might pose special difficulties for Crossan is suggested by the uneven progress of his thought between *Interval* (1975) and *Cliffs* (1980); e.g., "Polyvalence," the final essay in *Cliffs*, is the least orthodox but also the earliest (1977) essay in it.

sower 'was at his best a onestone parable, a rude breathing on the void of to be, a venter hearing his own brauchspeech in backwords, or, more strictly, but tristurned initials, the cluekey to a worldroom beyond the roomworld'" (64)?[15] (Post)modernist poets and novelists join with (post)-modernist theoreticians in the chorus of citations that is *Cliffs of Fall.* Crossan's own lead solos are lyrical, exuberant, and celebrative. There is a fit between the subject matter (Jesus' parables) and the way in which it is written up that helps to account for Crossan's considerable prestige within (certain sections of) the guild and that covers a multitude of ex-egetical sins. Foremost among these sins is the way the sifting of the Sower parable for the *ipsissima structura,* summarized earlier, is handled. Most conventional exegetes would concur with Kee's judgment that "the refine-ments of his [Crossan's] redactional assignments to editorial stages and the criteria by which those decisions are made are highly subjective" ("Polyvalence," 57).

A sin of a more subtle order, one that is instructive for us to consider here, concerns that same redactional sifting in "Sower and Seed." Later in that essay, at the beckoning of Roland Barthes, Crossan reads the par-able as an unsettling "text of bliss." For Barthes, however, the text of bliss—an exotic, mythic object that does not necessarily correspond to any actual text—is coupled with the reproductive activity of a hedonistic reader, who "takes his pleasure with the text," writing it as he reads, and matching his own particular "reading neurosis" to the "hallucinated form of the text" (Barthes, *Pleasure,* 63). At a minimum, the text of bliss resists the final word, the official reading, the foreclosure of multiple meanings in favor of a privileged meaning, and Crossan himself is well aware of this. He quotes Barthes on the "writerly text," which, in the freedom it ascribes to the reader, can be seen as the text of bliss in embryo: "the writerly text is *ourselves writing,* before the infinite play of the world . . . is traversed, intersected, stopped, plasticized by some singular system (Ideology, Ge-nus, Criticism) which reduces the plurality of entrances, the opening of networks, the infinity of languages" (*Cliffs,* 61, quoting Barthes, *S/Z,* 5). All the more surprising, therefore, is his contradictory handling of the Sower. His sifting of the competing versions of the parable in the synoptics and Thomas to get back to the bedrock version—a version suspiciously

15. Crossan's tongue-in-cheek subversion of discursive conventions—other, more sub-tle examples might be listed—interestingly parallels the strategic literariness of a certain brand of deconstruction associated with Derrida and Hartman that brazenly crosses the line sep-arating critical from creative writing, though these latter take it very much further than Crossan.

well-suited in its detail for the allegory of interpretation that he will go on to spin—strikes one as but a common or garden variant of the long-standing scholarly attempt to subordinate the cacophony of voices in the gospel tradition to some univocal, authoritative voice (that of Jesus, for example, as here). Indeed, in terms of Barthes' typology of readers in *The Pleasure of the Text,* the particular reading neurosis afflicting Crossan here must be said to be that of the fetishist, whom Barthes couples "with the divided-up text, the singling out of quotations, formulae, turns of phrase" (*Pleasure,* 63). "Sower and Seed," and by extension *Cliffs of Fall,* are thus as paradoxical as the Sower parable itself. The parable is used to make the point that univocity is perpetually dissolving into plurivocity. But the reciprocally undermining relations between theory and practice in the "Sower and Seed" essay, between various affirmations of the unavailability of correct interpretations and the unblushing attempt to supply one, exhibit a plurivocity of premises on the part of its author that subverts the univocity of his own argument. Indeed, one is tempted to add, extending *Cliffs of Fall*'s own logic, that it successfully illustrates its major tenet (the ubiquity of polyvalence and paradox) only by subverting the coherence of its author.[16]

Crossan was fated from the outset to be snarled in these or similar contradictions. In the neighboring field of literary criticism, the more-deconstructionist-than-thou game I have just played with him is one which has been popular since at least 1975—that is, since J. Hillis Miller's "Deconstructing the Deconstructors," and the deconstructive rejoinder ("A Miller's Tale") it provoked from Joseph Riddel, the critic being deconstructed on that occasion. The game has also caught on in the biblical guild. In 1986 in Atlanta, Gary Phillips presented "Deconstruction and the Parables of Jesus," a deconstructive analysis of a book by Jack Kingsbury, to the Literary Aspects Group of the Society of Biblical Literature, to which Mary Ann Tolbert responded with "Deconstructing 'Deconstruction and the Parables of Jesus' by Gary Phillips, or Does the Cat Perpetually Chase Its Tail?" The game is an easy one to play because to be rigorously deconstructive is a remarkably difficult thing. Deconstruction, as has often been said, is at its most vulnerable whenever it poses as a theory or a repeatable method. Derrida's general target is metaphysical thought in all its hydra-like manifestations, and it presupposes Heidegger's

16. Other attempts to tackle Crossan on his own turf include Aichele, *Limits,* 114–18; Brown and Malbon, "Parabling," 535ff.; Cobb, "Theology," 153–60; Tolbert, "Polyvalence," 66–67; and cf. Atkins, *Reading,* 46–47, 73–76; McKenna, "Biblioclasm"; and Tracy, "Reflections."

related attempt to "overcome metaphysics." But metaphysics is also a target on which Derrida himself is spreadeagled, as he is aware. The overcoming or end of metaphysics cannot even be envisioned, much less brought about, any more than can a reality without origin or end, foundations or center, presence, hierarchy, identity—all metaphysical concepts. Deconstruction's critique of metaphysical fundamentalism can be undertaken only from within the edifice that metaphysics provides. However, it can not simply take the form of an alternative master theory, which would certainly admit through the back door what has been summarily banished through the front. Derrida has always worked to circumvent this, turning a malleable strategy of reading against traditional forms of philosophical reasoning. Rather than construct a general system, block by block, on certain fundamental master-terms, he has preferred to give strategic, but generally transitory roles instead to words taken from the texts which he reads. Such terms as do recur, moreover (*différance, trace,* etc.), are strenuously presented as "nonconcepts," and designed to resist attempts at definition. By these and other means, Derrida has attempted to prevent, or at least postpone, the hardening of deconstruction into a theory with central concepts and repeatable methods. But he has only succeeded in deferring the inevitable. Over time, certain terms have taken on "talismanic value, undergoing circular repetition and assuming ever-growing mantric value till finally the mere mention of such holy words brings on a knowing and fanatic nod or grin common to the true believer" (Leitch, *Deconstructive Criticism,* 70).[17] Armies of advocates and critics alike have ransacked Derrida's earlier works for the elements of a general philosophy. Crossan, though not intent on wringing a systematics from Derrida, nonetheless feels for solid ground in his redactional analysis of the Sower parable, when, by his own logic and Derrida's, "it is play that should be affirmed" instead (*Cliffs,* 10, quoting Derrida, *Writing,* 297).[18]

However, much of Derrida's output since the early 1970s makes even his tortuously oblique earlier work (what we have been citing up to now) seem pellucid by comparison. The propositional diction of traditional philosophical discourse has been dropped altogether on occasion to be

---

17. Leitch is referring to Heidegger's terminology, but he could just as easily be referring to Derrida's.

18. Note that the way the term "(free)play" (*le jeu*) sounds to American ears—Crossan's included, one suspects—as connoting "playfulness," "freedom," and other qualities centered on individual subjects is quite at variance with the resonance it has in Derrida's writings, where it connotes an irreducible quality of movement in language that produces subjects as one of its effects (see Berman, *Reception,* 207; Ulmer, *Grammatology,* xi–xii).

replaced by a dense interlace of allegory and etymology, pun and allusion, trope and countertrope, combined in certain instances with Talmud-like multicolumned graphics. (The paramount example is *Glas* [1974]. Other works, preeminently, *The Post Card* [1980], are less startling graphically but no less arresting stylistically.) To shatter the protective shield separating philosophy from literature, allowing the latter to irradiate the former— or rather, to show that the former is already contaminated, and always has been—accounts in part for Derrida's strategy, but there is more. Whereas philosophy has traditionally been content merely to arrange and rearrange the *inferential connections* between sentences, thereby building and rebuilding the temple of ontotheology on the same restricted site, Derrida would seem to see his own project as a Promethian attempt to drastically shift the site of discourse altogether ("'beyond' absolute knowledge—*unheard of* thoughts are required, sought for across the memory of old signs" [*Speech,* 102]) by constructing a rigorous philosophical program based on *noninferential associations*—structural features of language that have been traditionally excluded from philosophy (cf. Rorty, "Deconstruction," 13). "In this respect Derrida resembles the nineteenth-century mathematicians who, challenged by the axiomatic absoluteness of Euclid's principles, were able to prove that it was possible to devise a geometry that Euclid's system held to be impossible. Considered at first to be playful monstrosities or abstract exercises, these non-Euclidean geometries eventually provided the mathematics of relativity (just as Derrida's non-Aristotelian grammatology is providing the writing of relativity)" (Ulmer, "Op Writing," 32; see further Ulmer, *Grammatology*).[19]

Large claims indeed, and more than a little removed from the waking concerns of the average biblical scholar. The capital-P Poststructuralist (Derrida, Foucault, Lacan, the later Barthes, Deleuze and Guattari, Baudrillard et al.) tends to be a creature of fabulous and exquisite extremes, and the environs of biblical studies will hardly prove to be his or her optimal breeding ground. The closing sentences of George Aichele's *Limits of Story* (1985), a deconstructive variation on narrative theology and biblical criticism, encapsulate the predicament rather well: "It is my hope that this book will be understandable and thought-provoking. Yet the very comprehensibility of this book must be, paradoxically, its most serious limitation" (139). Now, whatever else can be said of *Limits of Story,* by no stretch of the imagination is it a popular work. I found little provocation

---

19. Simultaneously in the 1970s, Derrida's writing began to take an explicit political turn, one that has become increasingly important for American poststructuralism in the 1980s. See, e.g., Derrida, "No Apocalypse," "Principle," and "Last Word."

in it to charge its author with being too readily comprehensible. His anxiety is understandable, nonetheless. As is very frequently remarked, many of Derrida's American progeny (literary critics in the main) have failed to attend with requisite rigor to the status of their own discourse, which cannot but claim knowledge implicitly at the same time as it calls knowledge about texts (structures, sources, intentionality, etc.) into question. This is not to say that American deconstructors have been a mild-mannered lot. Crossan's *Cliffs of Fall*, say, would seem sickly indeed if set against the voracious rigor of some, or the unbridled playfulness of others.[20] Measured against common, biblical scholarly sobriety, however, *Cliffs of Fall* is excessive, outrageous, and—some would say—irresponsible.

Crossan straddles two stools awkwardly in *Cliffs of Fall*. The rift between the practical and theoretical sections of the book, noted earlier, suggests that he is backing out of the poststructuralist labyrinth—the one without exits on extralinguistic reality—at the same time as he is edging into it. But let us consider, before moving on, a salient aspect of that attempted entry—Crossan's intermittent reflections on negative theology, mentioned earlier. Derrida plays a strategic role in these reflections: "Just as there is a negative theology, there is a negative atheology. An accomplice of the former, it still pronounces the absence of a center, when it is play that should be affirmed. But is not the desire for a center . . . the indestructible itself "? (*Cliffs*, 10, quoting Derrida, *Writing*, 297). For Crossan, the project of a negative theology knowingly allows itself to be caught up in the larger impossibility that has long obsessed Derrida—that of overcoming metaphysics while pinioned beneath its weight.[21]

In "Difference and Divinity" (1982) we find Crossan deeper within the labyrinth than before and gingerly feeling his way:

> there can certainly be little communication between Derrida and negative theology if that is conceived as a simple alternative strategy

20. De Man, *Allegories,* is considered exemplary of analytic deconstruction at its most rigorous (cf. Waters and Godzich, eds., *de Man*), while Hartman, *Saving the Text* is (or was) a leading American example of deconstruction "on the wild side": punning, playful, "nonserious," literary.

21. Lynn Poland, in her otherwise excellent critique of Crossan (*Literary Criticism*, 108–20), concludes that Crossan's project is incommensurably at odds with Derrida's. However, in his *Semeia* "Letter" Derrida himself gives the nod of approbation to Crossan's circumspect attempts to theologize negatively: "I found these texts [Crossan's "Difference" and others] lucid and rigorous; and in any case, I believe I have no objection to make to them, not even against some reservation or other regarding . . . negative theology" (61). Ricoeur anticipated Poland's conclusion on Crossan in "A Reply," 74 (Poland does not mention this, if she knows it) to which Crossan responded in "Stages," 59–61.

within onto-theology. If negative theology means no more than slaying the Minotaur by creeping up on it backwards while waving goodbye, it is hardly worth distinguishing it from an open and frontal assault. But surely the fact that negative theology has usually been held on the fringes of our tradition and has normally been suspect of unorthodoxy at best and of atheism at worst, may well indicate that something more profound is going on within that marginal but magnificent strand of our tradition. (38–39)

The essay concludes with a cunning reframing of the classic theistic question "What is the nature of God?," in which the question—which *as* question bespeaks the all-too-glib assumption that this matter, like any other, can be handled "within the simple rhetorics of question and answer, the questions now and the answers later"—is itself interrogated by the displacement of its question mark with a colon: "Certain questions beget not so much answers as different ways of phrasing themselves. What, then is . . .:" (39).

In the early 1980s, at that time still the only biblical scholar to have wrestled seriously with the Minotaur, and just beginning to become a cunning strategist, Crossan exited the labyrinth to enter a new research phase with a conventional historical emphasis, centered on the aphorisms of Jesus and noncanonical gospel traditions,[22] at about the same time that the first faint trickle of gospel studies informed by poststructuralism and deconstruction began to appear.[23] It is not to the close, deconstructive reading of individual gospel texts that Crossan's poststructuralist oeuvre points one, however, so much as to theology in the deconstructive mode—the Sisyphean task of rethinking theology after the end of philosophy (in Mark Taylor's Sisyphean prose, "to struggle to think the unthinkable, say

22. See Crossan, *Cross, Other Gospels*, and *In Fragments*. Crossan's latent postmodernism is still liable to provoke highly unusual readings of the Jesus tradition, e.g., his "Living Earth."

23. The trickle is still faint; diverse examples to date include: Castelli et al., *Power*; Belo, *Reading* (draws marginally on poststructuralism); Berg, "In/to Mark" (psychoanalytic deconstruction); Bloom, "Before"; Foster, "John" (a Bloomian analysis); Kelber, *Eclipse*, "Authority," "Beginning," and "Fleischwerdung" (all four combine Ong and Derrida); O'Leary, *Questioning*, 221–25 (Heideggerian *Destruktion* applied to John); Phillips, "Deconstruction" and "History" (Derrida and Foucault); and cf. Aichele, *Limits*; Altizer, "Demythologizing" and *Total Presence*; Bloom, *Ruin*; Detweiler, ed., "Derrida"; Fisher and Jobling, eds., "Ethics"; Güttgemanns, *Fragmenta*; Kristeva, *Horror*, 90–132; and Phillips, ed., "Text, Context." More than many of the foregoing, certain recent readings in the Hebrew Bible have served to convince me of deconstruction's aptitude for gospel interpretation; see esp. Miscall, *1 Samuel* and *Workings*, and cf. Moore, "Commentaries," 49–53. Less convinced are, inter alia, Frei, "'Literal Reading,'" and Via, *Ethics*, 210ff.

the unsayable, name the unnameable" [*Altarity,* xxvii]). And indeed the Crossan of *The Dark Interval* and its successor volumes can justly be regarded, with others such as Thomas Altizer, as a forerunner of "negative atheology"—the wide, deep swath cut by deconstruction in philosophical theology of the 1980s.[24]

Before moving on to matters exegetical there is a final question to be raised. What are the implications for religious belief of the sorts of developments that we have been reviewing? For instance, what does one say to the charge that deconstruction should be rejected a priori by biblical scholars "as a total skepticism denying any metaphysics or God behind words"? (Kurtz, "Narrative," 198, n. 10).[25] One might respond by pointing out that what Deconstruction (the rare, capital-D kind) faces biblical scholars with, if they happen to be persons of faith, is simply a recent expression of a challenge that has always faced the theological disciplines:

> The Presence of God in Scripture is stated by Scripture, a circular argument acceptable only to those who already accept Scripture as God's Word (as I do). Deconstruction calls us away from rationalistic attempts to "prove" God or God's Word, for scientific and philosophical inquiry will lead only to absence, difference, deferring.
>
> This conclusion, moreover, merely recasts deconstruction as one more step in the noumena/phenomena problem, back through . . . Kant to Plato at least. How does one find the Real? What discourse can one create which will prove the existence or presence of God? Deconstruction . . . demonstrates the failure of all . . . theories that seek to pin down the Absolute. Philosophy has been disproving the proofs of God for millennia. (Underwood, "Derrida," 11–12; cf. Walhout, "Christianized")

Narrowing our reflections to the New Testament and its claims, what deconstruction forces us to face as biblical scholars is a reiteration in a new register of Rudolf Bultmann's historically based challenge to the preceding generation, namely, that the Christian believer "has nothing in his hand on which to base his faith. He is suspended in mid-air, and cannot

24. Works to date include: Altizer et al., *Deconstruction*; Caputo, *Hermeneutics*; O'Leary, *Questioning*; Raschke, *Alchemy* and *Thinking*; Raschke, ed., *Dimensions,* 71–126; Taylor, *Altarity, Deconstructing,* and *Erring*; Winquist, *Epiphanies*; Winquist, ed., "Text"; and cf. Brown, *Philosophy,* and Jennings, *Beyond Theism.*

25. Cf. Greenwood, "Biblical Studies," 278 ("virulently anti-Christian, with its assault on the Logos-idea"). Less alarmist, though no less dismissive, are Kee, "Polyvalence," 59–61, and Staley, *First Kiss,* 48 n. 138. For a marginally better informed dismissal, see Thiemann, "Radiance," 21ff.

demand proof " (*Kerygma,* 211).[26] Statements such as these were, of course, the corollary of Bultmann's radical skepticism concerning the recoverability of the historical Jesus, a skepticism that would be judged excessive today by most who specialize in Christian origins. But questions of historicity are no longer the only major ones facing us. For this realization to properly hit home we should perhaps need a postmodernist Bultmann, or several such, capable of taking up where the modernist Bultmann left off—for there is considerably less in the Christian believer's hand than even Bultmann allowed. In any case, what needs to be stressed again today is that responsible exegesis is not obtained by a propitiatory sacrifice of the intellect, but only by facing up to the intellectual challenges necessarily incurred in academic biblical study. And the main challenge at present is occasioned not by poststructuralism, nor deconstructionism, nor any other -ism exactly, but by the reduction of disciplinary walls and the beginning of the end of the situation whereby biblical studies is something one does secure behind a door bearing that name, whereas sociology, anthropology, women's studies, literary criticism, and philosophy are other things someone else does down the hall.

The Incarnation of the *Logos* in the Body of the Fourth Gospel

Deconstructive reading of the Gospels is far less a *Glas*-like affair at present than an attempt to stretch conventional gospel criticism to, or perhaps beyond, its limits. Two readings are presented. The first is a distillation of Werner Kelber's recent reading of the Fourth Gospel; the second is my own attempt to extend part of that reading. Both are of the softer deconstructive variety, the kind that is content (or simply condemned) to apply a method straightforwardly—though capable of an unexpected turn now and then—as opposed to the extremely cunning variety that is able to

26. With the irruption of deconstruction in theology, parallel statements are not uncommon. Mackey ("Bethlehem," 270), for example, writes: "Perhaps deconstruction has done what Kant claimed to have done: it has (perhaps) destroyed knowledge so as to make room for faith. It does not destroy knowledge *in order* to make room for faith. The teleology in that formulation dissembles and disguises yet one more *defense* of faith." This statement, like many by deconstructive theologians (Caputo, Raschke, O'Leary et al.), invites a charge of fideism (the position that faith precedes reason with respect to knowledge of God.) A reappraisal of fideism might well begin on the following note: derived from Kant's objections in the first *Critique* to the possibility of rational arguments for God, fideism was condemned in 1840 by Gregory XVI, who forced its main proponent, Abbé Louis Bautain, to sign a recantation affirming that reason "can prove with certitude the existence of God and the infinity of His perfections." Today, of course, this statement might be judged a good deal more problematic than the error it was designed to refute (see further Runzo, *Reason*).

"appropriate the privilege of history" by putting its own conclusions into question repeatedly, almost before they have been reached (cf. Ray, *Meaning,* 191), that austere brand of deconstruction associated with the late Paul de Man.

To begin in media res, Kelber, reflecting on the residual orality of primitive Christian culture and its implications for the interpretation of the Fourth Gospel, argues in a forthcoming essay, "In the Beginning Were the Words," that the Johannine *Logos* represents the apotheosis of the spoken word.[27] Speech enforces a sense of "presentness" (presence), for Kelber, as writing never does. And so the Johannine *Logos* is the primacy and presence of the spoken word elevated to a transcendent status—an understandable development, perhaps, in a residually oral culture. But what is not explicable by reference to orality, according to Kelber, is the univocity of the *Logos* concept against the plurivocity of oral communication—the enactment of *logoi* and still more *logoi* in an ongoing process of supplementation and modification. In his absolute singularity, therefore, the Johannine *Logos* "stands unmasked as textually reinvented speech," as "individualized, monumentalized, fantasized orality" ("Beginning").

The Johannine narrative thus enacts "the apotheosis of the *Logos,*" the elevation of Jesus to the primordial position of a transcendental signified. The latter term, as will be remembered from our introduction to Derrida, refers to any order of meaning conceived as primary or foundational. A second, related term begs inclusion in the discussion—*logocentrism,* coined by Derrida, as Kelber explains, to refer "to the Greco-Christian or Platonic-Johannine tradition according to which . . . true knowledge and being pertain to the plane of the immutable forms or the preexistent, personified *Logos*" ("Authority," 119–20).[28] But the Fourth Gospel, far from dwelling on the apotheosis of the *Logos* or on the possibility of the believer's ascent to him, narrates the descent of the *Logos* instead into the world and human flesh. And the incarnation is not fleshly only; the *Logos* is doubly incarnated "through the materiality of written communication. His entry into the flesh is dramatically executed in the body of the text" ("Beginning"). This most logocentric of texts, therefore,

27. This essay is a trial balloon for Kelber's forthcoming *Eclipse.* I am indebted to Professor Kelber for allowing me to discuss it. Two companion essays, "The Authority of the Word" and "Die Fleischwerdung des Wortes," overlap with "In the Beginning" but give a less prominent role to deconstruction.

28. At its most inclusive, *logos* in Derrida's usage brings together "in a single concept the inward rational principle of verbal texts, the inward rational principle of human beings, and the inward rational principle of the natural universe" and combines "all these meanings with a further meaning: 'the Law'" (Harland, *Superstructuralism,* 146).

is at the same time markedly alogocentric. The text disseminates the *Logos* even as it centers and elevates him. Indeed, argues Kelber, only in doing so can it exist as a narrative text. An unremitting fixation on the transcendent *Logos* would not translate into narrative textuality. It is only "in dislodging the *Logos* from his transcendental position that the text narrates the *raison d'être* of its own written existence. . . . What generates the written gospel is not the preexistent *Logos,* but rupture with the logocentric origin" (ibid.). This enmeshes the text in a profound double bind. To exist as written gospel is to displace the transcendent *Logos*—to incarnate, distend, and scatter him in an extended, plotted narrative. Yet the more the demotion of the *Logos* is extended narratively in the Fourth Gospel, the more information is divulged about his preexistent status—one thinks of the frequent references, whether by Jesus or the narrator, to Jesus' preexistence. This double bind manifests itself theologically in the tension between an incarnational and an epiphanic christology. The more the narrative is expanded to absorb the *Logos* incarnationally, the more it enlarges his metaphysical profile. (Kelber seems to imply that the Johannine text resists the intention that gave birth to it.) This is to confirm, concludes Kelber, quoting Derrida, that there "is no sense in doing without the concepts of metaphysics in order to shake metaphysics" (ibid., quoting *Writing,* 280). This dilemma dogged the philosophical projects of Nietzsche, Heidegger, and Derrida himself, but "[i]n antiquity it announced itself prominently in the fourth gospel. For the story which it dramatizes is that of the history of metaphysics and the perpetually parallel history of the deconstruction of metaphysics" (ibid.).[29]

As in Crossan's *Cliffs of Fall,* the fit between topic and treatment in Kelber's essay is satisfying (for some, however, his speculations will have an abstruse Hegelian ring to them). Given the historic roles that the *Logos* has played in the philosophical and Judeo-Christian tradition of the West—the latest being its role as whipping boy in Derrida's onslaught on logocentrism—Kelber's decision to rethink the Johannine *Logos* in a Derridean register seems to me to be an irreproachably logical one (no pun intended). A sustained encounter between Ong and the Johannine *Logos,*

29. A parallel version of the dilemma, which, in antiquity, announced itself so prominently in the Fourth Gospel as Kelber reads it, is adumbrated in another yet more elemental ancient "text" as read by de Man: "The most familiar and general of all linguistic models, the classical *trivium,* which considers the sciences of language as consisting of grammar, rhetoric, and logic (or dialectics), is in fact a set of unresolved tensions powerful enough to have generated an infinitely prolonged discourse of endless frustration of which contemporary literary theory, even at its most self-assured, is one more chapter" (*Resistance,* 13).

of the kind staged by Kelber, was also long overdue. Ong's *Orality and Literacy* contains some observations Kelber could aptly have cited:

> In Christian teaching orality-literacy polarities are particularly acute, probably more acute than in any other religious tradition, even the Hebrew. For in Christian teaching the Second Person of the One Godhead, who redeemed mankind from sin, is known not only as the Son but also as the Word of God. In this teaching God the Father utters or speaks His Word, his Son. He does not inscribe him. The very Person of the Son is constituted as the Word of the Father. Yet Christian teaching also presents at its core the written word of God, the Bible, which . . . has God as author. . . . In what way are the two sense of God's "word" related to one another? (179)

Elsewhere Ong has argued that "the Bible is very likely the most variegated orality-literacy mix we have in any text" ("Orality-Literacy," 381). But within the Bible it is surely in the Fourth Gospel that these contrasts are manifested most starkly. And Kelber's recent Johannine work suggests intriguingly how such contrasts—and tensions—might be conceptualized and explored.

Kelber's reading of plot and character in *Mark's Story of Jesus* interfuses with his reading of Mark's *Sitz im Leben,* until Mark's story becomes an elaborate allegory of the historical situation that occasioned it. A similar fusion occurs in Kelber's recent Johannine research. His reflections on the *Logos* are embedded in a historical framework—one that I have bracketed hitherto for clarity's sake but that must now be sketched in turn. The oral circumstances of Jesus' original proclamation were extended in the early Christian communities, despite the absence of the charismatic speaker himself. From the perspective of emerging orthodoxy, the oral-prophetic phenomenon was troublesome; the rapid propagation of charismatic *logoi* "took on the features of a veritable explosion," which eventually elicited the "control mechanism" of a written gospel that functioned to "implode" the dispersive forces of the oral tradition. A second factor of disruption concerned the capacity of oral-prophetic speech to represent Jesus in a powerfully immediate and alive way to its audience—but a curiously disembodied Jesus unconnected to a concrete, historical past. The written narrative gospel succeeded in restabilizing the oral-prophetic Jesus by binding him firmly to a past that encompassed not only his resurrection but his physicality and his death as well. "By elevating the earthly Jesus to normative significance, the evangelist introduces a historicizing dimension and a sense of pastness that is not directly translatable into pleromatic presence" ("Authority," 116).[30]

The pull and tug between residual oral presentness in John, and the simultaneous narrative suppression of it, fascinates Kelber. He notes the massive amount of sayings material in the Fourth Gospel and draws a series of parallels between it and the noncanonical sayings Gospels, *Thomas* in particular. He concludes that what we encounter in the Fourth Gospel is a notion of the presence and efficacy of words as a *life-or-death force* (cf. John 5:24; 6:68; 8:51–52; 10:19; 12:48), which has to do with a perception of language deeply rooted in oral sensibilities. But these pleromatic, efficacious *logoi* are now inserted into a narrative framework that defuses the immediacy of meaning once derived from the oral context. In their new, narrative context the *logoi* are subordinated to "a plotted sequentiality wherein meaning unfolds progressively" ("Beginning"). Immediacy of meaning is thus dispersed narratively. Most of all, however, the oral-prophetic situation with its unstable, crisis-eliciting features is now countered and contained by the elevation of Jesus as the preexistent and transcendent *Logos,* for in this capacity Jesus orders and governs all *logoi* and *logoi* clusters. His apotheosis as unique *Logos* is his seal of authority over the disruptive plurality of the *logoi.* Kelber's deconstructive reflections on the Fourth Gospel, then, are infused with a reconstructive intent. The immediate, conceptual roots of the Johannine *Logos* lie, for him, in the tension-fraught community setting that he describes.

These essays of Kelber will likely be read as an appendix to *The Oral and the Written Gospel,* an attempt to extend his revisionary history of primitive Christianity, centered hitherto on Paul and the synoptic tradition, to the Fourth Gospel also. To me, these essays partake in the path-breaking originality of the book. However, the details of Kelber's historical reconstruction in the essays are no less challengeable than those of the book.[31] Such sifting I leave to the specialists, though I shall venture a few comments of a general sort. Although the Jewish myth of Wisdom's heavenly origin and descent (cf. Wisdom 9:1–2, 10; Proverbs 8:22–23; Sirach 24:8ff.; Enoch 42:2) has been the leading candidate in genetic explanations of the *Logos* in recent Johannine studies, it begs a perplexing question, in Kelber's view. Why replace Wisdom with the *Logos* ("Authority," 109; cf.

---

30. In Kelber, *Written Gospel,* the Gospel of Mark was paradigmatic of a written counterform to the oral gospel.

31. There have been many critiques of Kelber's book. Williams, *Gospel,* 143–54, assesses Kelbler's theses within a literary-critical as well as a historical framework and may be of special interest to readers of this book.

"Beginning")? Now, Kelber seems to be asking the right question here—but is he really? At a minimum it might be objected that since Wisdom (*Sophia/Chokmah*) was a female figure in Jewish tradition, direct transference of her name to the male Jesus might have jarred (*logos,* of course, is a masculine noun).[32] But of course the question persists nonetheless: why *Logos,* specifically? Less problematic than Kelber's precise framing of that much asked question is the presupposition that informs his handling of it. To hypothesize some situation of tension, conflict, or crisis within the Johannine community as the immediate seedbed of *Logos* christology is but to echo and amplify the tenor of much recent Johannine research. Indeed, Kelber's Johannine work, especially should it issue in a book-length study, as planned, could be seen as giving renewed momentum to the ball that J. Louis Martyn set rolling in earnest two decades ago with his attempt to crack the veneer of the Fourth Gospel and "define the particular circumstances in response to which [it] was written" (*History,* 17). In the wake of Martyn, Brown et al., genetic explanations of the *Logos,* which, however faintly, conjure up the image of a Johannine tradition, community, or evangelist disinterestedly fashioning a *Logos* christology, seem more anachronistic than at any time in the past.

But does Kelber's preoccupation with Johannine *Sitz im Leben,* like Crossan's preoccupation with the *ipsissima structura* of the Sower parable, cause him to fall heavily between two stools: between the deconstructor's retreat from logocentrism and the historian's pursuit of solid, logocentric ground—ground on which the roving contours of the Fourth Gospel might settle in some enduring and reassuring configuration? Unquestionably he does so fall; the lion will not eat straw with the ox, nor will poststructuralism lie down with historical criticism. As Derrida tersely puts it: "the movement of any archaeology, like that of any eschatology . . . always attempts to conceive of structure on the basis of a full presence which is beyond play" (*Writing,* 279).[33] But in fairness to Kelber, he is a

32. I am indebted here to a suggestion made to me by Richard B. Hays.

33. Kelber argues, possibly in defense of his own retention of traditional historical concerns, that "opposites such as . . . literary versus historical readings, and mirror versus window views of language dissolve into the single overriding reality of interpretation" ("Narrative," 127). But for Derrida the force of that "overriding reality" is "a certain pure and infinite equivocality which gives signified meaning no respite, no rest . . . it always signifies again and differs" (*Writing,* 25). Nothing could be further from Kelber's positivistic delineation of Johannine community history. In *Positions,* 57–60, Derrida discusses alternative ways of conceiving history (cf. *Grammatology,* 158–59). Other poststructuralists, notably Foucault, have been far more preoccupied with history—though with a version largely drained of transhistorical absolutes that a historical critic might have trouble recognizing. Foucault's "Genealogy" is his most concise statement on history. Further on Foucault and history, see

good deal less concerned to repudiate logocentrism per se than to explore its simultaneous affirmation and suppression in the Fourth Gospel. For Kelber, the conviction of Ernst Käsemann that underpins his influential *Testament of Jesus,* that the *"praesentia Christi* is the centre of [John's] proclamation," is simply inadequate to the complexity of the *Logos*'s position in the Fourth Gospel ("Authority," 127, quoting *Testament,* 15).

But the most damaging charge that might issue from the deconstructionist camp is a still more general one. Kelber's hypothesis concerns the immediacy and presentness of the oral tradition and its displacement by the written gospel. Exposing his hypothesis to Derrida's Gorgonian gaze, however, Kelber's "In the Beginning Were the Words" asks whether all such talk of immediacy and presentness might not be highly suspect from the start as a mere craving for original simplicity, and whether the preoccupation with orality against literacy in scholars such as Ong and himself might not merely be the latest in a long series of oppositions (transcendent/immanent, intelligible/sensible, nature/culture, male/female, object/representation, content/form, text/interpretation, history/fiction, etc.—I am adding to Kelber's text here) that eloquently bespeak the power and allure of Western mythology but that blinker our thinking on history and language? (Could Ong and Derrida meet without hostility?)[34] Derrida is deeply suspicious of all reflection built on a speech/writing binarism. He contends that from Plato down through Saussure, with remarkable regularity, such reflection has tended to privilege speech over writing as a pleromatic and diaphanous medium: "My words are 'alive' because they seem not to leave me: not to fall outside me, outside my breath . . . not to cease to belong to me" (*Speech,* 76; cf. *Grammatology,* 166). Writing has tended in contrast to be seen as an orphaned medium, no sooner born than separated from its father, a "mediation of mediation," and "a fall into . . . exteriority" (*Margins,* 316; *Grammatology,* 12–13). But for Derrida, the substitutive and dispersive traits of writing "always already" infect the spoken word, sabotaging the apparently simple, intuitive self-identity of even the most immediate-seeming speech event. Signification occurs, whether uttered or written,

> only if each so-called "present" element, each element appearing on
> the scene of presence, is related to something other than itself, thereby

---

Descombes, *French Philosophy,* 110–17; Harland, *Superstructuralism,* 101–20, 155–66; and White, "Foucault." Finally, see Attridge, ed., *Question,* and Stempel, "History," and cf. n. 15 to chapter 7 above.

34. For another recent attempt to bring Ong and Derrida into dialogue, see Kennedy, "'Voice,'" and cf. Tyler, *Unspeakable,* 89–102.

> keeping within itself the mark of the past element, and already letting itself be vitiated by the mark of its relation to the future element . . . and constituting what is called the present by means of this very relation to what it is not. . . . An interval must separate the present from what it is not in order for the present to be itself, but this interval must, by the same token, divide the present in and of itself, thereby also dividing, along with the present, everything that is thought on the basis of the present. (*Margins*, 13).

Thus, if "nonpresence and otherness are internal to presence" (*Speech*, 66), speech's very condition of possibility (despite its apparent immediacy) is that same deferral of full presence that is the precise condition of writing: "speech . . . is already in itself a writing" (*Grammatology*, 46). The study of orality-literacy contrasts would be rendered immeasurably more complex were it to acknowledge this generalized writing, characterized by absence and displacement, relative to which presence, consciousness, and the speech system itself could appear only as effects (cf. *Margins*, 329).

Derrida's critique of phonocentrism also menaces the opposition mediated versus unmediated narrative. We said that the former depends on the transmitting activity of a narrator and necessitates an indirect (or imagined) perception of the story world, whereas the latter pertains to drama, film, opera, ballet, and mime and affords a direct perception of the story-world. However, the notion of immediate or direct perception hardly needs a Derrida to discredit it; like the tabula rasa on which experience writes, it has been lacking advocates for quite some time. But let us see how Kelber handles Derrida. Kelber's retort, echoing Ong and others (cf. Ong, *Orality*, 168–70), is that Derrida is dominated by typographic concepts. To think of oral speech as a differential web endlessly deferring meaning smacks too much of written textuality. "Even if it is admitted that speech already exhibits alienating features, displacement and deferral will not get us to the heart of orality" ("Beginning"; cf. "Authority," 127). But one could easily respond that Derrida takes us to "the heart of orality" in a way that Kelber and Ong do not; what orality endures at Derrida's hands is nothing short of open heart surgery. Still, Kelber has a point. He is objecting that, Derrida notwithstanding, we still experience oral communication to be more immediate than written, and that that too is of account—if not paramount. By the same commonsense token, dramatic and other varieties of scenic narrative have the feel of direct perception, whereas written narrative does not. But a comment by Christopher Norris, made in another connection, does much to curb my complacency:

"What he [Derrida] calls into question is the right of philosophy to erect a wholesale theory of mind and language on the basis of commonsense notions that work well enough for all practical purposes but take on a different, more doctrinaire aspect when applied as a matter of philosophic principle" (*Derrida*, 179). And indeed the charge of Kelber and Ong that deconstruction's critique of phonocentrism is a textcentric one seems somehow beside the point given the main thrust of that critique: what speech conceals (i.e., the absence internal to every presence), writing reveals.

What we find in Kelber's Johannine essays, then, are not the tactics and sensibilities of a hyperrigorous deconstruction, but an attempted demonstration of deconstruction's exegetical aptitude in at least one area of gospel research—a demonstration that, while it amounts to a significant extension of the traditional parameters of such research, would undoubtedly be seen by others (for whom those parameters would have been eminently extendible to begin with) as a crude appropriation of Derrida's dispute with philosophy, "its reduction to a few sturdy devices for the critic's use" (Gasché, "Deconstruction," 180).[35]

The Failure of Johannine Irony

With the verdict on Kelber above I tar myself with the same brush used on him; for rather than conclude with an appeal for a more sophisticated handling of Derrida in gospel studies, I shall take hold of "a few sturdy devices" myself and venture a reading of some scenes in John—recklessly, no doubt, for I am not a licensed Johannine scholar, much less a licensed deconstructor. Certain comments on John 4, 7, and 19 in Kelber's "In the Beginning Were the Words" form a springboard for my own reading. I extend his insights as much as space and competence allow by amplifying the general deconstructive subtext on which they rely. I should mention that Kelber's reading of these episodes is considerably less detailed than mine (it spans only two pages of his essay), is rather differently nuanced, and is closely bound up with orality-literacy concerns that play no part in my own reading.

Like those surveyed in chapter 6, mine too is a story of reading and

35. Increasingly in the 1980s expositors of deconstruction have been at pains to situate it philosophically, resulting in a kind of "second wave" of highly sophisticated introductions. See, inter alia, Caputo, *Hermeneutics*; Berman, *Reception*; Gasché, *Tain*; Harvey, *Economy*; Llewelyn, *Threshold*; Norris, *Derrida*; Staten, *Derrida*; and cf. Taylor, ed., *Context*, and Ulmer, *Grammatology*.

is susceptible to several of the ailments there diagnosed (the reader is encouraged to play physician to my own attempt—at least until I offer a self-diagnosis). Where it differs from the story of reading that a reader-response critic typically tells is that it meanders into terrain where the ability of a narrative to achieve its ostensible aim of leading an audience through complications and deferrals to a climactic, completed understanding—the ability that reader-oriented exegesis celebrates—is precisely what is thrown into question. The Johannine narrative, if submitted to a certain kind of grilling, tells a particular story of reading indeed. Finally, my interpretation is also an interrogation of more traditional ones, and I am tempted to say (very recklessly, I fear) that its aim is "to outdo the closeness of reading that has been held up to [it] and to show, by reading [previous] close readings more closely, that they were not nearly close enough" (de Man, "Introduction," 242).

In John 4, Jesus dialogues with a Samaritan woman around the theme of water. Jesus breaks with the literal sense of water drawn from the well to introduce the superseding "living water" that he himself dispenses and that prevents those who drink it from ever thirsting again, becoming a spring in them that wells up to eternal life (4:10, 13–14). But the woman, incapable of distinguishing the literal and material from the figural and spiritual, says, "Sir, give me this water, that I may not thirst, nor come here to draw" (4:15; cf. 4:11). A two-storey ironic structure is erected. "Below" is the apparent meaning, which the woman as unwitting victim reads. "Above" is a higher level of meaning of which the woman is unaware, in sharp contrast to the reading or listening audience.[36]

As it transpires, however, the complete meaning of the figure has also been withheld from the wider audience, deferred, it seems, to a later time. For on the last day of the feast of Tabernacles, "the great day," Jesus again speaks of thirst, drinking, and the supramundane living water (7:37–38), and in an aside by the Johannine narrator (7:39) this figure is now interpreted as being "about the Spirit, which those who believed in him were to receive." Again the reader-listener is positioned on a perceptual level superior to that of Jesus' audience within the narrative. But now there is a second deferral. The figure of living water being imbibed is interpreted as the receiving of the Spirit, but its narrative representation is postponed until later: "as yet the Spirit had not been given, because Jesus was not

---

36. Others would add that the ironic interchange between Jesus and the woman is compounded by echoes of the Old Testament betrothal type-scene (Gn 24, 29; Ex 2; cf. 1 Sm 9). See, most recently, Eslinger, "Wooing"; Plunkett, "Samaritan" (though for Plunkett, the Samaritan woman is *not* the victim of irony); and Staley, *First Kiss*, 98–102.

yet glorified" (7:39) (cf. Kelber, "Beginning"). And subsequently Jesus' glorification is itself interpreted in its turn as the hour of his exaltation on the cross, an exaltation that will prefigure his resurrection (12:23–24, 28; 13:31–32; 17:1, 5; cf. 3:14; 12:32).

At the scene of crucifixion, the themes of thirsting and drinking recur once more in a way that strangely echoes their first occurrence in chapter 4. There are suggestions of completion and closure: "Jesus, knowing that all was now finished, said (to fulfill the scripture), 'I thirst'" (19:28). But by this utterance, far from seeming to satisfy the desire for living water (and should we not expect some such satisfaction on the basis of 7:37–39?), Jesus is depicted as thirsting himself for the literal earthly water, just as he was first depicted at the Samaritan well ("Jesus said to her, 'Give me a drink'"). Expectations have been steadily raised and redirected from 4:10ff. from the mundane to the supramundane. Jesus, source of the figural water, is now thrust into the very condition of the literal thirst that his discourse has led the audience to transcend (ibid.). And the satiation of Jesus' physical thirst, an event peculiarly linked to the fulfillment of Scripture (19:28), elicits the climactic announcement from Jesus himself that "It is finished" (19:30)—at which point he yields up—what? His spirit? The Spirit? (Greek simply has *to pneuma*.). Raymond Brown's double reading is attractive: "In vii 39 John affirmed that those who believed in Jesus were to receive the Spirit once Jesus had been glorified, and so it would not be inappropriate that at this climactic moment in the hour of glorification there would be a symbolic reference to the giving of the Spirit. . . . [T]his symbolic reference is evocative and *proleptic,* reminding the reader of the *ultimate* purpose for which Jesus has been lifted up on the cross. In Johannine thought the actual giving of the Spirit does not come now but in xx 22 after the resurrection" (*John [XIII–XXI]*, 931). Now, the satiation of Jesus' physical thirst in 19:30 is an arrestingly strange precondition for the symbolic yielding up of that which is designed to satiate the supraphysical thirst of the believer. (The source of living water himself cries out in thirst; some have read this as an instance of irony, as Brown notes [930].) But the sequence is a good deal stranger still when one begins to rethink it deconstructively. The literal, material, earthly level, hierarchically superseded in John 4:7–14 and shifted into the background, is reinstated in John 19:28–30 as the very condition (physical thirst, physical death) that enables the Spirit itself, emblem and token of the supramundane order (cf. 14:17), to effectively come into being. The hierarchy established in chapter 4 is thus curiously inverted (the ostensibly superior, pleromatic term is shown to depend for its effective existence on the inferior, insufficient term), an inversion prefigured in 7:39: "the Spirit had not been given [lit., there was as yet no Spirit], because Jesus was not yet glorified" (cf. 12:24).[37] And the inversion of the hierarchy by the death scene—an inversion that the larger context precludes, incidentally[38]—is followed by the reappearance of water (the flow from Jesus' side), this time as an equivocal term that inhabits both levels simultaneously, suspending the hierarchy altogether.

Let me unpack the latter part of the preceding sentence, adding that I am as interested in what might be out of the control of the Johannine writers at this point as in anything that has traditionally been said to be within their control.[39] Jesus expires and yields up his spirit (19:30). This symbolic predonation of the Spirit, which is to say, the living water, is followed by the reappearance of material water as Jesus' side is pierced and blood and water issue forth (19:34). The detail of the issue of water is unusual enough to demand supraliteral interpretation (Schnackenburg, *St. John,* 3:289–90, in particular, leaves little doubt of this). Many would posit a connection between 7:37–39 and the flow of water in 19:34, but 19:34 itself has been read in a wide variety of ways (sacramentally, antidocetically, in light of 1 John 5:6, Zechariah 13:1 and 14:8, etc.), which we need not go into here. But let us venture that, given the previous associations of earthly water with living water and Spirit, the flow of water is (at a minimum) another symbolic token of the promised living water, which has now become available in the form of the Spirit with Jesus' glorification. That leaves us with a symbol (the flow of water) of a metaphor (living water) for the Spirit. But does this figural skid come to a halt with the Spirit? What if the Spirit were itself a further substitution? Brown, sounding uncannily deconstructive, defines the Johannine Paraclete as "another Jesus . . . the presence of Jesus when Jesus is absent" with the Father (*John [XIII–XXI],* 1141). Not surprisingly, the convoluted route of the water imagery in John empties out on the very absence (that of Jesus) that occasioned the emission of substitutions in the first place. But is this substitutive, figural weave self-consistent in its pattern? Retracing the design yet again, we see that the initial, earthly water at the Samaritan well was declared superseded by figural living water (4:13–14), which was in-

37. No distinction is made between ontology and soteriology in 7:39b, as has often been noted; thus the Spirit is presented as though it had no effective existence prior to Jesus' glorification.

38. See John 1:13; 3:5–6, 31; 4:13–14, 24, 33–34; 6:26–27, 31–33, 49–50, 58, 63; 8:23; 12:25; 17:2.

39. See the quotation from Genette, *Narrative Discourse,* in chapter 4 above, and the Derridean quotation that follows it.

terpreted as the Spirit (7:39) that has now been made available (19:30), and the making available of which is symbolized by water (19:34) that is neither simply literal nor yet fully figural—a "literal figure," so to speak. We can not keep the literal cleanly separated from the figural in the end. The narrative, then, has forced a "sublime simplicity" (cf. de Man, *Allegories,* 9) on us that it led us earlier to transcend—that of the woman of Samaria who desired the living water so that she might no longer have to come to the well to draw (4:15), or of Nicodemus perplexed that he should have to reenter the womb in order to be born anew (3:4), or of the crowd who would fill their bellies with the imperishable bread (6:26–27, 34), or of the disciples unable to distinguish plain speech from figural (16:25, 29 [*en parrēsia/en paroimiais*]). In each case, two levels of meaning are collapsed that should have been kept apart. The ironic structure that positioned us on a level above these characters depended on our being able to keep the literal and figural levels clearly separate. But the events of the death scene have elided the levels and disallowed their separation. The result is a kind of cognitive paralysis, an acute symptom of which erupts within the story-world itself in the subsequent resurrection appearance to Mary Magdalen (20:11–18)—as though the ontological divide separating reader from character has been annulled in turn. Wayne Meeks, drawing categories from cultural anthropology, perceptively interprets Jesus' difficult injunction to Mary Magdalen, "Do not touch me, for I have not yet ascended to the father" (20:17), as an effect of the "compression of exaltation and crucifixion motifs into one" that leaves the traditional resurrection appearances "in a kind of limbo." Jesus' "strange statement imparts to that limbo a sacred liminality" (neither one thing nor the other, neither here nor there). He "is no longer in the world, but not yet ascended; he belongs to the intermediate zone that violates these categories and renders him untouchable" ("Heaven," 159). But the compression of exaltation and crucifixion motifs into one has already consigned the hierarchical structure of Johannine irony to a liminal zone, annulling it. Irony—which depended on the clean separation of flesh and glory, earthly and heavenly, material and spiritual, literal and figural, water and "water"—is now collapsed in paradox (cf. Kelber, "Beginning").

To Tear the Text or to Cast Lots for It?

> This coherence, which readers desire much more than texts exhibit.
> —Mieke Bal, *Death and Dissymmetry*

Before we proceed to the second part of our reading—our reading of the preceding reading—let us pause to take stock and speculate a little. Ultimately the paradox just spoken of (the one that unravels Johannine irony) is the result of an oscillatory pull and tug within the Fourth Gospel between an epiphanic and an incarnational christology—a christological opposition toward which a deconstructive reading would be irresistibly drawn, given the powerful resistance to synthesis it might expect to find manifested therein. Here I find Brown's very different reading illuminating. For Brown, as for many others, "the Johannine view of salvation is both vertical and horizontal." The vertical dimension pertains to Johannine dualism (heavenly/earthly, above/below, descent/ascent, with the Father/in the world, Spirit/flesh, glory/flesh, "water"/water, "bread"/bread, etc.), whereas the horizontal dimension pertains to the incarnation of the Word in human flesh and human history. "The blending of the vertical and the horizontal may be said (perhaps too facilely) to represent a blending of the Hellenistic and the Hebrew approaches to salvation, but such a blending occurred long before the Fourth Gospel was written" (*John [I–XII]*, cxvi). However, from our angle, it is not the identification of the vertical and the horizontal with Hellenism and Judaism that seems facile, so much as the blithe assumption that the two planes do in fact blend in the Fourth Gospel. It may be instead, as our reading suggested, that the (impracticable) attempt to synthesize the planes has backlashed in a severe disruption of the gospel's internal logic. Robert Kysar, surveying the range of positions adopted on the relationship of flesh to glory in John, similarly fails to consider the possibility that the relationship might be one defiant of noncontradictory expression (*Evangelist*, 195–99)—though he does drop a bare, tantalizing hint in a later section that the coming together of flesh and glory in the gospel might not be without a certain pain (218; his "Recent Research" [1985] contains no further clues).

A means to diagnose such pain might be offered by deconstructive criticism as a variable strategy of reading that entails "scrupulous attention to what seems ancillary or resistant to understanding" and is suspicious, in dealing with previous readings, of attempts to convert the strange into the familiar that seem to elide, conceal, or circumvent whatever stands in the way of coherence. "What would happen if, for once, one were to reverse the ethos of explication [i.e., explication at any cost] and try to be really precise," to rigorously examine every resistance to meaning?[40] Interestingly, to adopt a close-reading strategy of this sort would be to place oneself broadly in the tradition of source-centered gospel scholarship,

40. De Man, "Foreword," ix–x, quoted and paraphrased in Culler, *On Deconstruction*, 242–43.

which could be said to have prefigured deconstruction in its often scrupulous attention to minute tears in the ostensibly smooth fabric of the
text. (I use the past tense, but this form of gospel scholarship could bury
its successors—though it is wilting in the holistic climate of current research.) To give single illustration of the older approach, Ernst Haenchen
commenting on John 19:28–29 notes that "the clause 'to fulfill the scripture'
does not go with the preceding remark of Jesus, 'When Jesus knew that
all was now finished,'—if everything is finished, there is nothing left to
follow. [Moreover, h]olding a sponge filled with vinegar up to Jesus'
mouth does not conform to the Johannine picture of the death of Jesus,
to which elements of affliction and agony are alien and in which there
remain only the victorious overcoming and consummation" (*John 2*, 193–
94). The detail of the vinegar seems amiss precisely because of the
compression of the exaltation and crucifixion motifs. However—and this
is typical of the approach—Haenchen draws attention to these resistances
to coherence only to declare them insertions by the "ecclesiastical redactor." (The difficult 19:34b, also, has often been suspected of being an
editorial addition.) In source criticism's more ambitious manifestations
(Bultmann, Fortna et al.; see most recently Fortna, *Fourth Gospel*), close
reading is a device that enables one (or so one hopes) to separate out the
redactional layers in the gospel and to provide a chronological account of
its composition. Not surprisingly, these layers have proved most elusive.
(It is correspondingly difficult to specify the extent to which redactional
fault lines are responsible for the logical rift opened up by the Johannine
crucifixion scene. The paradox of the crucified Word resists easy resolution.)

Interestingly, a reading strategy that would accord special attention
to whatever is resistant to sense in a gospel might have a valuable function
other than a historical one. It can be expected in the years ahead, particularly in North America, that composition criticism and narrative criticism
will continue to mount their challenge to source-centered gospel criticism
(I have source-centered redaction criticism particularly in mind here). The
verse-by-verse style of close reading, epitomized by the traditional commentary, will continue its slow decline in favor of more holistic and para-
phrastic approaches that attempt to center on larger sense units within the
received text. But there is no obvious reason why a disgruntlement with
the quest for sources, coupled with the decision to center one's energies
on the received text, might not issue in a reading style other than the
holistic ones—a style characteristically sensitive to inconsistencies. Haenchen, for example, implies but omits to spell out that the ecclesiastical

redactor (if there was one) all but sabotaged the evangelist's careful prep-
aration of his audience to hear/read the crucifixion episode as the resurrection prefiguring elevation of Jesus. The case is similar with respect to
our own earlier reading: if the thirst motif in the crucifixion scene is a
redactional addition, and if the issue of blood and water is too, then the
redactor is responsible for finally bringing down the two-storey ironic
structure that the evangelist had so carefully erected, a structure rendered
dangerously unstable, in any case, once the crucifixion and exaltation motifs were compressed. But what if our diachronic accounts of the building
up and tearing down in John, and in the other Gospels, were to be given
a synchronic twist (we invoke that opposition reservedly)? This would be
done not to drown out the undercurrent of cacophony, of difference in
the text, in the manner of holistic reading, but to listen in on it more
closely instead, and not to ascribe what we overhear to different inten-
tionalities within our account of the gospel's composition history, but to
tease out "the warring forces of signification within the text itself " (Johnson, *Difference*, 5) in as rigorous a manner as possible.

Attention to the forces of difference within the text would extend not
only to differences between one textual unit and another (the kind of
perspectival differences resulting, for example from redactional activity),
but to the possibility that the text might also differ from itself; in de Man's
terms, "simultaneously assert and deny the authority of its own rhetorical
mode" (*Allegories*, 17). This more than anything marks deconstruction's
own difference from biblical source-criticism. Our earlier reading of John
was preoccupied with this second kind of difference. Exemplary (i.e., im-
mensely intricate) analyses of the phenomenon occur in de Man's *Allegories
of Reading* and Johnson's *Critical Difference*, but there is a more elementary
example. Robert Fowler reads Mark 16:8 ("and they said nothing to any
one, for they were afraid") as saying "that the discovery of the empty tomb
was never reported. . . . Mark's Gospel, unlike the other canonical Gospels,
comes to a halt [assuming that Mark 16:8 originally ended the gospel]
before it narrates circumstances in which one could imagine something
like the Gospel of Mark being narrated. The story *in* Mark's Gospel seems
to preclude the telling *of* Mark's Gospel" ("Reading Matthew," 14). Generally speaking, something will always elude a text's capacity for self-
reflexivity and remain unnoticed or unknown. Consequently, the relationship between the text's structural unconscious on the one hand, as analysis
discloses it, and its self-interpretation or self-presentation on the other,
can be nonidentical or askew.

The pendulum has swung heavily in recent years against reading methods that treat the Gospels as parted garments. The tendency more recently is to find them, if not without seams, at least without serious rents, woven from top to bottom, so that composition critics are now saying to narrative critics "Let us not tear it, but cast lots for it to see whose it shall be" (John 19:24). But narrative criticism may be founded unsteadily on the suppression of the older paradigm of the fragmentary, source-spliced text and may depend heavily for its success on an effective blocking out of the more disruptive data that the supplanted paradigm would bring into view (cf. Moore, "Gospels," and "Commentaries," 52–53). (Composition criticism invites similar suspicions.) Deconstructive criticism, in contrast, enables a detailed tracing of the weave of figure and trope within the fabric of the gospel text—a tracing attentive to any tears in that fabric or to any inconsistencies in its pattern.

My own reading of the opposition between figural and literal water in John, amplifying certain insights of Werner Kelber, is offered as a dim illustration of what a more thorough reading of Johannine figurality— one that would feel for fault lines through a wide range of oppositions— might reveal. But in offering tribute to deconstructive *techne* we flirt with illusion, as though the secrets of the text's hidden divisions are to be extracted from it by the skill of an interrogator—secrets that the text managed to conceal through the ages but that can no longer be withheld now that certain pressures have been brought to bear on it. Are we really in the inquisitional business of extracting shameful secrets from the text— secrets of deep inner division? In the preceding chapter, I argued in some detail that we tend to fall victim in biblical studies to a stubbornly lingering essentialism. Do our biblical texts *have* innate properties and meanings that may be extracted if only the right techniques are found? Or is what we find purely a function of how we frame the text—our frames being less individual creations, of course, than corollaries of our different locations? Traditionally as exegetes, we have detracted attention from the frame, effaced it, buried it within the text so that what the frame yields up as data appears to be self-evidently there within the text. The more effective the frame is, the less attention it draws to itself (cf. Phillips, "Deconstruction"). My earlier reading of the water opposition held fast to this traditional way of working. But we can reenact our reading, this time with an altered script, one specifically designed to draw attention to the workings of the frame itself, as opposed to the data framed. Indeed, such a reading would enable us to bring our divergent concerns into dialogue: deconstructive criticism, interpretation theory, and reader-response criticism.

The Retreat of the Reader

The interpretation narrated earlier culminated in the conclusion that Johannine irony, instigated by the supersession of literal water by living, must eventually collapse in paradox. The question it implicitly raises is whether irony must always work on behalf of story recipients at the expense of story participants, enabling the recipients to comprehend what the participants do not. Are we, the recipients of the story, never the victims of its irony? The reading I enacted did indeed imply that the recipients of the Fourth Gospel are the ultimate victims of its irony.[41] But the question such a conclusion raises in turn is, Who precisely is perceived as the victim of the irony in such an instance, and who is doing the perceiving? "Irony is a matter of perception and it must, to become manifest, be seen by an observer or it does not exist" (Amante, "Theory," 81; cf. Muecke, *Irony,* 69). In the scene at the Samaritan well, for example, it was the reader who perceived the irony in the interchange between Jesus and the woman. Later at the crucifixion scene the tables were turned, uncannily, on the canny reader,[42] who is extended the same sublime incapacity as the woman (and Nicodemus, the crowd in John 6, the disciples in John 16, etc.) to cleanly and confidently separate the literal from the figural, a separation on which the irony at the well depended. But who perceives the reader's ironic dilemma at the death scene?

The reason I press this question is because it touches on something vital with regard to stories of reading. We noted how the "virginal" reader of most reader-oriented gospel criticism, exposed to the text for the first time, is to be distinguished from the more experienced reader with whom the redaction critic identifies. This was a useful distinction, certainly, but it should be qualified. Stories of reading, most especially those utilizing the construct of a first-time reader, are necessarily limited in their claims by the irreducible "secondariness" of the reading experience. That experience must be mediated and have its contours fixed by the matrix of factors (relating to conventions, beliefs, institutions, etc.) that regulate reading in the social formations of which the reader is a part or a product. Consequently, our experience of interpreting a text—the Fourth Gospel, for example—will never be a simple, immediate, given one. Rather, it will be

41. Cf. Kelber, "Beginning." Staley, *First Kiss,* 95–118, arrives at a similar conclusion, though by a very different route.

42. Duke, *Irony,* 113–14, following MacRae and others, argues that the death scene turns the tables on Jesus' opponents.

a cultural product, necessarily blind to the intricacy of the factors that empower and delimit it at once, to its own structural unconscious.

This prompts us to rephrase and to reframe our reading of Johannine irony. The most we can do, incidentally, is exchange frames or lenses; we can not dispense with them altogether. Whichever lens we settle on, our precise situation as we focus, as through the eye of a camera, will necessarily exceed our range of vision. But if we earlier read John with a zoom lens, let us now refocus that reading with a wide-angle lens.

In the scene at the Samaritan well, the reader who perceives the irony in the interchange between Jesus and the woman is not really the present author (myself), nor even the "ideal reader" (given the usual masterful connotations of that term), so much as the one scripted to play the straight man in the exegetical drama to follow, on whom the irony will eventually rebound—though my reader will not yet know that. The straight man (stand-in for anyone who has ever read Johannine irony "naively") is further set up, or framed, in the Tabernacles scene, being the seeming beneficiary of the narrator's explanatory aside (7:39). Later at the scene of crucifixion, as the ironic levels teeter and begin to crumble, a startling denouement occurs. It transpires that this persona is not the true reader after all. Her/his role, as is now disclosed, has been simply that of forerunner to a second reader, able to smile superciliously at the straight man (or dupe), as the dupe once smiled at the Samaritan woman, and able to comprehend the instability of the literal/figural dichotomy, while the dupe reels helplessly in the throes of the reversal. It transpires, furthermore, that this second reader is in fact the ideal reader, in relation to whom the first is merely a "reader." This ideal reader must have stood, a dim wraith or ghostly trace, in the wings in the scenes with Nicodemus, the woman, the crowd, and the disciples, identifying not with the less-than-ideal "reader," but with these inhabitants of the story-world instead—inhabitants whose "sublime simplicity" has now been thoroughly vindicated. But, of course, this second, usurper reader is no more the present author than the first one. Rather, as I read or interpret his or her role, he or she becomes a "reader" in his or her turn relative to the role-playing reader-critic that I have become, while the original reader (the straight man) becomes a "'reader'" in his or her turn, and so on.

I am aware that the preceding rereading could prompt my own readers to take my earlier interpretation of Johannine irony even less seriously than they might otherwise have been disposed to do, but certain risks are worth the taking. In rereading the earlier reading the way I have done, I hope to suggest some of the involutions that can lurk beneath a calm exegetical surface—some of the involutions only, for that reading was necessarily oblivious in turn to its own enabling conditions. We can swing the camera around to focus on the spot we just occupied, but in doing so we merely move to another position, itself invisible until we repeat the maneuver. But what has become of the Johannine text in the course of this hermeneutical photographic session? Which text has our reading vindicated: Kermode's opaque and secretive text, or Fish's insubstantial and empty one? Has our detour through the mirrored corridors of deconstruction returned us "to a new respect for the text's integrity and impenetrability" (Freund, *Return,* 154)? For how could a text empty of all signifying properties account for such significative complexity? Or is it merely that our "analytic discourse is as self-differing, its truths as slippery, as any literary work" (Ray, *Meaning,* 206)? But is it not precisely the distinction implied by that formulation—that between the literary work and its analysis—that is in question? In this case the poststructuralist detour has led us, not deeper into the heart of the text, but deeper into the heart of reading (cf. Barthes, *Essays,* 89). But of reading what? The circle seems endless. Reading "create[s] and disclose[s] at the same time, disclose[s] by creating and create[s] by disclosing. . . . [F]or the reader everything is to be done and everything is already done."[43] And this is the seemingly irreducible paradox around which contemporary reading theory seems fated to wheel, until centrifugal force sets it spinning off again in some as yet unknowable direction.

43. Sartre, *Literature,* 30, 32, quoted in Culler, *On Deconstruction,* 76. See Culler's discussion of the paradox (64–83 passim) and especially Ray's book-length discussion of it (*Meaning*).

Conclusion: New Testament Criticism and Mythology: Demythologizing Today

> Either we are foundationalists, and thus stand within the tradition called Cartesian, or we define ourselves in opposition to all that. These are just two ways of having the same father.
> —Jeffrey Stout, *The Flight from Authority*

> There was a man who had two sons; and the younger of them said to his father, "Father, give me the share of property that falls to me." And he divided his living between them. Not many days later, the younger son gathered all he had and took his journey into a far country.
> —Luke 15:11–13

Our retrospective-prospective survey has taken us all the way from critical readings that bring the Gospels into focus as self-consistent wholes to readings that bring them into precisely the opposite focus. The phenomenon is a hermeneutic "domino effect"—the dominoes in question being different working models of, or ways of framing, the gospel texts. Alternatively we could say that the phenomenon was less one of different working models bent shoulder-to-shoulder in the joint labor of exegesis than of competing models jostling for position, some light-framed, some heavily muscled, each capable of shouldering a weaker competitor off-balance. Or yet again we could say that the movement traced has been an ever outward one, from a relatively narrow focus on story (chapters 1, 2), through a wider focus on narrative rhetoric (chapters 3, 4, 5), through a focus on the roles of reading elicited by such rhetoric (chapter 6), through a focus on the shared interpretive premises that operate through readers to generate texts (chapter 7), to a focus on the intractable paradoxes in which focusing or interpreting sooner or later seems to entangle us (chapter 8). And each new method, or set of methods, was ideally positioned to interrogate the preceding one, if not to topple it altogether. (*Focus* can also mean the place of origin of seismic activity.) The payoff, however, was not the final unveiling of some "supermethod" that would render all previous methods obsolete.[1] Narrative theory and interpretation are not amenable to the teleology of a supermethod:

1. Paradoxically, the more rigorous deconstruction becomes, the more it is obliged to forfeit posturing as a supermethod (cf. chapter 8).

Just as one might verify a scientific theory that applies to a limited range of phenomena and then expand it by identifying variables that would account for other classes of events, so by considering more and more features in the narrative situation, we should be able to produce theories of increasing generality and precision. Unfortunately, however, the analogy does not seem to hold. Theories of narrative do not fit together in a neat, hierarchic relationship; taking more features into account can overturn the conclusions derived from a simpler model rather than subsume them. (Martin, *Recent Theories,* 174; cf. Freund, *Return,* 1–2).[2]

As biblical literary criticism pushes deeper into literary theory, far from gaining an ever more secure footing in the biblical text, it can expect its footing to become ever more precarious (cf. chapter 8). Why bother at all, then?

Let us wax apocalyptic for a moment, to speak of what is and what may be hereafter. Today, it is biblical criticism itself that cries out for demythologizing. And whereas the modernist demythologizer, Bultmann, found it necessary to wrestle critically with the New Testament's rendering of the metaphysical in terms of the contingent, "the other side in terms of this side" ("New Testament," 10), the postmodern demythologizer will find it necessary to address the New Testament critic's propensity to render "this side in terms of the other side," contingent *physis* (here, semantic instability) in terms of idealist (or metaphysical) presuppositions—preeminently, the three hypostases widely assumed to preexist the interpreter's activity: transcendentalized textual content, assumed to be independent in principle of attempts to paraphrase it; transcendentalized *Sitz im Leben,* assumed to be independent in principle of attempts to reconstruct it; and transcendentalized authorial intention, assumed in principle to be a kind of Procrustean bed to which virtually all features of the text can some day be adapted. (The arguments for this rather sweeping statement, which might not be entirely innocent of caricature, were advanced in chapters 3, 5, 7 and 8).

Bultmannian demythologizing was "the radical application of the doctrine of justification by faith to the sphere of knowledge and thought. Like the doctrine of justification, demythologizing destroys every longing for security" (*Jesus Christ,* 84). But while the Marburg *Prediger*'s compulsion to vindicate Luther's Paul could hardly be the driving force of a

2. Scientific theories are not themselves immune to such collapse; relative to scientific theories, however, literary theories reach their level of overload with disconcerting rapidity.

postmodern demythologizing, the destruction of illusory security would be stepped up beyond anything that he might have foreseen. (Bultmann and Gadamer took the high, confident road out of the early Heidegger of *Being and Time,* but Derridean deconstruction takes the skeptical low road out of late Heidegger's disenchantment with his early work and his obsession with the overcoming of metaphysics.)[3]

New Testament exegetes have adapted well to the harsh light of modernity refracted more pitilessly in the twentieth century by Bultmann than by any other biblical scholar. Indeed, exegetes have learned to bask quite comfortably in it. Far from being blighted by its glare, their faith boasts a suntan. And over the last three decades, the historical Jesus, helped to his feet initially by the post-Bultmannians and the New Quest, has made an impressive recovery from the beatings inflicted on him by earlier scholarship[4]—a hypermodernist, skeptical scholarship, which might be said, schematically, to have been noisily ushered in with Strauss' *Das Leben Jesu kritisch untersucht* (1835–36), and to have climaxed with Bultmann's dogmatic insistence on the irrecoverability of "Christ after the flesh." But paradoxically, over the same three decades, modernity itself, having all but consumed Jesus of Nazareth in its flames ("I calmly let the fire burn, for I see that what is consumed is only the fanciful portraits of Life-of-Jesus theology, and that means nothing other than 'Christ after the flesh'" [Bultmann, *Faith,* 132]) came under increasingly harsh suspicion and was dragged out in turn to be interrogated:

> Postmodernism at its deepest level represents not just another crisis within the perpetual cycle of boom and bust, exhaustion and renewal, which has characterized the trajectory of modernist culture. It rather represents a new type of crisis *of* that modernist culture itself . . . that we are not bound to *complete* the project of modernity (Habermas' phrase) and still do not necessarily have to lapse into irrationality or apocalyptic frenzy. . . . Rather than being bound to a one-way history of modernism which interprets it as a logical unfolding toward some imaginary goal . . . we are beginning to explore its contradictions and

3. The Gadamer-Derrida relationship is frequently articulated as two divergent paths, each of which has passed through Heidegger, e.g., Caputo, *Hermeneutics,* 95–119. Bultmann, it need hardly be said, stands closer to Gadamer than to Derrida. Further on Bultmann's philosophical location, see Hobbs, ed., *Bultmann,* 13–34 passim, and Jaspert, ed., *Werk,* 211–300 passim.

4. As recent evidence of that recovery, witness "The Jesus Seminar" (1985–), comprising more than a hundred American gospel scholars, which represents a new, cautious but optimistic chapter in the quest for the historical Jesus.

contingencies, its tensions and internal resistances to its own "forward" movement. (Huyssen, *Great Divide,* 217)

Does the modernist project in biblical studies—broadly, the attempt to retrieve the original meanings of the biblical texts (authorial intentions objectified in textual features)—even admit of completion? What, at a minimum, should be necessary in order that it might be completed? An objective biblical text whose fixed, innate properties admit of cumulative retrieval? A sleeping text that awaits our kiss? Chapter 7 showed this text-model, the product of a stubborn, lingering essentialism in biblical studies, to be illusory. It represents the dream that drives the biblical scholar incessantly upward, erecting a massive interpretive edifice that would ascend to heaven—or, at any rate, to that Platonic sphere in which the text's primordial semantic content is thought to inhere (cf. chapter 5). But major developments in neighboring fields (philosophy, literary criticism, even theology) send shock waves through our tower and set its foundations trembling.

The first demythologizing performed for faith "the supreme service of recalling it to a radical reconsideration of its own nature" (Bultmann, *Kerygma,* 210) by letting the flame kindled by the Enlightenment in New Testament scholarship purge faith of its dross. Through the long night that follows, faith must hear "the voice of God in the rumble of the flux" and feel "the hand of God in its tremors." It must grow "accustomed to the lack of evidence and to living without assurances" (Caputo, *Hermeneutics,* 279). Bultmann could certainly have written those words; he did, after all, write, "faith is security where no security can be seen . . . the readiness to enter confidently into the darkness of the future" (*Jesus Christ,* 40–41). But Caputo's next sentence, echoing late Heidegger as refracted by Derrida, suggests what a demythologizing of New Testament criticism itself, which would amount to a principled refusal to unabashedly render "this side in terms of the other side," might entail: "I reject all forms of privileged positions above the flux. . . . I write . . . from below, and I ask all who do otherwise how they acquired their elevated position" (*Hermeneutics,* 279).[5] This will do for a postmodern creed. "The aim is always to avoid the illusion that our institutions and practices, that our reason and our faith have dropped from the sky" (272). (And our solid-seeming biblical text also? I am reminded of Acts 19:35: "what man is there who does not know that the city of the Ephesians is temple keeper of . . . the

---

5. Caputo does not himself refer to biblical interpretation, but his book helps set chapters 7 and 8 in theological perspective.

sacred stone that fell from the sky?" Certain members of the biblical guild may echo Demetrius the shrine-maker's complaint to his fellow guildsmen on seeing that sacred object threatened: "Men, you know that from this business we have our wealth" [Acts 19:25]. Understandably, the most resolute opposition to change within the biblical guild tends to come from established scholars whose prestige derives from interpretive consensuses that their hard labor helped consolidate [cf. Ray, *Meaning*, 207].) Caputo continues: "Radical hermeneutics is a sustained attempt to write from below, without celestial, transcendental justifications" (*Hermeneutics*, 272).[6] Which is why, if a radical Lutheranism was the logical theological correlate of a skeptical, hypermodernist biblical criticism (at any rate, for its most skeptical practitioner, Bultmann), deconstructive theology, or some other, presently unforeseeable form of nontranscendental theology, would be the logical correlate of its postmodernist successor. And without doubt, at the site on which Bultmann opted to build, his successors will feel obliged to dig. For Bultmann hedged his bets, and certain of his expositors hedged enthusiastically with him:

> He [Bultmann] puts forward a view of theology which calls for radical demythologizing, and the translation of all transcendent statements into statements about the understanding of the self. Yet at the same time he believes that God has acted decisively in Christ, and he does not appear to realize the incompatibility of the two positions. We do not find fault with him for holding to the latter position. Rather we might say . . . that Bultmann's greatness here shows itself in his steadfast refusal to follow out his own ideas to the bitter end. But we can readily imagine that some disciple of his, with more consistency and less insight than his master, might run straight into the dangers we have indicated. [Macquarrie, *Theology*, 243]

But today it is less Bultmann's theological progeny who manifest that "deficiency of insight" (or surfeit of intellectual rigor) that registered high on Macquarrie's heresy-monitor in 1955 than the theological progeny of Heidegger and Derrida.[7] Macquarrie's dangers have indeed irrupted with a vengeance (he was even to flirt with danger himself in *God-Talk*), though

6. Elsewhere Caputo shows himself cognizant of the difficulty of "writing from below" (e.g., 271, 288) and of deconstruction's critique of hermeneutics (146–47).

7. Christology among postmodernist theologians has (predictably) tended to take a postmetaphysical (or "radically incarnational") turn. See, e.g., Taylor, *Erring,* 103ff. For an excellent introduction to Altizer's many writings on the subject, see Winquist, *Epiphanies,* 108–23.

traces of the existentialism that he helped to popularize have persisted in radical theology. For example: "Radical hermeneutics makes a pass at formulating . . . the human situation. I do not mean by this to incite another wave of the 'humanism' which deconstruction has tried to put down but to evoke the notion of 'facing up' to the limits of our situation, to the illusions of which we are capable, to the original difficulty of our lives. And I call this 'hermeneutics' just because I think there is something liberating about all this" (Caputo, *Hermeneutics,* 97). Even though a de-mythologized biblical criticism must know that it can only ever be a re-mythologized biblical criticism, striding forward on enabling myths that lie concealed beneath the soles of its feet, it can lay claim to a redoubtable self-reflexivity nonetheless (cf. chapter 8). This is a nomadic reflexivity that goes out like a Kierkegaardian Abraham not knowing where to, except that it cannot be to "a city which has foundations"; rumors abound across the span of academic disciplines that no such city lies en route (cf. chapter 7).

How one will respond to such rumors is largely a matter of temper-ament—one's way "of feeling the whole push, and seeing the whole drift of life, forced on one by one's total character and experience, and on the whole *preferred*—there is no other truthful word—as one's best working attitude."[8] Some are troubled by the implications of a postmodern skep-ticism for traditional religious belief—modern skepticism was bad enough! —and they respond with "a defiant rejection of every critique of foun-dational beliefs," while others devour the rumors hungrily like "children unbound from the rule of a domineering father." But there is in addition "a large, and . . . growing, group of people who find themselves caught in the middle of such extremes. Suspended between the loss of old cer-tainties and the discovery of new beliefs, these marginal people constantly live on the border that both joins and separates belief and unbelief " (Tay-lor, *Erring,* 4–5).[9] In that group I count myself. Historical criticism sent my strapping but flabby faith to boot camp over a decade ago, but after a grueling survival course it slipped little by little into the anesthesia of a desk job, adrift in the sea of paperwork that is the mainstay of biblical studies in peace time: the thousands of small-scale jobs collectively under-taken, which issue in thousands of small-scale findings. My successive ef-forts to get back into the field again are obliquely narrated in this book. Convinced now of the necessity of an iconoclastic moment in biblical

8. William James from an unspecified work, quoted in Bernstein, "Difference," 343.
9. Cf. Tracy, *Imagination,* 30: "Many have come to recognize the presence of real doubt in authentic contemporary faith."

studies (for myself, at any rate)—a revision, though not a rejection, of foundational concepts such as Bible and exegesis (a conviction that animates several of my chapters)—I feel a spring-like quickening of my intellectual *and* spiritual sap such as I have not felt since historical criticism's first rude accostation mated my quest for Reality (I was a Cistercian monk at the time, and much taken with *The Cloud of Unknowing*) with a questioning. "For to begin thinking such thoughts is to approach the boundaries of faith" (Kierkegaard, *Fear,* 269).

What are the prospects, actually, for a demythologized, postmodernist, or philosophical biblical criticism? Unwanted by so many, will it dare crawl forth from the womb—or will it scuttle back into the darkness? More specifically, what are the chances of gospel literary criticism taking a broad philosophical turn? Literary criticism of the Gospels at present, while it does manifest a variety of forms, clusters around a few preferred foci (plot and character, point of view, "the reader in the text"), as we have seen. Narrative criticism (cf. chapters 1–4), with reader-in-the-gospel criticism (chapter 6) leaning on its arm, seems to be the most successful literary approach. New Testament scholars are not converting en masse to narrative criticism, but significant numbers, epitomized by the interested onlookers ("God-fearers") who fill the back rows in the Society of Biblical Literature's literary critical seminars, give tentative credence to certain of narrative criticism's holistic precepts and practices (mainly in North America, as we said earlier), while retaining their belief in historical method. But if narrative criticism sometimes presents the aspect of a genial reform movement within historical criticism, philosophical or poststructuralist biblical criticism—for now they amount to the same thing—presents the forbidding aspect of a millenarian sect and has had as little general appeal. This imbalance in drawing power is not at all surprising. The narrativist approach, centered on plot, character, point of view, and reader-response, is one with considerable pedagogic potential. It can admirably prepare beginning New Testament students, who may be quite unfamiliar with the details of the gospel narratives, for the deeper mysteries of redaction criticism. Neither is its appeal for scholars surprising. With remarkably little extracurricular reading, one can get sufficient grasp of the story-centered approach to integrate it with one's customary approaches. But to gain a thorough grasp of current literary theory, however, particularly where it shades over into continental philosophy, takes years of toil and tears. In this respect, literary criticism "is rather like a laboratory in which some of the staff are seated in white coats at control panels, while others are throwing sticks in the air or spinning coins. Genteel amateurs jostle with hard-nosed professionals" (Eagleton, *Literary Theory,* 199). Some of us, to be sure, attempt to pass for white-coated professionals, while the funny hat that we forgot to remove shows us up for the amateurs that we really are. Yet, if we are not to remain perpetual dilettantes in our literary criticism of the Bible, we must be prepared to read long and hard in critical theory.

Literary critics wield one particular premise with considerable effect in the arena of gospel criticism. The premise is that participation in the form of a literary work (specifically, its narrative form) is indispensible to its adequate interpretation (cf. chapter 5, on what that premise would look like if wielded in a poststructuralist arc). This is an old premise, one especially associated with the New Criticism. However, the sort of premise that it is leveled against—for example, that the biblical text is fundamentally a vehicle of, or opening onto, some historical or theological reality in principle independent of it—represents even older, and hence more vulnerable, influences from the secular disciplines. To keep the ideas that animate it, and that give it this power, intact—the idea of the holistic text, especially—the newer literary criticism of the Gospels must turn a blind eye to much that has passed under the bridge since the New Criticism or else draw very selectively from it (see chapter 4). Relative to the cutting edge of secular literary study, historical criticism occupies one time warp, narrative criticism another. The question thus remains, What happens in gospel studies and in biblical studies generally once biblical scholars finally dispense with freeze-frames and action replays in order to participate fully in literary study in its high-risk present forms? What would happen were we to take leave of our father (see the epigraph from Stout for his true identity—Bultmann was merely his deputy) to journey to that perilous country where he holds progressively less sway? We should have to travel by night, certainly, and learn to live by our wits. But soon we would find ourselves prodigally devouring our living, defiant of famine or want, as at the dawn of our critical enterprise—or better still, like chaste Ruth (less an illegal immigrant than a permanent resident) "agleaning in strange and alien fields, in places we have not seen before, among companions we have not met before, but with gains we have not known before" (Crossan, "Ruth," 210).

Glossary

Composition criticism: As used in recent gospel studies, particularly in the United States, it denotes a holistic variation of redaction criticism in which the gospel itself (or Luke-Acts), viewed rigorously and persistently in its entirety, becomes the primary context for interpreting any part of it.

Discourse analysis (or *textlinguistics*): In the biblical studies context, an appropriation for purposes of exegesis of the attempts in contemporary linguistics to describe how units of utterance greater than the sentence cohere and communicate.

Deconstruction: "A deconstruction always has for its target to reveal the existence of hidden articulations and fragmentations within assumedly monadic totalities" (de Man, *Allegories,* 249). "'What's the bottom line?' What deconstruction does is to teach you to ask: 'What does the construction of the bottom line leave out? What does it repress? . . . What does it put in the margins?'" (Johnson, "Barbara Johnson," 164). "[D]econstruction is a form of what has long been called a *critique. . . .* It is an analysis that focuses on the grounds of [a] system's possibility. . . . Every theory starts somewhere; every critique exposes what that starting point conceals, and thereby displaces all the ideas that follow from it" (Johnson, "Introduction," xv). "Deconstruction is not a critical operation. The critical is its object; the deconstruction always bears . . . on the confidence invested in the critical . . . process . . . in the act of decision, in the ultimate possibility of the decidable" (Derrida, "Ja," 103). "All sentences of the type 'deconstruction is X' . . . a priori miss the point" (Derrida, "Japanese," 4).

Demythologizing: Concerned that "it is no longer possible for anyone seriously to hold the New Testament view of the world," Rudolf Bultmann announced, preeminently in "New Testament and Mythology" (1941), a demythologizing program which would aim, not to jettison the gospel myth and the understanding of existence which it enshrines, but to reexpress it in a contemporary register (in effect, Heidegger's existential language of freedom, *Angst,* and authenticity), which would enable it to speak to modern humanity.

Diachronic analysis: The study of changes within a system (e.g., a system of language, or of texts) over time.

Formalism: A methodological attitude in which the meaning of a literary work is located in the details of its structure.

Form criticism: First applied systematically to the Gospels by Dibelius, Schmidt, and Bultmann in Germany in the period 1919–21, its principal aims were (1) to classify (in such categories as paradigms, tales, legends, myths, exhortations, etc.) the units of tradition of which the Gospels were said to be composed, units that circulated independently during the oral period preceding the written gospels, and (2) to assign these units a situation and function (catechesis, parenesis, apologetic, worship, etc.) in the life of the early Christian communities.

Historical criticism: A panoply of methods developed (1) to recover the meanings that the biblical texts would have had in their original historical contexts and (2) to uncover ancient Israelite history and Christian origins.

Implied author: "[A] core of norms and choices" immanent in a work that "we infer as an ideal, literary, created version of the real [author]" (Booth, *Rhetoric,* 74–75).

Implied reader: "[T]he term . . . incorporates both the prestructuring of the potential meaning by the text, and the reader's actualization of the potential through the reading process" (Iser, *Implied Reader,* xii).

Narratee: "[T]he encoded or inscribed 'you' . . . in any narrative text [that] may or may not coincide with the ostensible addressee of that text and/ or with the receiver of it" (Prince, "Narratee Revisited," 302).

Narrative criticism: A form of biblical criticism, mainly holistic in thrust and associated with the study of the Gospels, that appropriates narrative theory to analyze plot, character, point of view, setting, narrative time, and other features of gospel narrative including the intratextual reader (at which point it shades over into *reader-response criticism*).

Narratology (or *narrative poetics*): With its recent roots in French structuralism, narratology searches for the general principles that manifest themselves in narrative discourse (see *structuralism*). As it has developed outside of France, narratology has tended to concern itself less with the regularities of narrative's deep structures (the static logical relations among elements) than with the regularities and irregularities of surface structures (governed by temporal and causal relations—plot, characterization, narrative perspective, etc.).

New Criticism: The dominant mode of Anglo-American literary criticism in the 1940s and 1950s, it arose in reaction to an earlier literary scholarship preoccupied with the biographies and psychologies of authors, social background, and literary history, gradually displacing such scholarship with a conception of the poetic work as an autonomous, internally unified organism, with a meaning to be validated first and foremost by the context of the poem itself, and with a method of "close reading" developed to elucidate the poem's intricate structure. The New Criticism's effects are still evident in the way literature is taught and studied.

Point of view: The perspective of a narrator or character on a story-world. More precisely, the rhetorical activity of an author as he or she attempts, from a position within some socially shared system of assumptions and convictions, to impose a story-world upon an audience by the manipulation of narrative perspective.

Postmodernism: Represents, among other things, a discontent within modernity and an incredulity toward its legitimizing "metanarratives" (Lyotard, *Condition*, xxiv); an extension of the crisis of representation that marked the emergence of modernist art and literature to the critical text (Krauss, "Paraliterary"); a "criticism which would include in its own discourse an implicit (or explicit) reflection upon itself " (Hutcheon, *Postmodernism*, 13); "a desire to think in terms sensitive to difference (of others without opposition, of heterogeneity without hierarchy)" (Foster, "Preface," xv); "an acceptance of the challenge that other religious options present to the Judeo-Christian tradition . . . a sense of the displacement of the white Western male and the rise of those dispossessed due to gender, race, or class" (McFague, *Theology*, x–xi).

Poststructuralism: A heterogeneous, multidisciplinary discourse that emerged from the environs of French structuralism (e.g., Derrida's deconstruction), or from within structuralism (e.g., later Barthes). In American literary criticism, scene of poststructuralism's most obvious success, it has been transmuted so as to say: "Structuralism offered criticism its last chance to make a science out of theorizing literature. . . . Criticism after structuralism is impotent in so far as it is unable to produce further and greater structuralisms. . . . Post-structuralism . . . opens [literature] up to a practice of . . . reading that can take in philosophy, history or psychoanalysis, [though] *not* on the reckoning that these are . . . ultimate sources of truth. . . . No longer is it a question of theory setting up as some kind of ultimate explanatory method that would seek to comprehend literary texts through application of scientific principles. . . . Indeed there is a strange reversal of roles whereby . . . 'theory' becomes the straight-man or foil of a literary language that everywhere outwits its powers of conceptual command" (Machin and Norris, "Introduction," 1–2, 18).

Pragmatism: "[A]nti-essentialism applied to notions like 'truth,' 'knowledge' . . . and similar objects of philosophical theorizing" (Rorty, *Consequences*, 162).

Rhetorical criticism: In the study of the Hebrew Bible, the term is principally associated with analysis of the techniques of Hebrew poetic composition. More recently, within the context of New Testament studies, the term has come to designate the reading of the New Testament texts as they "would be read by an early Christian, by an inhabitant of the Greek-speaking world in which rhetoric was the core subject of formal education and in which even those without formal education necessarily developed cultural preconceptions about appropriate discourse" (Kennedy, *Rhetorical Criticism*, 5).

Source criticism: In the biblical studies context, the attempt to specify, by attention to breaks and dislocations of sequence and stylistic and theological inconsistencies, the nature of the literary dependence between two or more extant texts where such dependence is suspected to exist (the classic New Testament case being that of Matthew, Mark, and Luke) or the attempt to specify or recreate nonextant sources where these are suspected to underlie given texts (e.g., Acts, John). (Source criticism has been an integral feature both of *form criticism* and *redaction criticism*.)

Structuralism: The application of explanatory principles derived from linguistics to such fields as anthropology, psychoanalysis, political theory, and literary theory. For example: "Faced with the impossibility of commanding all the sentences of a language, linguists agree to establish a *hypothetical descriptive model*, from which they can explain how the infinite sentences of a language are generated. . . . There is no reason not to try to apply such a method to works of literature. These works are themselves comparable to immense sentences, derived from a general language of symbols. . . . [L]inguistics can give literature that generative model which is the basis of all science" (Barthes, *Criticism*, 74). Thus, biblical structuralism attempts to analyze biblical texts in terms of the transhistorical and transcultural generative systems on which they are assumed to depend.

Reader-response criticism: Not a unified theory or method but a spectrum of contrasting positions, some focused on the roles of reading implied or encoded in literary texts (New Testament reader-response critics have favored this focus in which interpretation becomes an account of the successive experiences of an intratextual reader), others more concerned with how actual readers read, and others centered on the factors (institutional, sociocultural, linguistic) that enable and delimit reading in the first place—at which point we move out of reader-response criticism, narrowly conceived, and into the more general preoccupation with reading and interpretation that has characterized recent theory and criticism, particularly since the advent of *poststructuralism*.

Redaction criticism: First applied to the Gospels by Bornkamm, Conzelmann, and Marxsen in Germany in the 1950s, it marks a decisive shift from a view of the evangelists as compilers of traditional material to a view of the evangelists as creative reshapers of tradition with consistent theological viewpoints. It attempts (1) to isolate the unique theological perspective of each gospel by analysis of the evangelist's selection, modification, and expansion of his source material (e.g., Matthew and Luke's redaction of Mark, generally assumed to be their principal source) and (2) to identify the specific circumstances in the sociohistorical context of the evangelist that he intended to address by means of his particular reframing of the tradition.

Signified: The conceptual constituent of the linguistic sign (e.g., the concept *tree*).

Signifier: The sensible (acoustic, graphic) constituent of the linguistic sign (e.g., the sound *tree*).

Sitz im Leben ("setting in life," "life situation"): A technical term denoting the situation within the early Christian communities in response to which a given gospel, or unit of gospel tradition, assumed a certain form. It is associated with *form criticism* and *redaction criticism*.

Synchronic analysis: The study of a system (e.g., a language or a text) as it appears at a given point in time.

Synoptic Gospels: Matthew, Mark, and Luke, so called because of their many agreements in subject, order, and language.

Targums: Aramaic translations of the Jewish Scriptures, characterized by paraphrase and dating from the last centuries B.C.E. and the early centuries C.E.

Bibliography

The list of works cited has been supplemented with further literary-biblical works, mainly gospel studies with a narrative or readerly focus.

Achtemeier, Paul J., ed. *Society of Biblical Literature 1980 Seminar Papers*. Chico, Calif.: Scholars Press, 1980.

Adam, A. K. M. "The Sign of Jonah: A Fish-Eye View." In Phillips, "Text, Context."

Ades, J. I. "Literary Aspects of Luke." *Papers on Language and Literature* 15 (1979): 193–99.

Aichele, George, Jr. *The Limits of Story*. Atlanta: Scholars Press, 1985.

Alonso-Schökel, Luis. *The Inspired Word: Scripture and Tradition in the Light of Language and Literature*. Translated by Francis Martin. New York: Herder & Herder, 1965.

Alter, Robert. *The Art of Biblical Narrative*. New York: Basic Books, 1981.

———. "Biblical Narrative." *Commentary* 61 (1976): 61–67.

———. "Biblical Type-Scenes and the Uses of Convention." *Critical Inquiry* 5 (1978): 355–68.

———. "Character in the Bible." *Commentary* 66 (1978): 58–65.

———. "How Convention Helps Us Read: The Case of the Bible's Annunciation Type-Scenes." *Prooftexts* 3 (1983): 115–30.

———. "A Literary Approach to the Bible." *Commentary* 60 (1975): 70–77.

Alter, Robert, and Frank Kermode, eds. *The Literary Guide to the Bible*. Cambridge: Belknap Press, Harvard University Press, 1987.

Altizer, Thomas J. J. "Demythologizing as the Self-Embodiment of Speech." In Spencer, *Orientation*, 139–50.

———. *Total Presence: The Language of Jesus and the Language of Today*. New York: Seabury Press, 1980.

Altizer, Thomas J. J. et al. *Deconstruction and Theology*. New York: Crossroad, 1980.

Amante, David J. "Theory of Ironic Speech Acts." *Poetics Today* 2 (1981): 77–96.

Anderson, Janice Capel. "Double and Triple Stories, the Implied Reader, and Redundancy in Matthew." In Detweiler, "Reader Response," 71–90.

———. "Mary's Difference: Gender and Patriarchy in the Birth Narratives." *Journal of Religion* 67 (1987): 183–202.

———. "Matthew: Gender and Reading." *Semeia* 28 (1983): 3–28.

———. "Matthew: Sermon and Story." In Lull, *1988 Seminar Papers,* 496–507.

———. "Over and Over and Over Again: Repetition in the Gospel of Matthew." Ph.D. diss., University of Chicago, 1985.

Arac, Jonathan, Wlad Godzich, and Wallace Martin, eds. *The Yale Critics: Deconstruction in America.* Minneapolis: University of Minnesota Press, 1983.

Ash, B. S. "Jewish Hermeneutics and Contemporary Theories of Textuality: Hartman, Bloom, and Derrida." *Modern Philosophy* 85 (1987): 65–80.

Atkins, G. Douglas. *Reading Deconstruction/Deconstructive Reading.* Lexington: University Press of Kentucky, 1983.

Attridge, Derek, ed. *Post-Structuralism and the Question of History.* Cambridge: Cambridge University Press, 1987.

Auerbach, Erich. *Mimesis: The Representation of Reality in Western Literature.* Translated by Willard Trask. Princeton: Princeton University Press, 1953.

Aune, David E. *The New Testament in Its Literary Environment.* Philadelphia: Westminster Press, 1987.

Bagwell, J. Timothy. *American Formalism and the Problem of Interpretation.* Houston: Rice University Press, 1986.

Bakhtin, Mikhail M. *The Dialogic Imagination: Four Essays.* Edited by Michael Holquist. Translated by Caryl Emerson. Austin: University of Texas Press, 1981.

Bal, Mieke. *Death and Dissymmetry: The Politics of Coherence in Judges.* Chicago: University of Chicago Press, 1988.

———. *Femmes imaginaires: L'ancien Testament au risque d'une narratologie critique.* Montreal: HMH, 1986.

———. "The Laughing Mice, or: On Focalization." *Poetics Today* 2 (1981): 202–10.

———. *Lethal Love: Literary Feminist Readings of Biblical Love-Stories.* Bloomington: Indiana University Press, 1987.

———. *Murder and Difference: Gender, Genre and Scholarship on Sisera's Death.* Bloomington: Indiana University Press, 1988.

———. "The Narrating and the Focalizing: A Theory of the Agents of Narrative." Translated by Jane E. Lewin. *Style* 17 (1983): 235–69.

———. *Narratology: Introduction to the Theory of Narrative*. Translated by Christine van Boheemen. Toronto: University of Toronto Press, 1985.

———. "Tell-Tale Theories." *Poetics Today* 7 (1986): 555–64.

Barnouw, Dagmar. "Critics in the Act of Reading." *Poetics Today* 1 (1980): 213–22.

Barr, David L. "The Apocalypse as a Symbolic Transformation of the World: A Literary Analysis." *Interpretation* 38 (1984): 39–50.

———. "The Apocalypse of John as Oral Enactment." *Interpretation* 40 (1986): 243–56.

———. "Elephants and Holograms: From Metaphor to Methodology in the Study of John's Apocalypse." In Richards, *1986 Seminar Papers*, 400–11.

———. *New Testament Story: An Introduction*. Belmont: Wadsworth, 1987.

Barta, Karen A. "Mission in Matthew: The Second Discourse as Narrative." In Lull, *1988 Seminar Papers*, 527–35.

Barthes, Roland. *Criticism and Truth*. Edited and translated by Katrine Pilcher Keunemen. Minneapolis: University of Minnesota Press, 1987.

———. "The Death of the Author." In *Image—Music—Text*, edited and translated by Stephen Heath, 142–48. New York: Hill & Wang, 1977.

———. *New Critical Essays*. Translated by Richard Howard. New York: Hill & Wang, 1980.

———. *The Pleasure of the Text*. Translated by Richard Miller. New York: Hill & Wang, 1975.

———. "The Structural Analysis of Narrative: Apropos of Acts 10–11." In *The Semiotic Challenge*, edited and translated by Richard Howard, 217–45. New York: Hill & Wang, 1988.

———. *S/Z*. Translated by Richard Miller. New York: Hill & Wang, 1974.

———. "Textual Analysis of a Tale by Edgar Allan Poe." In *Semiotic*, 261–93.

———. "Wrestling with the Angel: Textual Analysis of Genesis 32:23–33." In *Semiotic*, 246–60.

Bassler, Jouette M. "The Parable of the Loaves." *Journal of Religion* 66 (1986): 157–72.

Beardslee, William A. *Literary Criticism of the New Testament*. Philadelphia: Fortress Press, 1970.

———. "Parable Interpretation and the World Disclosed by the Parable." *Perspectives in Religious Studies* 3 (1976): 123–39.

———. "Parable, Proverb, and Koan." *Semeia* 12 (1978): 151–71.

Beavis, Mary Ann. "The Trial before the Sanhedrin (Mark 14:53–65): Reader Response and Greco-Roman Readers." *Catholic Biblical Quarterly* 49 (1987): 581–96.

Belo, Fernando. *A Materialist Reading of the Gospel of Mark*. Translated by Matthew J. O'Connell. Maryknoll, N.Y.: Orbis Books, 1981.

Berg, Temma F. "Psychologies of Reading." In Natoli, *Tracing,* 248–77.
———. "Reading in/to Mark." In McKnight, "Reader."
Berlin, Adele. *Poetics and Interpretation of Biblical Narrative.* Sheffield: Almond Press, 1983.
Berman, Art. *From the New Criticism to Deconstruction: The Reception of Structuralism and Post-Structuralism.* Urbana: University of Illinois Press, 1988.
Bernstein, Richard J. "What Is the Difference That Makes a Difference?: Gadamer, Habermas, and Rorty." In *Hermeneutics and Modern Philosophy,* edited by Brice R. Wachterhauser, 343–76. Albany: State University of New York Press, 1986.
Blackwell, John. *The Passion as Story: The Plot of Mark.* Philadelphia: Fortress Press, 1986.
Blank, G. Kim. "Deconstruction: Entering the Bible through Babel." *Neotestamentica* 20 (1986): 61–67.
Bleich, David. *Readings and Feelings: An Introduction to Subjective Criticism.* Urbana: National Council of Teachers of English, 1975.
———. *Subjective Criticism.* Baltimore: Johns Hopkins University Press, 1978.
Bloom, Harold. " 'Before Moses Was, I Am': The Original and the Belated Testaments." In Harold Bloom, *Poetics of Influence,* edited by John Hollander, 387–404. New Haven: Schwab, 1988.
———. *Kabbalah and Criticism.* New York: Continuum, 1983.
———. *Ruin the Sacred Truths: Poetry and Belief from the Bible to the Present.* Cambridge: Harvard University Press, 1989.
Boers, Hendrikus. *Neither on This Mountain Nor in Jerusalem: A Study of John 4.* Atlanta: Scholars Press, 1988.
Boomershine, Thomas E. "Biblical Megatrends: Towards a Paradigm for the Interpretation of the Bible in Electronic Media." In Richards, *1987 Seminar Papers,* 144–55.
———. "Peter's Denial as Polemic or Confession: The Implications of Media Criticism for Biblical Hermeneutics." In Silberman, "Orality," 47–68.
———. "Mark 16:8 and the Apostolic Commission." *Journal of Biblical Literature* 100 (1981): 225–39.
———. "Mark, the Storyteller: A Rhetorical-Critical Investigation of Mark's Passion and Resurrection Narrative." Ph.D. diss., Union Theological Seminary, 1974.
———. *Story Journey: An Invitation to the Gospel as Storytelling.* Nashville: Abingdon Press, 1988.
Boomershine, Thomas E., and Gilbert L. Bartholomew. "The Narrative Technique of Mark 16:8." *Journal of Biblical Literature* 100 (1981): 213–23.

Booth, Wayne C. *The Rhetoric of Fiction*. 2d ed. Chicago: University of Chicago Press, 1983.

Bové, Paul A. "Variations on Authority: Some Deconstructive Transformations of the New Criticism." In Arac, *Yale Critics*, 3–19.

Brawley, Robert L. "Paul in Acts: Aspects of Structure and Characterization." In Lull, *1988 Seminar Papers*, 90–105.

Breech, James. *Jesus and Postmodernism*. Philadelphia: Fortress Press, 1989.

Breytenbach, Cilliers. "Das Problem des Übergangs von mündlicher zu schriftlicher Überlieferung." *Neotestamentica* 20 (1986): 47–58.

Brinker, Menachem. "Two Phenomenologies of Reading: Ingarden and Iser on Textual Indeterminacy." *Poetics Today* 1 (1980): 203–12.

Brooke Rose, Christine. "Round and Round the Jakobson Diagram: A Survey." *Hebrew University Studies in Literature* 8 (1980): 153–82.

Brooks, Peter. *Reading for the Plot: Design and Intention in Narrative*. New York: Vintage Books, 1985.

Brooks, Cleanth. "The Formalist Critics." *Kenyon Review* 13 (1951): 72–81.

————. "The Heresy of Paraphrase." In *The Well Wrought Urn*, 176–96. New York: Reynal & Hitchcock, 1947.

Brown, David. *Continental Philosophy and Modern Theology*. Oxford and New York: Basil Blackwell, 1987.

Brown, Frank Burch, and Elizabeth Struthers Malbon. "Parabling as a *Via Negativa*: A Critical Review of the Work of John Dominic Crossan." *Journal of Religion* 64 (1984): 530–38.

Brown, Raymond E. *The Birth of the Messiah: A Commentary on the Infancy Narratives in Matthew and Luke*. Garden City: Doubleday, 1977.

————. *The Gospel According to John*. 2 vols. Garden City: Doubleday, 1966, 1970.

————. "Gospel Infancy Narrative Research from 1976 to 1986: Part II (Luke)." *Catholic Biblical Quarterly* 48 (1986): 660–80.

Brown, Schuyler. "John 3 and the Resistant Reader: The Fourth Gospel after Nicea and the Holocaust." Paper presented at a joint session of the Johannine Seminar and the Role of the Reader in the Interpretation of the New Testament Seminar. Annual meeting of the *Studiorum Novi Testamenti Societas*, Cambridge, England, August 1988.

————. "Reader Response: Demythologizing the Text." *New Testament Studies* 34 (1988): 232–37.

————. "The Role of the Prologues in Determining the Purpose of Luke-Acts." In *Perspectives on Luke-Acts*, edited by Charles H. Talbert, 99–111. Danville: Association of Baptist Professors of Religion, 1978.

————. "The True Light (Jn 1:9–12)." *Toronto Journal of Theology* 1 (1985): 222–26.

Bultmann, Rudolf. *Faith and Understanding*. Translated by Louise Pettibone Smith. London: SCM Press, 1966.

————. "Is Exegesis without Presuppositions Possible?" In *Existence and Faith: The Shorter Writings of Rudolf Bultmann,* edited and translated by Schubert M. Ogden, 289–96. New York: Living Age Books, 1960.

————. *Jesus Christ and Mythology.* New York: Charles Scribner's Sons, 1958.

————. *Kerygma and Myth.* Edited by Hans Werner Bartsch. Translated by R. H. Fuller. New York: Harper & Row, 1961.

————. "New Testament and Mythology." In Bartsch, *Kerygma,* 1–44.

Burnett, Fred W. "Characterization in Matthew: Reader Construction of the Disciple Peter." *McKendree Pastoral Review* 4 (1987): 13–43.

————. "Postmodern Biblical Exegesis: The Eve of Historical Criticism." In Phillips, "Text, Context."

————. "Prolegomenon to Reading Matthew's Eschatological Discourse: Redundancy and the Education of the Reader in Matthew." In Detweiler, "Reader Response," 91–110.

Cahill, Joseph P. "Narrative Art in John IV." *Religious Studies Bulletin* 2 (1982): 41–48.

Cain, William E. *The Crisis in Criticism: Theory, Literature, and Reform in English Studies.* Baltimore: Johns Hopkins University Press, 1984.

Caird, G. B. *The Language and Imagery of the Bible.* Philadelphia: Westminster Press, 1980.

Camery-Hoggatt, Jerry Alan. "Word Plays: Evidence of Dramatic Irony in the Gospel of Mark." Ph.D. diss., Boston University, 1985.

Canary, Robert, and Henry Kozicki, eds. *The Writing of History: Literary Form and Historical Understanding.* Madison: University of Wisconsin Press, 1978.

Caputo, John D. *Radical Hermeneutics: Repetition, Deconstruction, and the Hermeneutic Project.* Bloomington: Indiana University Press, 1987.

Cassel, Jay Frank. "The Reader in Mark: The Crucifixion." Ph.D. diss., University of Iowa, 1984.

Castelli, Elizabeth, James Butts, Robert Miller, and David Seeley. *Power, Language, and the Sacred: Poststructuralism and the New Testament.* Forthcoming.

Chatman, Seymour. *Story and Discourse: Narrative Structure in Fiction and Film.* Ithaca: Cornell University Press, 1978.

Clévenot, Michel. *Materialist Approaches to the Bible.* Translated by William J. Nottingham. Maryknoll, N.Y.: Orbis Books, 1985.

Cobb, John B., Jr. "A Theology of Story: Crossan and Beardslee." In Spencer, *Orientation,* 153–60.

Cohen, Ralph, ed. "Philosophy of Science and Literary Theory." *New Literary History* 17, no. 1 (1985).

Cohn, Dorrit. *Transparent Minds: Narrative Modes for Presenting Consciousness in Fiction.* Princeton: Princeton University Press, 1978.

Coleridge, Samuel Taylor. "Letter to Joseph Cottle." In *Unpublished Letters of Samuel Taylor Coleridge,* edited by Earl Leslie Griggs, 128. New Haven: Yale University Press, 1933.

Collins, Adela Yarbro, ed. *Feminist Perspectives on Biblical Scholarship.* Chico, Calif.: Scholars Press, 1985.

Collins, John J. "The Rediscovery of Biblical Narrative." *Chicago Studies* 21 (1981): 45–58.

Combrink, H. J. B. "The Structure of the Gospel of Matthew as Narrative." *Tyndale Bulletin* 34 (1983): 61–90.

Conzelmann, Hans. *Die Mitte der Zeit: Studien zur Theologie des Lukas.* Tübingen: Mohr-Siebeck, 1954. Translated by Geoffrey Buswell as *The Theology of St. Luke.* New York: Harper & Row, 1961.

Cox, Harvey. *Religion in the Secular City: Toward a Postmodern Theology.* New York: Simon and Schuster, 1984.

Croatto, J. Severino. *Biblical Hermeneutics: Toward a Theory of Reading as the Production of Meaning.* Translated by Robert R. Barr. Maryknoll, N.Y.: Orbis Books, 1987.

Cronjé, J. van W. "Defamiliarization in the Letter to the Galatians." In Petzer and Hartin, *Perspective,* 214–27.

Crossan, John Dominic. *Cliffs of Fall: Paradox and Polyvalence in the Parables of Jesus.* New York: Seabury Press, 1980.

———. *The Cross That Spoke: The Origins of the Passion Narrative.* San Francisco: Harper & Row, 1988.

———. *The Dark Interval: Towards a Theology of Story.* 2d ed. Sonoma: Polebridge Press, 1988.

———. "Difference and Divinity." In Detweiler, "Derrida," 29–40.

———. *Finding Is the First Act: Trove Folktales and Jesus' Treasure Parable.* Missoula, Mont.: Scholars Press, 1979.

———. "A Form for Absence: The Markan Creation of Gospel." *Semeia* 12 (1978): 41–56.

———. *Four Other Gospels: Shadows on the Contours of Canon.* New York: Winston, 1985.

———. *In Fragments: The Aphorisms of Jesus.* San Francisco: Harper & Row, 1983.

———. *In Parables: The Challenge of the Historical Jesus.* New York: Harper & Row, 1973.

———. "Literary Criticism and Biblical Hermeneutics." *Journal of Religion* 57 (1977): 76–80.

———. "Living Earth and Living Christ: Thoughts on Carol P. Christ's 'Finitude, Death, and Reverence for Life.'" In Winquist, "Text," 109–18.

———. *Raid on the Articulate: Comic Eschatology in Jesus and Borges.* New York: Harper & Row, 1976.

————. "Ruth Amid the Alien Corn." In *The Biblical Mosaic: Changing Perspectives,* edited by Robert M. Polzin and Eugene Rothman, 199–210. Chico, Calif.: Scholars Press, 1982.

————. "Stages in Imagination." In *The Archaeology of the Imagination,* edited by Charles E. Winquist, 49–62. Chico, Calif.: Scholars Press, 1981.

————. "Waking the Bible: Biblical Hermeneutic and Literary Imagination." *Interpretation* 23 (1978): 269–85.

Crossan, John Dominic, ed. "Polyvalent Narration." *Semeia* 9 (1977).

Crossan, John Dominic, comp. "Basic Bibliography for Parables Research." *Semeia* 1 (1974): 236–74.

Culler, Jonathan. *On Deconstruction: Theory and Criticism after Structuralism.* Ithaca: Cornell University Press, 1982.

————. "Prolegomena to a Theory of Reading." In Suleiman and Crosman, *Reader,* 46–66.

————. *The Pursuit of Signs: Semiotics, Literature, Deconstruction.* Ithaca: Cornell University Press, 1981.

————. *Structuralist Poetics: Structuralism, Linguistics, and the Study of Literature.* Ithaca: Cornell University Press, 1975.

Culpepper, R. Alan. *Anatomy of the Fourth Gospel: A Study in Literary Design.* Philadelphia: Fortress Press, 1983.

————. "Commentary on Biblical Narratives: Changing Paradigms." *Forum* (forthcoming).

————. "Mark 10:50: Why Mention the Garment?" *Journal of Biblical Literature* 101 (1982): 131–32.

————. "The Narrator in the Fourth Gospel: Intratextual Relationships." In Richards, *1982 Seminar Papers,* 81–96.

————. "Story and History in the Gospels." *Review and Expositor* 81 (1984): 71–85.

Darr, John A. *Characters and Characterization in Luke-Acts: A Reader-Response Approach.* Nashville: Abingdon Press, forthcoming.

————. "Glorified in the Presence of Kings: A Literary-Critical Study of Herod the Tetrarch in Luke-Acts." Ph.D. diss., Vanderbilt University, 1986.

Dawsey, James M. "The Literary Function of Point of View in Controlling Confusion and Irony in the Gospel of Luke." Ph.D. diss., Emory University, 1983.

————. *The Lukan Voice: Confusion and Irony in the Gospel of Luke.* Macon: Mercer University Press, 1986.

————. "What's in a Name? Characterization in Luke." *Biblical Theology Bulletin* 16 (1986): 143–47.

Dean, William. "The Challenge of the New Historicism." *Journal of Religion* 66 (1986): 261–81.

De Beaugrande, Robert. "Surprised by Syncretism: Cognition and Literary Criticism Exemplified by E. D. Hirsch, Stanley Fish, and J. Hillis Miller." *Poetics* 12 (1983), 83–138.

De Man, Paul. *Allegories of Reading: Figural Language in Rousseau, Nietzsche, Rilke, and Proust.* New Haven: Yale University Press, 1979.

———. *Blindness and Insight: Essays in the Rhetoric of Contemporary Criticism.* 2d ed. Minneapolis: University of Minnesota Press, 1983.

———. "Foreword." In *The Dissimulating Harmony: The Image of Interpretation in Nietzsche, Rilke, Artaud, and Benjamin,* by Carol Jacobs, vii–xiii. Baltimore: Johns Hopkins University Press, 1978.

———. "Introduction." *Studies in Romanticism* 18 (1979): 495–99.

———. *The Resistance to Theory.* Minneapolis: University of Minnesota Press, 1986.

Derrida, Jacques. *Edmund Husserl's "Origin of Geometry": An Introduction.* Translated by John P. Leavey, Jr. Stony Brook: Nicholas Hays, 1978.

———. *Dissemination.* Translated by Barbara Johnson. Chicago: University of Chicago Press, 1981.

———. *Glas.* Translated by John P. Leavey, Jr., and Richard Rand. Lincoln: University of Nebraska Press, 1986.

———. "Ja, ou le faux bond." *Digraphe* 11 (1977): 84–121.,

———. "Letter to a Japanese Friend." Translated by David Wood and Andrew Benjamin. In *Derrida and Différance,* edited by David Wood and Robert Bernasconi, 1–5. Evanston: Northwestern University Press, 1988.

———. "Letter to John P. Leavey, Jr." In Detweiler, "Derrida," 61–62.

———. "Limited Inc abc." *Glyph* 2 (1977): 162–254.

———. "Living On: Border Lines." Translated by James Holbert. In Harold Bloom et al., *Deconstruction and Criticism,* 75–176. New York: Seabury Press, 1979.

———. *Margins of Philosophy.* Translated by Alan Bass. Chicago: University of Chicago Press, 1982.

———. "No Apocalypse, Not Now (full speed ahead, seven missiles, seven missives)." Translated by Catherine Porter and Philip Lewis. *Diacritics* 14 (1984): 20–31.

———. "Of an Apocalyptic Tone Recently Adopted in Philosophy." Translated by John P. Leavey, Jr. In Detweiler, "Derrida," 63–97.

———. *Of Grammatology.* Translated by Gayatri Chakravorty Spivak. Baltimore: Johns Hopkins University Press, 1976.

———. "The Original Discussion of 'Différance.'" Translated by David Wood, Sarah Richmond, and Malcolm Bernard. In Wood and Bernasconi, *Derrida,* 83–95.

———. *Positions.* Translated by Alan Bass. Chicago: University of Chicago Press, 1981.

————. *The Post Card: From Socrates to Freud and Beyond.* Translated by Alan Bass. Chicago: University of Chicago Press, 1987.

————. "The Principle of Reason: The University in the Eyes of Its Pupils." Translated by Catherine Porter and Philip Lewis. *Diacritics* 13 (1983): 3–20.

————. "Racism's Last Word." Translated by Peggy Kamuf. In *"Race," Writing and Difference,* edited by Henry Louis Gates, Jr., 329–38. Chicago: University of Chicago Press, 1986.

————. *Speech and Phenomena and Other Essays on Husserl's Theory of Signs.* Translated by David B. Allison. Evanston: Northwestern University Press, 1973.

————. "Des Tours de Babel." In *Difference in Translation,* edited by Joseph F. Graham, 165–248. Ithaca: Cornell University Press, 1986.

————. *Writing and Difference.* Translated by Alan Bass. Chicago: University of Chicago Press, 1978.

De Saussure, Ferdinand. *Course in General Linguistics.* Translated by Roy Harris. London: Duckworth, 1983.

Descombes, Vincent. *Modern French Philosophy.* Translated by L. Scott-Fox and J. M. Harding. Cambridge: Cambridge University Press, 1980.

Detweiler, Robert. *Story, Sign, and Self: Phenomenology and Structuralism as Literary-Critical Methods.* Missoula, Mont: Scholars Press, 1978.

————. "What Is a Sacred Text?" In Detweiler, "Reader Response," 213–30.

Detweiler, Robert, ed. "Derrida and Biblical Studies." *Semeia* 23 (1982).

————. "Reader Response Approaches to Biblical and Secular Texts." *Semeia* 31 (1985).

De Villiers, Pieter G. R. "Configuration and Plot in Mt 19–22: Aspects of the Narrative Character of the Gospel of Matthew." In de Villiers, "Structure," 56–73.

De Villiers, Pieter G. R., ed. "Reading a Text: Source, Reception, Setting." *Neotestamentica* 18 (1984).

————. "Structure and Meaning in Matthew 14–28." *Neotestamentica* 16 (1982).

Dewey, Joanna. *Markan Public Debate: Literary Technique, Concentric Structure, and Theology in Mark 2:1–3:6.* Chico, Calif.: Scholars Press, 1980.

————. "Mark as Interwoven Tapestry: Forecasts and Echoes for a Listening Audience." *Catholic Biblical Quarterly* (forthcoming).

————. "Oral Methods of Structuring Narrative in Mark." *Interpretation* 43 (1989): 32–44.

————. "Point of View and the Disciples in Mark." In Richards, *1982 Seminar Papers,* 97–106.

Dillon, Richard J. "Previewing Luke's Project from His Prologue (Luke 1:1–4)." *Catholic Biblical Quarterly* 43 (1981): 205–27.

Dodd, C. H. *The Interpretation of the Fourth Gospel*. Cambridge: Cambridge University Press, 1953.

Doložel, Lubomír. "Eco and His Model Reader." *Poetics Today* 1 (1980): 181–88.

Donahue, John R. *The Gospel in Parable: Metaphor, Narrative, and Theology in the Synoptic Gospels*. Philadelphia: Fortress Press, 1988.

————. *The Theology and Setting of Discipleship in the Gospel of Mark*. Milwaukee: Marquette University Press, 1983.

Duke, Paul D. *Irony in the Fourth Gospel*. Atlanta: John Knox Press, 1985.

Du Rand, J. A. "The Characterization of Jesus as Depicted in the Narrative of the Fourth Gospel." *Neotestamentica* 19 (1985): 18–36.

————. "Die Leser in die Evangelie volgens Johannes." *Fax Theologica* 4 (1984): 45–63.

————. "Plot and Point of View in the Gospel of John." In Petzer and Hardin, *Perspective*, 149–69.

————. "A Syntactical and Narratological Reading of John 9–10." In *Studies in John 10*, edited by J. Beutler and R. T. Fortna. Cambridge: Cambridge University Press, forthcoming.

Eagleton, Terry. *Literary Theory: An Introduction*. Minneapolis: University of Minnesota Press, 1983.

Edwards, O. C., Jr. *Luke's Story of Jesus*. Philadelphia: Fortress Press, 1981.

Edwards, Richard A. *Matthew's Story of Jesus*. Philadelphia: Fortress Press, 1985.

————. "Uncertain Faith: Matthew's Portrait of the Disciples." In *Discipleship in the New Testament*, edited by Fernando F. Segovia, 47–61. Philadelphia: Fortress Press, 1985.

Ehrmann, Jacques. "Homo Ludens Revisited." *Yale French Studies* 41 (1968): 31–57.

Ellis, John. *The Theory of Literary Criticism: A Logical Analysis*. Berkeley and Los Angeles: University of California Press, 1974.

Ellis, E. Earle. "Present and Future Eschatology in Luke." *New Testament Studies* 12 (1965–66): 27–41.

Eslinger, Lyle. "The Wooing of the Woman at the Well: Jesus, the Reader and Reader-Response Criticism." *Literature and Theology* 1 (1987): 167–83.

Fackre, Gabriel. "Narrative Theology: An Overview." *Interpretation* 37 (1983): 340–52.

Faur, José. *Golden Doves with Silver Dots: Semiotics and Textuality in Rabbinic Tradition*. Bloomington: Indiana University Press, 1986.

Felman, Shoshana. "Turning the Screw of Interpretation." In *Literature and Psychoanalysis. The Question of Reading: Otherwise,* edited by Shoshana Felman, 94–207. Baltimore: Johns Hopkins University Press, 1982.

Felperin, Howard. *Beyond Deconstruction: The Uses and Abuses of Literary Theory*. New York: Oxford University Press, 1985.

Fish, Stanley E. *Change, Rhetoric, and the Practice of Theory.* Durham, N.C.: Duke University Press, forthcoming.

———. "Consequences." *Critical Inquiry* 11 (1985): 433–58.

———. *Is There a Text in This Class? The Authority of Interpretive Communities.* Cambridge: Harvard University Press, 1980.

———. *Surprised by Sin: The Reader in Paradise Lost.* New York: St. Martin's Press, 1967.

———. "Theory and Consequences: An Interview with Stanley Fish, Part I." Conducted by James Buzard and Joseph Childers. *Critical Text* 2 (1984): 1–6.

———. "Why No One's Afraid of Wolfgang Iser." *Diacritics* 11 (1981): 2–13.

Fisher, David H. "The Phenomenology of Displacement: Tradition, Anti-Tradition, and Liberal Theology." *Religious Studies Review* 13 (1987): 314–17.

Fisher, David H., and David Jobling, eds. "The Ethics of Reading." *Semeia* (forthcoming).

Fitzmyer, Joseph A. *The Gospel according to Luke (I–IX).* Garden City: Doubleday, 1981.

Foley, John Miles. *Oral-Formulaic Theory and Research: An Introduction and Annotated Bibliography.* New York: Garland, 1985.

Forster, E. M. *Aspects of the Novel.* London: Edward Arnold, 1927.

Fortna, Robert T. *The Fourth Gospel and Its Predecessor: From Narrative Source to Present Gospel.* Philadelphia: Fortress Press, 1988.

Foster, Donald. "John Come Lately: The Belated Evangelist." In McConnell, *Bible,* 113–31.

Foster, Hal. "Postmodernism: A Preface." In Foster, *Anti-Aesthetic,* ix–xvi.

Foster, Hal, ed. *The Anti-Aesthetic: Essays on Postmodern Culture.* Seattle: Bay Press, 1983.

Foucault, Michel. *The Archaeology of Knowledge.* Translated by A. M. Sheridan Smith. New York: Pantheon, 1972.

———. "Nietzsche, Genealogy, History." In *Language, Counter-Memory, Practice: Selected Essays and Interviews.* Edited by Donald F. Bouchard. Translated by Donald F. Bouchard and Sherry Simon. Ithaca: Cornell University Press, 1977.

———. "What Is an Author?" Translated by Josué V. Harari. In *Textual Strategies: Perspectives in Post-Structuralist Criticism,* edited by Josué V. Harari, 141–60. Ithaca: Cornell University Press, 1979.

Fowl, Stephen. "The Ethics of Interpretation or What's Left Over after the Elimination of Meaning." In Lull, *1988 Seminar Papers,* 69–81.

Fowler, Robert M. "Irony and the Messianic Secret in the Gospel of Mark." *Proceedings: Eastern Great Lakes Biblical Society* 1 (1981): 26–36.

―――. *"Let the Reader Understand."* Philadelphia: Augsburg Fortress, forthcoming.

―――. *Loaves and Fishes: The Function of the Feeding Stories in the Gospel of Mark.* Chico, Calif.: Scholars Press, 1981.

―――. "Postmodern Biblical Criticism." In *Proceedings: Eastern Great Lakes and Midwest Biblical Societies* 8 (forthcoming).

―――. "Reading Matthew Reading Mark: Observing the First Steps toward Meaning-as-Reference in the Synoptic Gospels." In Richards, *1986 Seminar Papers,* 1–16.

―――. "The Rhetoric of Direction and Indirection in the Gospel of Mark." In McKnight, "Reader."

―――. "Thoughts on the History of Reading Mark's Gospel." In *Proceedings: Eastern Great Lakes Biblical Society and Midwest Society of Biblical Literature* 4 (1984): 120–30.

―――. "Using Literary Criticism on the Gospels." *The Christian Century* (26 May 1982): 626–29.

―――. "Who Is 'the Reader' in Reader Response Criticism?" In Detweiler, "Reader Response," 5–23.

―――. "Who Is 'the Reader' of Mark's Gospel?" In Richards, *1983 Seminar Papers,* 31–53.

Frei, Hans W. *The Eclipse of Biblical Narrative: A Study in Eighteenth and Nineteenth Century Hermeneutics.* New Haven: Yale University Press, 1974.

―――. *The Identity of Jesus Christ: The Hermeneutical Bases of Dogmatic Theology.* Philadelphia: Fortress Press, 1975.

―――. "The 'Literal Reading' of Biblical Narrative in the Christian Tradition: Does It Stretch or Will It Break?" In McConnell, *Bible,* 36–77.

Freund, Elizabeth. *The Return of the Reader: Reader-Response Criticism.* New York: Methuen, 1987.

Freyne, Sean. *Galilee, Jesus and the Gospels: Literary Approaches and Historical Investigations.* Philadelphia: Fortress Press, 1988.

Friedemann, Kate. *Die Rolle des Erzählers in der Epik.* Leipzig: Haessel, 1910.

Frye, Northrop. *Anatomy of Criticism.* Princeton: Princeton University Press, 1957.

―――. *The Great Code: The Bible and Literature.* New York: Harcourt Brace Jovanovich, 1982.

Frye, Roland Mushat. "The Jesus of the Gospels: Approaches through Narrative Structure." In *From Faith to Faith: Essays in Honor of Donald G. Miller,* edited by Dikran Y. Hadidian, 75–89. Pittsburgh: Pickwick Press, 1979.

―――. "Literary Criticism and Gospel Criticism." *Theology Today* 36 (1979): 207–19.

————. "A Literary Perspective for the Criticism of the Gospels." In *Jesus and Man's Hope: Essays from the Pittsburgh Festival on the Gospels,* edited by Donald G. Miller and Dikran Y. Hadidian, 2:193–221. Pittsburgh: Pittsburgh Theological Seminary, 1971.

————. "Metaphors, Equations and the Faith." *Theology Today* 37 (1980): 59–67.

————. "On the Historical Critical Method in New Testament Studies: A Reply to Professor Achtemeier." *Perspective* 14 (1973): 28–33.

————. "The Synoptic Problem and Analogies in Other Literatures." In Walker, *Relationships,* 261–302.

Funk, Robert W. *Jesus as Precursor.* Missoula, Mont.: Scholars Press, 1975.

————. *Language, Hermeneutic, and the Word of God.* New York: Harper & Row, 1966.

————. *Parables and Presence: Forms of the New Testament Tradition.* Philadelphia: Fortress Press, 1982.

————. *The Poetics of Biblical Narrative.* Sonoma: Polebridge Press, 1989.

Gasché, Rodolphe. "Deconstruction as Criticism." *Glyph* 6 (1979): 177–216.

————. *The Tain of the Mirror: Derrida and the Philosophy of Reflection.* Cambridge: Harvard University Press, 1986.

Gaventa, Beverly Roberts. "Toward a Theology of Acts: Reading and Rereading." *Interpretation* 42 (1988): 146–57.

Genette, Gérard. *Figures III.* Paris: Seuil, 1972.

————. *Narrative Discourse: An Essay in Method.* Translated by Jane E. Lewin. Ithaca: Cornell University Press, 1980.

Gerhart, Mary, and James G. Williams, eds. "Genre, Narrativity, and Theology." *Semeia* 43 (1988).

Gillespie, Gerald. "Bible Lessons: The Gospel according to Frye, Girard, Kermode, and Vogeling." *Comparative Literature* 38 (1986): 289–97.

Girard, René. "Scandal and the Dance: Salome in the Gospel of Mark." *New Literary History* 15 (1984): 311–24.

————. *The Scapegoat.* Translated by Yvonne Freccero. Baltimore: Johns Hopkins University Press, 1986.

————. *Things Hidden since the Foundation of the World.* Trans. Stephen Bann and Michael Metteer. Stanford: Stanford University Press, 1987.

Goodheart, Eugene. *The Skeptic Disposition in Contemporary Criticism.* Princeton: Princeton University Press, 1985.

Gottcent, John H. *The Bible: A Literary Study.* Boston: Twayne, G. K. Hall, 1986.

————. *The Bible as Literature: A Selected Bibliography.* Boston: G. K. Hall, 1979.

Goulder, Michael. "The Pauline Epistles." In Alter and Kermode, *Guide,* 479–502.

Graham, William A. *Beyond the Written Word: Oral Aspects of Scripture in the History of Religion.* New York: Cambridge University Press, 1987.

Greenwood, D. S. "Poststructuralism and Biblical Studies: Frank Kermode's *The Genesis of Secrecy*." In *Gospel Perspectives: Studies in Midrash and Historiography,* edited by R. T. France and David Wenham, 3:263–88. Sheffield: JSOT Press, 1983.

Gros Louis, Kenneth R. R. "Some Methodological Considerations." In Gros Louis, *Interpretations,* 2:13–34.

Gros Louis, Kenneth R. R., ed. *Literary Interpretations of Biblical Narratives.* 2 vols. Nashville: Abington Press, 1974, 1982.

Güttgemanns, Erhardt. *Candid Questions Concerning Gospel Form Criticism: A Methodological Sketch of the Fundamental Problematics of Form and Redaction Criticism.* Translated by William G. Doty. Pittsburgh: Pickwick Press, 1979.

———. *Fragmenta Semiotico-Hermeneutica: Eine Texthermeneutik für den Umgang mit der Hl. Schrift.* Bonn: Linguistica Biblica, 1983.

———. "Generative Poetics." Edited by Norman R. Petersen and translated by William G. Doty. *Semeia* 6 (1976).

———. "Die Semiotik des Traums in apokalyptischen Texten am Beispiel von Apokalypse Johannis 1." *Linguistica Biblica* 59 (1987): 7–54.

———. "Zur Normativität des Historischen." *Linguistica Biblica* 57 (1985): 7–60.

Habermas, Jürgen. "Modernity—An Incomplete Project." In Foster, *Anti-Aesthetic,* 3–15.

Hadas, Moses. *Ancilla to Classical Reading.* New York: Columbia University Press, 1954.

Haenchen, Ernst. *John 2: A Commentary on the Gospel of John Chapters 7–21.* Edited and translated by Robert W. Funk with Ulrich Busse. Philadelphia: Fortress Press, 1984.

———. *Der Weg Jesu: Eine Erklärung des Markus-Evangeliums und der kanonischen Parellelen.* 2d ed. Berlin: Walter de Gruyter, 1968.

Handelman, Susan. "Jacques Derrida and the Heretic Hermeneutic." In Krupnik, *Displacement,* 98–129.

———. *The Slayers of Moses: The Emergence of Rabbinic Interpretation in Modern Literary Theory.* Albany: State University of New York Press, 1982.

Harland, Richard. *Superstructuralism: The Philosophy of Structuralism and Post-Structuralism.* New York: Methuen, 1987.

Harnisch, Wolfgang. *Die Gleichniserzählungen Jesu: Eine hermeneutische Einführung.* Göttingen: Vandenhoeck & Ruprecht, 1985.

Harnisch, Wolfgang, ed. *Die neutestamentliche Gleichnisforschung im Horizont von Hermeneutik und Literaturwissenschaft.* Darmstadt: Wissenschaftliche Buchgesellschaft, 1982.

Hartman, Geoffrey. *Criticism in the Wilderness: The Study of Literature Today.* New Haven: Yale University Press, 1980.

———. *Saving the Text: Literature/Derrida/Philosophy*. Baltimore: Johns Hopkins University Press, 1981.

———. "The Struggle for the Text." In Hartman and Budick, *Midrash*, 3–18.

Hartman, Geoffrey, and Sanford Budick, eds. *Midrash and Literature*. New Haven: Yale University Press, 1986.

Hartman, Lars. "An Attempt at a Text-Centered Exegesis of John 21." *Studia Theologica* 38 (1984): 29–45.

Harvey, Irene. *Derrida and the Economy of Différance*. Bloomington: Indiana University Press, 1986.

———. "The Wellsprings of Deconstruction." In Natoli, *Tracing*, 127–47.

Hassan, Ihab. *The Postmodern Turn: Essays in Postmodern Theory and Culture*. Columbus: Ohio State University Press, 1987.

Hays, Richard B. *Echoes of Scripture in the Letters of Paul*. New Haven: Yale University Press, 1989.

———. *The Faith of Jesus Christ: An Investigation of the Narrative Substructure of Galatians 3:1–4:11*. Chico, Calif.: Scholars Press, 1983.

Hedrick, Charles W. "Narrator and Story in the Gospel of Mark: *Hermeneia* and *Paradosis*." *Perspectives in Religious Studies* 14 (1987): 239–58.

———. "Parables and the Kingdom: The Vision of Jesus in Fiction and Faith." In Richards, *1987 Seminar Papers*, 368–93.

———. "What Is a Gospel? Geography, Time and Narrative Structure." *Perspective in Religious Studies* 10 (1983): 255–68.

Heil, John Paul. *Paul's Letter to the Romans: A Reader-Response Commentary*. Mahwah, N.J.: Paulist Press, 1987.

Heiny, Stephen B. "2 Corinthians 2:14–4:6: The Motive for Metaphor." In Richards, *1987 Seminar Papers*, 1–22.

Hellholm, David. "The Problem of Apocalyptic Genre and the Apocalypse of John." *Semeia* 36 (1986): 13–64.

Hobbs, Edward C., ed. *Bultmann, Retrospect and Prospect: The Centenary Symposium at Wellesley*. Philadelphia: Fortress Press, 1985.

Hoffman, John C. *Law, Freedom and Story: The Role of Narrative in Therapy, Society, and Faith*. Waterloo: Wilfred Laurier University Press, 1986.

Holland, Norman N. *The Dynamics of Literary Response*. New York: Oxford University Press, 1968.

———. *Five Readers Reading*. New Haven: Yale University Press, 1975.

———. *The I*. New Haven: Yale University Press, 1985.

———. *Poems in Persons: An Introduction to the Psychoanalysis of Literature*. New York: Norton, 1973.

———. "Unity Identity Text Self." *Proceedings of the Modern Language Association* 90 (1975): 813–22.

Holub, Robert C. *Reception Theory: A Critical Introduction*. New York: Methuen, 1984.

Horton, Fred L., Jr. "Authorial Presence in the Gospel of Matthew and the Question of Genre." In *Essays in Ancient Historiography,* edited by John van Seters, Fred L. Horton, Jr., and James Moyer. Winston-Salem: Wake Forest University Press, forthcoming.

————. "Parenthetical Pregnancy: The Conception and Birth of Jesus in Matthew 1:18–25." In Richards, *1987 Seminar Papers,* 175–89.

Horton, Susan R. *Interpreting Interpreting: Interpreting Dickens' Dombey.* Baltimore: Johns Hopkins University Press, 1979.

Hunter, J. H. "Deconstruction and Biblical Texts: Introduction and Critique." *Neotestamentica* 21 (1987): 125–40.

Hutcheon, Linda. *A Poetics of Postmodernism: History, Theory, Fiction.* New York: Routledge, 1988.

Huyssen, Andreas. *After the Great Divide: Modernism, Mass Culture, Postmodernism.* Bloomington: Indiana University Press, 1986.

Ingarden, Roman. *The Cognition of the Literary Work of Art.* Translated by Ruth Ann Crowley and Kenneth Olson. Evanston: Northwestern University Press, 1973.

————. *The Literary Work of Art: An Investigation on the Borderlines of Ontology, Logic, and the Theory of Literature.* Translated by George G. Grabowicz. Evanston: Northwestern University Press, 1973.

Iser, Wolfgang. *The Act of Reading: A Theory of Aesthetic Response.* Baltimore: Johns Hopkins University Press, 1978.

————. *The Implied Reader: Patterns of Communication in Prose Fiction from Bunyan to Beckett.* Baltimore: Johns Hopkins University Press, 1974.

————. "Interaction between Text and Reader." In Suleiman and Crosman, *Reader,* 106–19.

————. "Talk Like Whales." *Diacritics* 11 (1981): 82–87.

Jacobson, Richard. "Absence, Authority and the Text." *Glyph* 3 (1978): 137–47.

Jameson, Fredric. *The Political Unconscious: Narrative as a Socially Symbolic Act.* Ithaca: Cornell University Press, 1981.

Jasper, David. *The New Testament and the Literary Imagination.* London: Macmillan, 1987.

————. "The New Testament and Literary Interpretation." *Religion and Literature* 17 (1985): 1–10.

Jaspert, Bernd. *Rudolf Bultmanns Werk und Wirkung.* Darmstadt: Wissenschaftliche Buchgesellschaft, 1984.

Jauss, Hans Robert. "Levels of Identification of Hero and Audience." Translated by Benjamin Bennett and Helga Bennett. *New Literary History* 5 (1974): 283–317.

Jeanrond, Werner. *Text and Interpretation as Categories of Theological Thinking.* Translated by Thomas Wilson. New York: Crossroad-Continuum, 1988.

Jennings, Theodore W., Jr. *Beyond Theism: A Grammar of God-Language*. New York: Oxford University Press, 1985.

Johanson, Bruce C. *To All the Brethren: A Text-Linguistic and Rhetorical Approach to 1 Thessalonians*. Stockholm: Almqvist & Wiksell, 1987.

Johnson, Alfred M., Jr. *A Bibliography of Semiological and Structural Studies of Religion*. Pittsburgh: Clifford E. Barbour Library, Pittsburgh Theological Seminary, 1979.

Johnson, Barbara. "Barbara Johnson." In *Criticism in Society: Interviews with Jacques Derrida, Northrop Frye, Harold Bloom, Geoffrey Hartman, Frank Kermode, Edward Said, Barbara Johnson, Frank Lentricchia, and J. Hillis Miller,* conducted and introduced by Imre Salusinszky, 150–75. New York: Methuen, 1987.

———. *The Critical Difference: Essays in the Contemporary Rhetoric of Reading*. Baltimore: Johns Hopkins University Press, 1980.

———. "The Frame of Reference: Poe, Lacan, Derrida." In Johnson, *Difference,* 110–46.

———. Translator's Introduction. In *Dissemination,* by Jacques Derrida, vii–xxxiii. Chicago: University of Chicago Press, 1981.

Josipovici, Gabriel. *The Book of God: A Response to the Bible*. New Haven: Yale University Press, 1988.

Karris, Robert J. *Luke: Artist and Theologian. Luke's Passion Account as Literature*. Mahwah, N.J.: Paulist Press, 1985.

———. "Windows and Mirrors: Literary Criticism and Luke's *Sitz im Leben*." In *Society of Biblical Literature 1979 Seminar Papers,* edited by Paul J. Achtemeier, 1:47–58. Missoula: Scholars Press, 1979.

Käsemann, Ernst. *The Testament of Jesus: A Study of the Gospel of John in the Light of Chapter 17*. Translated by Gerhard Krodel. Philadelphia: Fortress Press, 1968.

Kea, Perry V. "Discipleship in the Great Sermon: A Literary-Critical Approach." Ph.D. diss., University of Virginia, 1983.

Keck, Leander. "Will the Historical-Critical Method Survive? Some Observations." In Spencer, *Orientation,* 115–28.

Kee, Howard Clark. *Community of the New Age: Studies in Mark's Gospel*. Philadelphia: Westminster Press, 1977.

———. "Polyvalence and Parables: Anyone Can Play. A Response to J. D. Crossan's *Cliffs of Fall*." In Achtemeier, *1980 Seminar Papers,* 57–61.

Keegan, Terence J. *Interpreting the Bible: A Popular Introduction to Biblical Hermeneutics*. Mahwah, N.J.: Paulist Press, 1985.

Kelber, Werner H. "The Authority of the Word in St. John's Gospel: Charismatic Speech, Narrative Text, Logocentric Metaphysics." *Oral Tradition* 2 (1987): 108–31.

———. "Biblical Hermeneutics and the Ancient Art of Communication: A Response." In Silberman, "Orality," 97–106.

————. *The Eclipse of Presence: Transparency and Opacity in the Fourth Gospel*. Madison: University of Wisconsin Press, forthcoming.

————. "Die Fleischwerdung des Wortes in der Körperlichkeit des Textes." In *Materialität der Kommunikation*, edited by H. U. Gumbrecht and K. L. Pseisser. Frankfurt: Suhrkamp Verlag, forthcoming.

————. "Gospel Narrative and Critical Theory." *Biblical Theology Bulletin* 18 (1988): 130–36.

————. "In the Beginning Were the Words: The Apotheosis and Narrative Displacement of the *Logos*." Forthcoming.

————. "Mark and Orality." *Semeia* 16 (1979): 7–55.

————. *Mark's Story of Jesus*. Philadelphia: Fortress Press, 1979.

————. "Narrative and Disclosure: Mechanisms of Concealing, Revealing, and Reveiling." In Gerhart and Williams, "Genre," 1–20.

————. "Narrative as Interpretation and Interpretation of Narrative: Hermeneutical Reflections on the Gospels." In Silberman, "Orality," 107–34.

————. *The Oral and the Written Gospel: The Hermeneutics of Speaking and Writing in the Synoptic Tradition, Mark, Paul, and Q*. Philadelphia: Fortress Press, 1983.

Kelber, Werner H., ed. *The Passion in Mark: Studies on Mark 14–16*. Philadelphia: Fortress Press, 1976.

Kennedy, George A. *New Testament Interpretation through Rhetorical Criticism*. Chapel Hill: University of North Carolina Press, 1984.

Kennedy, William J. "'Voice' and 'Address' in Literary Theory." *Oral Tradition* 2 (1987): 214–30.

Kermode, Frank. "Anteriority, Authority, and Secrecy: A General Comment." In Gerhart and Williams, "Genre," 155–67.

————. "The Argument about Canons." In McConnell, *Bible*, 78–96.

————. *The Art of Telling: Essays on Fiction*. Cambridge: Harvard University Press, 1983.

————. *The Genesis of Secrecy: On the Interpretation of Narrative*. Cambridge: Harvard University Press, 1979.

————. "Institutional Control of Interpretation." In *Art*, 168–84.

————. "John." In Alter and Kermode, *Guide*, 440–66.

————. "Matthew." In Alter and Kermode, *Guide*, 387–401.

————. "St. John as Poet." *Journal for the Study of the New Testament* 28 (1986): 3–16.

————. "The Plain Sense of Things." In Hartman and Budick, *Midrash*, 179–94.

Kieffer, René. "Was heisst das, einen Text zu kommentieren?" *Biblische Zeitschrift* 20 (1976): 212–16.

Kierkegaard, Søren. *"Fear and Trembling" and "Repetition."* Edited and translated by Howard V. Hong and Edna H. Hong. Princeton: Princeton University Press, 1983.

Kingsbury, Jack Dean. *The Christology of Mark's Gospel*. Philadelphia: Fortress Press, 1983.

———. "The Developing Conflict between Jesus and the Jewish Authorities in Matthew's Gospel: A Literary-Critical Study." *Catholic Biblical Quarterly* 49 (1987): 57–73.

———. "The Figure of Jesus in Matthew's Story: A Literary-Critical Probe." *Journal for the Study of the New Testament* 21 (1984): 3–36.

———. "The Figure of Jesus in Matthew's Story: A Rejoinder to David Hill." *Journal for the Study of the New Testament* 25 (1985): 61–81.

———. *Matthew*. 2d ed. Philadelphia: Fortress Press, 1986.

———. *Matthew as Story*. 2d ed. Philadelphia: Fortress Press, 1988.

———. "The Parable of the Wicked Husbandmen and the Secret of Jesus' Divine Sonship in Matthew: Some Literary-Critical Observations." *Journal of Biblical Literature* 105 (1986): 643–55.

———. "The Place, Structure, and Meaning of the Sermon on the Mount within Matthew." *Interpretation* 41 (1987): 131–43.

———. "Reflections on 'the Reader' of Matthew's Gospel." *New Testament Studies* 34 (1988): 442–60.

Klauck, Hans-Josef. "Die erzählerische Rolle der Junger im Markusevangelium: Eine narrative Analyse." *Novum Testamentum* 24 (1982): 1–26.

Klein, Günther. "Lukas 1:1–4 als theologisches Programm." In *Zeit und Geschichte: Dankesgabe an R. Bultmann zum 80. Geburtstag,* edited by Erich Dinkler, 193–216. Tübingen: Mohr, 1964.

Knapp, Steven, and Walter Benn Michaels. "Against Theory." *Critical Inquiry* 8 (1982): 723–42.

Kort, Wesley A. *Story, Text, and Scripture: Literary Interests in Biblical Narrative*. University Park: Pennsylvania State University Press, 1988.

Kotzé, P. P. A. "John and Reader's Response." *Neotestamentica* 19 (1985): 50–63.

Krauss, Rosalind. "Poststructuralism and the 'Paraliterary.'" *October* 13 (1980): 36–40.

Krentz, Edgar. "New Testament Commentaries: Their Selection and Use." *Interpretation* 36 (1982): 372–81.

Krieg, Robert A. *Story-Shaped Christology: The Role of Narratives in Identifying Jesus Christ*. Mahwah, N.J.: Paulist Press, 1988.

Krieger, Murray. *A Window to Criticism: Shakespeare's Sonnets and Modern Poetics*. Princeton: Princeton University Press, 1964.

Kristeva, Julia. *Powers of Horror: An Essay on Abjection*. Translated by Leon S. Roudiez. New York: Columbia University Press, 1982.

Krupnik, Mark, ed. *Displacement: Derrida and After*. Bloomington: Indiana University Press, 1983.

Krupnik, Mark. "Introduction/Sensible Language." In Krupnik, *Displacement,* 1–28.

Kümmel, Werner Georg. *The New Testament: The History of the Investigation of Its Problems.* Translated by S. McLean Gilmour and Howard C. Kee. Nashville: Abingdon Press, 1972.

Kurz, William S. "Narrative Approaches to Luke-Acts." *Biblica* 68 (1987): 195–220.

Kysar, Robert. *The Fourth Evangelist and His Gospel: An Examination of Contemporary Scholarship.* Minneapolis: Augsburg, 1975.

———. "The Fourth Gospel: A Report on Recent Research." In *Aufstieg und Niedergang der römischen Welt: Geschichte und Kultur Roms im Spiegel der neuren Forschung,* vol. 2, edited by H. Temporini and W. Haase, 25.3:2391–480. New York: de Gruyter, 1985.

———. *John's Story of Jesus.* Philadelphia: Fortress Press, 1984.

LaFargue, Michael. "Are Texts Determinate? Derrida, Barth and the Role of the Biblical Scholar." *Harvard Theological Review* 81 (1988): 341–57.

Lanser, Susan Sniader. *The Narrative Act: Point of View in Prose Fiction.* Princeton: Princeton University Press, 1981.

Lategan, Bernard C. "Coming to Grips with the Reader." In McKnight, "Reader."

———. "Current Issues in the Hermeneutical Debate." In de Villiers, "Reading," 1–17.

———. "Reader Clues and the Text of Galatians." *Journal of Literary Studies* 3 (1987): 47–59.

Lategan, Bernard C., and Willem S. Vorster. *Text and Reality: Aspects of Reference in Biblical Texts.* Atlanta: Scholars Press, 1985.

Leigh, David J. "Michel Foucault and the Study of Literature and Theology." *Christianity and Literature* 33 (1983): 75–85.

Leitch, Thomas M. *What Stories Are: Narrative Theory and Interpretation.* University Park: Pennsylvania State University Press, 1986.

Leitch, Vincent B. *Deconstructive Criticism: An Advanced Introduction.* New York: Columbia University Press, 1983.

Lentricchia, Frank. *After the New Criticism.* Chicago: University of Chicago Press, 1980.

Levinsohn, Stephen H. *Textual Connections in Acts.* Atlanta: Scholars Press, 1987.

Llewelyn, John. *Derrida on the Threshold of Sense.* London: Macmillan, 1986.

Lohfink, Gerhard. "Kommentar als Gattung." *Bibel und Leben* 15 (1974): 1–16.

Lord, Albert B. "The Gospels as Oral Traditional Literature." In Walker, *Relationships,* 33–91.

Louw, J. P. *A Semantic Discourse Analysis of Romans 1 and 2.* Pretoria: University of Pretoria Press, 1979.

Lull, David J., ed. *Society of Biblical Literature 1988 Seminar Papers*. Atlanta: Scholars Press, 1988.

Lyotard, Jean-François. *The Postmodern Condition: A Report on Knowledge*. Translated by Geoff Bennington and Brian Massumi. Minneapolis: University of Minnesota Press, 1984.

Machin, Richard, and Christopher Norris. "Introduction." In Machin and Norris, *Readings,* 1–19.

Machin, Richard, and Christopher Norris, eds. *Post-Structuralist Readings of English Poetry*. New York: Cambridge University Press, 1987.

Mack, Burton L., and Vernon K. Robbins. *Patterns of Persuasion in the Gospels*. Sonoma: Polebridge Press, forthcoming.

Mackey, Louis. "Slouching Toward Bethlehem: Deconstructive Strategies in Theology." *Anglican Theological Review* 65 (1983): 255–72.

Macky, P. W. "The Coming Revolution: The New Literary Approach to the New Testament." In *A Guide to Contemporary Hermeneutics: Major Trends in Biblical Interpretation,* edited by Donald K. McKim, 263–79. Grand Rapids: Eerdmans, 1986.

Macquarrie, John. *An Existentialist Theology: A Comparison of Heidegger and Bultmann*. London: SCM Press, 1955.

————. *God-Talk: An Examination of the Language and Logic of Theology*. New York: Harper & Row, 1967.

Maddox, Robert. *The Purpose of Luke-Acts*. Edinburgh: T & T Clark, 1982.

Magness, J. Lee. *Sense and Absence: Structure and Suspension in the Ending of Mark's Gospel*. Atlanta: Scholars Press, 1986.

Mailloux, Steven. *Interpretive Conventions: The Reader in the Study of American Fiction*. Ithaca: Cornell University Press, 1982.

————. "Rhetorical Hermeneutics." *Critical Inquiry* 11 (1985): 620–41.

Malbon, Elizabeth Struthers. "Disciples/Crowds/Whoever: Markan Characters and Readers." *Novum Testamentum* 28 (1986): 104–30.

————. "Fallible Followers: Women and Men in the Gospel of Mark." *Semeia* 28 (1983): 29–48.

————. "Galilee and Jerusalem: History and Literature in Marcan Interpretation." *Catholic Biblical Quarterly* 44 (1982): 242–55.

————. "The Jesus of Mark and the Sea of Galilee." *Journal of Biblical Literature* 103 (1984): 363–77.

————. "The Jewish Leaders in the Gospel of Mark: A Literary Study of Markan Characterization." *Journal of Biblical Literature* (forthcoming).

————. "Mark: Myth and Parable." *Biblical Theology Bulletin* 16 (1986): 8–17.

————. *Narrative Space and Mythic Meaning in Mark*. San Francisco: Harper & Row, 1986.

Margolis, Joseph. "The Threads of Literary Theory." *Poetics Today* 7 (1986): 95–100.

Marks, Herbert. "Pauline Typology and Revisionary Criticism." *Journal of the American Academy of Religion* 52 (1984): 71–92.

Marshall, I. Howard. *The Gospel of Luke: A Commentary on the Greek Text.* Grand Rapids: Eerdmans, 1978.

Martin, James P. "Toward a Post-Critical Paradigm." *New Testament Studies* 33 (1987): 370–85.

Martin, Wallace. *Recent Theories of Narrative.* Ithaca: Cornell University Press, 1986.

Martyn, J. Louis. *History and Theology in the Fourth Gospel.* Nashville: Abingdon Press, 1968.

Matera, Frank J. "The Plot of Matthew's Gospel." *Catholic Biblical Quarterly* 49 (1987): 233–53.

McConnell, Frank, ed. *The Bible and the Narrative Tradition.* New York: Oxford University Press, 1986.

McFague, Sallie. *Metaphorical Theology: Models of God in Religious Language.* 2d ed. Philadelphia: Fortress Press, 1985.

———. *Speaking in Parables: A Study in Metaphor and Theology.* Philadelphia: Fortress Press, 1975.

McGinn, Bernard. "Revelation." In Alter and Kermode, *Guide,* 523–44.

McKenna, Andrew J. "Biblioclasm: Joycing Jesus and Borges." *Diacritics* 8 (1978): 15–29.

McKnight, Edgar V. *The Bible and the Reader: An Introduction to Literary Criticism.* Philadelphia: Fortress Press, 1985.

———. *Meaning in Texts: The Historical Shaping of a Narrative Hermeneutics.* Philadelphia: Fortress Press, 1978.

———. *Postmodern Use of the Bible: The Emergence of Reader-Oriented Criticism.* Nashville: Abingdon Press, 1988.

McKnight, Edgar V., ed. "The Reader in the Text: Aspects of the Textually Defined Reader in New Testament Literature." *Semeia* (forthcoming).

Meeks, Wayne A. "The Man from Heaven in Johannine Sectarianism." In *The Interpretation of John,* edited by John Ashton, 141–73. Philadelphia: Fortress Press, 1987.

Messmer, Michael W. "Making Sense of/with Postmodernism." *Soundings* 68 (1985): 404–26.

Michaels, Walter Benn. "Against Formalism: The Autonomous Text in Legal and Literary Interpretation." *Poetics Today* 1 (1980): 23–34.

———. "Saving the Text: Reference and Belief." *Modern Language Notes* 93 (1978): 771–93.

Miller, J. Hillis. "Ariadne's Thread: Repetition and the Narrative Line." In *Interpretation of Narrative,* edited by Mario J. Valdés and Owen J. Miller, 148–66. Toronto: University of Toronto Press, 1978.

———. "Deconstructing the Deconstructors." *Diacritics* 5 (1975): 24–31.

———. *The Disappearance of God.* Cambridge: Harvard University Press, 1963.

———. *Fiction and Repetition: Seven English Novels.* Cambridge: Harvard University Press, 1982.

Miller, Joan M., comp. *French Structuralism: A Multidisciplinary Bibliography with a Checklist of Sources for Louis Althusser, Roland Barthes, Jacques Derrida, Michel Foucault, Lucien Goldmann, Jacques Lacan and an Update of Works on Claude Lévi-Strauss.* New York: Garland, 1981.

Minear, Paul S. "Dear Theo: The Kerygmatic Intention and Claim of the Book of Acts." *Interpretation* 27 (1973): 131–50.

———. "Luke's Use of the Birth Stories." In *Studies in Luke-Acts,* edited by Leander E. Keck and J. Louis Martyn, 111–30. Nashville: Abingdon Press, 1966.

———. *To Heal and To Reveal: The Prophetic Vocation According to Luke.* New York: Seabury Press, 1976.

Miscall, Peter D. *1 Samuel: A Literary Reading.* Bloomington: Indiana University Press, 1986.

———. *The Workings of Old Testament Narrative.* Chico, Calif.: Scholars Press, 1983.

Mitchell, W. J. T., ed. *Against Theory: Literary Studies and the New Pragmatism.* Chicago: University of Chicago Press, 1985.

Moore, Stephen D. "Are the Gospels Unified Narratives?" In Richards, *1987 Seminar Papers,* 443–58.

———. "Narrative Commentaries on the Bible: Context, Roots, and Prospects." *Forum* 3 (1987): 29–62.

———. "Narrative Homiletics: Lukan Rhetoric and the Making of the Reader." Ph.D. diss., University of Dublin (Trinity College), 1986.

Mosher, Harold F. "A New Synthesis of Narratology." *Poetics Today* 1 (1980): 171–86.

Muecke, D. C. *Irony and the Ironic.* New York: Methuen, 1982.

Muilenberg, James. "Form Criticism and Beyond." In *The Bible in Its Literary Milieu,* edited by Vincent L. Tollers and John R. Maier, 362–80. Grand Rapids: Eerdmans, 1979.

Natoli, Joseph, ed. *Tracing Literary Theory.* Urbana: University of Illinois Press, 1987.

Navone, John. *Themes of St. Luke.* Rome: Gregorian University Press, 1970.

Navone, John, and Thomas Cooper. *The Story of the Passion.* Rome: Gregorian University Press, 1986.

Nelson, Edwin S. "Paul's First Missionary Journey as Paradigm: A Literary-Critical Assessment of Acts 13–14." Ph.D. diss., Boston University, 1982.

Newton-De Molina, David, ed. *On Literary Intention.* Edinburgh: Edinburgh University Press, 1976.

Noll, Mark A. "Review: The Bible in America." *Journal of Biblical Literature* 106 (1987): 493–509.

Norris, Christopher. *The Contest of Faculties: Philosophy and Theory after Deconstruction*. New York: Methuen, 1985.

————. *Deconstruction: Theory and Practice*. New York: Methuen, 1982.

————. *Derrida*. Cambridge: Harvard University Press, 1987.

————. *Paul de Man: Deconstruction and the Critique of Aesthetic Ideology*. New York: Routledge, 1988.

Nuttall, Geoffrey F. *The Moment of Recognition: Luke as Story-Teller*. London: University of London, Athlone Press, 1978.

O'Day, Gail R. "Narrative Mode and Theological Claim: A Study in the Fourth Gospel." *Journal of Biblical Literature* 105 (1986): 657–68.

————. *Revelation in the Fourth Gospel: Narrative Mode and Theological Claim*. Philadelphia: Fortress Press, 1986.

————. *The Word Disclosed: John's Story and Narrative Preaching*. St. Louis: CBP, 1987.

O'Leary, Joseph Stephen. *Questioning Back: The Overcoming of Metaphysics in Christian Tradition*. New York: Winston Press, 1985.

O'Toole, Robert F. *The Unity of Luke's Theology: An Analysis of Luke-Acts*. Wilmington: Michael Glazier, 1984.

Olsson, Birger. "A Decade of Text-Linguistic Analyses of Biblical Texts at Uppsala." *Studia Theologica* 39 (1985): 107–26.

————. *Structure and Meaning in the Fourth Gospel: A Text-Linguistic Analysis of John 2:1–11 and 4:1–42*. Translated by Jean Gray. Lund: C. W. K. Gleerup, 1974.

Ong, Walter J. "Gospel, Existence, and Print." *Modern Language Quarterly* 35 (1974): 66–77.

————. *"Maranatha*: Death and Life in the Text of the Book." In *Interfaces of the Word: Studies in the Evolution of Consciousness and Culture*, 230–71. Ithaca: Cornell University Press, 1977.

————. *Orality and Literacy: The Technologizing of the Word*. New York: Methuen, 1982.

————. "Orality-Literacy Studies and the Unity of the Human Race." *Oral Tradition* 2 (1987): 371–82.

————. *The Presence of the Word: Some Prolegomena for Cultural and Religious History*. 2d ed. Minneapolis: University of Minnesota Press, 1986.

————. "The Psychodynamics of Oral Memory and Narrative: Some Implications for Biblical Studies." In *The Pedagogy of God's Image: Essays on Symbol and the Religious Imagination*, edited by Robert Masson, 55–73. Chico, Calif.: Scholars Press, 1982.

————. "Text as Interpretation: Mark and After." In Silberman, "Orality," 7–26.

Parsons, Mikeal C. "'Allegorizing Allegory': Narrative Analysis and Parable Interpretation." *Perspectives in Religious Studies* 15 (1988): 147–64.

————. *The Departure of Jesus in Luke-Acts: The Ascension Narratives in Context*. Sheffield: Sheffield Academic Press, 1987.

———. "The Making of 'Luke-Acts': The Unity of the Lucan Writings Reconsidered." Paper presented to the Society of Biblical Literature, Southwest Regional Meeting, Dallas, March 1988.

———. "Narrative Closure and Openness in the Plot of the Third Gospel: The Sense of an Ending in Luke 24:50–53. In Richards, *1986 Seminar Papers*, 201–23.

Patte, Daniel. *The Gospel According to Matthew: A Structural Commentary on Matthew's Faith*. Philadelphia: Fortress Press, 1987.

———. *Greimas's Structural Semiotics and Biblical Exegesis*. Philadelphia: Augsburg Fortress, 1989.

———. *Paul's Faith and the Power of the Gospel: A Structural Introduction to the Pauline Letters*. Philadelphia: Fortress Press, 1983.

———. "Speech Act Theory and Biblical Exegesis." In White, *Speech Act*, 85–102.

———. *What Is Structural Exegesis?* Philadelphia: Fortress Press, 1976.

Perrin, Norman. "The Evangelist as Author: Reflections on Method in the Study and Interpretation of the Synoptic Gospels and Acts." *Biblical Research* 17 (1972): 5–18.

———. "Historical Criticism, Literary Criticism, and Hermeneutics." *Journal of Religion* 52 (1972): 361–75.

———. *Jesus and the Language of the Kingdom: Symbol and Metaphor in New Testament Interpretation*. Philadelphia: Fortress Press, 1976.

———. "The Parables of Jesus as Parables, as Metaphors, and as Aesthetic Objects: A Review Article." *Journal of Religion* 47 (1967): 340–47.

———. *What Is Redaction Criticism*. Philadelphia: Fortress Press, 1969.

Pervo, Richard I. *Profit with Delight: The Literary Genre of the Acts of the Apostles*. Philadelphia: Fortress Press, 1987.

Petersen, Norman R. "The Composition of Mark 4:1–8:26." *Harvard Theological Review* 73 (1980): 194–217.

———. *Literary Criticism for New Testament Critics*. Philadelphia: Fortress Press, 1978.

———. "Literary Criticism in Biblical Studies." In Spencer, *Orientation*, 25–50.

———. "'Point of View' in Mark's Narrative." *Semeia* 12 (1978): 97–121.

———. "The Reader in the Gospel." In de Villiers, "Reading," 38–51.

———. *Rediscovering Paul: Philemon and the Sociology of Paul's Narrative World*. Philadelphia: Fortress Press, 1985.

———. "When Is the End Not the End?: Literary Reflections on the Ending of Mark's Narrative." *Interpretation* 34 (1980): 151–66.

Petzer, J. H., and P. J. Hartin, eds. *A South African Perspective on the New Testament: Essays by South African New Testament Scholars*. Leiden: E. J. Brill, 1986.

Phillips, Gary A. *Biblical Exegesis in a Postmodern Age*. Philadelphia: Augsburg Fortress, forthcoming.

————. "Biblical Exegesis in the Postmodern Age: Hearing Different Voices." *Journal of the American Academy of Religion* (forthcoming).

————. "Deconstruction and the Parables of Jesus: Framing the Critics and the Critical Frame." *Semeia* (forthcoming).

————. "Exegesis as Praxis: Reclaiming History and Text for a Postmodern Context." In Phillips, "Text, Context."

————. "History and Text: The Reader in Context in Matthew's Parables Discourse." In Detweiler, "Reader Response," 111–38.

————. "Intertextuality and the Reading of Biblical Texts: From Canon to Chaos." In *Intertextuality and the Human Sciences,* edited by Heinrich Plett. Munich: Kaiser, forthcoming.

————. "'This Is a Hard Saying. Who Can Be Listener to It?': Creating a Reader in John 6." *Semeia* 26 (1983): 32–56.

Phillips, Gary A., ed. "Text, Context, History: Biblical Exegesis in the Postmodern Context." *Semeia* (forthcoming).

Piwowarcyzk, Mary Ann. "The Narratee and the Situation of Enunciation: A Reconsideration of Prince's Theory." *Genre* 9 (1976): 161–77.

Plank, Karl A. *Paul and the Irony of Affliction.* Atlanta: Scholars Press, 1987.

Plunkett, Regina St. G. "The Samaritan Woman: Partner in Revelation." *The Anglican Theological Review* (forthcoming).

Poland, Lynn M. *Literary Criticism and Biblical Hermeneutics: A Critique of Formalist Approaches.* Chico, Calif.: Scholars Press, 1985.

————. "The New Criticism, Neoorthodoxy, and the New Testament." *Journal of Religion* 65 (1985): 459–77.

Praeder, Susan M. "Jesus-Paul, Peter-Paul, and Jesus-Peter Parallelisms in Luke-Acts: A History of Reader-Response." In Richards, *1984 Seminar Papers,* 23–40.

————. "Luke-Acts and the Ancient Novel." In *Society of Biblical Literature 1981 Seminar Papers,* edited by Kent Harold Richards, 269–92. Chico, Calif.: Scholars Press, 1981.

————. "Miracle Stories in Christian Antiquity: Some Narrative Elements." *Forum* 2 (1986): 43–54.

————. "The Narrative Voyage: An Analysis and Interpretation of Acts 27–28." Ph.D. diss., Graduate Theological Union, 1980.

————. *The Word in Women's Worlds: Four Parables.* Wilmington: Michael Glazier, 1988.

Pratt, Mary Louise. "Interpretive Strategies/Strategic Interpretations: On Anglo-American Reader Response Criticism." *Boundary 2* 11 (1982): 201–31.

Prince, Gerald. *A Dictionary of Narratology.* Lincoln: University of Nebraska Press, 1988.

————. "Introduction to the Study of the Narratee." In Tompkins, *Reader-Response,* 7–25.

————. "The Narratee Revisited." *Style* 19 (1985): 299–303.

————. *Narratology: The Form and Functioning of Narrative*. New York: Mouton, 1982.

Raschke, Carl A. *The Alchemy of the Word: Language and the End of Theology*. Missoula, Mont.: Scholars Press, 1979.

————. *Theological Thinking: An In-quiry*. Atlanta: Scholars Press, 1988.

Raschke, Carl A., ed. *New Dimensions in Philosophical Theology*. Chico, Calif.: Scholars Press, 1982.

Ray, William. *Literary Meaning: From Phenomenology to Deconstruction*. Oxford: Basil Blackwell, 1984.

Reese, James M. *Experiencing the Good News: The New Testament as Communication*. Wilmington: Michael Glazier, 1984.

Reiss, Timothy. *The Discourse of Modernism*. Ithaca: Cornell University Press, 1982.

Rendall, Steven. "Fish vs. Fish." *Diacritics* 12 (1982): 49–57.

Resseguie, James L. "John 9: A Literary-Critical Analysis." In Gros Louis, *Interpretations*, 2:295–303.

————. "Point of View in the Central Section of Luke (9:51–19:44)." *Journal of the Evangelical Theological Society* 25 (1982): 41–47.

————. "Reader-Response Criticism and the Synoptic Gospels." *Journal of the American Academy of Religion* 52 (1984): 307–24.

Rhoads, David. "Narrative Criticism and the Gospel of Mark." *Journal of the American Academy of Religion* 50 (1982): 411–34.

Rhoads, David, and Donald Michie. *Mark as Story: An Introduction to the Narrative of a Gospel*. Philadelphia: Fortress Press, 1982.

Richards, Kent Harold, ed. *Society of Biblical Literature 1982 Seminar Papers*. Chico, Calif.: Scholars Press, 1982.

————. *Society of Biblical Literature 1983 Seminar Papers*. Chico, Calif.: Scholars Press, 1983.

————. *Society of Biblical Literature 1984 Seminar Papers*. Chico, Calif.: Scholars Press, 1984.

————. *Society of Biblical Literature 1986 Seminar Papers*. Atlanta: Scholars Press, 1986.

————. *Society of Biblical Literature 1987 Seminar Papers*. Atlanta: Scholars Press, 1987.

Ricoeur, Paul. "Biblical Hermeneutics." *Semeia* 4 (1975): 29–148.

————. *Essays on Biblical Interpretation*. Edited by Lewis S. Mudge. Philadelphia: Fortress Press, 1980.

————. "A Reply." *Biblical Research* 24/25 (1979–80): 70–80.

————. *Time and Narrative*. 3 vols. Translated by Kathleen McLaughlin and David Pellauer. Chicago: University of Chicago Press, 1984–88.

Riddel, Joseph. "A Miller's Tale." *Diacritics* 5 (1975): 56–65.

Riekert, S. J. P. K. "The Narrative Coherence in Matthew 26–28." *Neotestamentica* 16 (1982): 118–36.

Rimmon, Shlomith. "A Comprehensive Theory of Narrative: Genette's *Figures III* and the Structuralist Study of Fiction." *PTL: A Journal for Descriptive Poetics and Theory of Literature* 1 (1976): 33–62.

Rimmon-Kenan, Shlomith. *Narrative Fiction: Contemporary Poetics*. New York: Methuen, 1983.

Robbins, Vernon K. *Jesus the Teacher: A Socio-Rhetorical Interpretation of Mark*. Philadelphia: Fortress Press, 1984.

Rogers, Robert. "Amazing Reader in the Labyrinth of Literature." *Poetics Today* 3 (1982): 31–46.

Rorty, Richard. *Consequences of Pragmatism (Essays: 1972–1980)*. Minneapolis: University of Minnesota Press, 1982.

———. "Deconstruction and Circumvention." *Critical Inquiry* 11 (1984): 1–21.

———. *Philosophy and the Mirror of Nature*. Princeton: Princeton University Press, 1979.

———. "Texts and Lumps." In Cohen, "Philosophy," 1–16.

Runzo, Joseph. *Reason, Relativism and God*. New York: St. Martin's Press, 1986.

Russell, Letty M., ed. *Feminist Interpretation of the Bible*. Philadelphia: Westminster Press, 1985.

Ryan, Michael. *Marxism and Deconstruction: A Critical Articulation*. Baltimore: Johns Hopkins University Press, 1982.

Ryken, Leland, ed. *The New Testament in Literary Criticism*. New York: Frederick Ungar, 1984.

Said, Edward W. "Opponents, Audiences, Constituencies, and Community." In *The Politics of Interpretation*, edited by W. J. T. Mitchell, 7–32. Chicago: University of Chicago Press, 1983.

Sartre, Jean-Paul. *What Is Literature?* London: Methuen, 1950.

Schenk, Wolfgang. *Evangelium—Evangelien—Evangeliologie: Ein "hermeneutisches" Manifest*. Munich: Kaiser, 1983.

———. *Die Phillipperbriefe des Paulus: Kommentar*. Stuttgart: Kohlhammer, 1984.

———. "Die Rollen der Leser oder der Mythos *des Lesers*?" *Linguistica Biblica* 60 (1988): 61–81. Translation by Edgar V. McKnight. In McKnight, "Reader."

———. *Die Sprache des Matthäus: Die Text-Konstituenten in ihren makro- und mikro-strukturellen Relationen*. Göttingen: Vandenhoeck & Ruprecht, 1987.

Schmidt, Daryl. "Tyson's Approach to the Literary Death of Luke's Jesus." *Perkins Journal* 40 (1987): 33–38.

Schmidt, Karl Ludwig. *Der Rahmen der Geschichte Jesu*. Darmstadt: Wissenschaftliche Buchgesellschaft, 1964.

Schmidt, Siegfried J. "Selected Bibliography on Interpretation (1970–1982)." *Poetics* 12 (1983): 277–92.

Schnackenburg, Rudolf. *The Gospel According to St. John*. 3 vols. Translated by Kevin Smyth et al. New York: Herder & Herder, 1968, 1979; New York: Crossroad, 1982.

Schneidau, Herbert N. "Biblical Narrative and Modern Consciousness." In McConnell, *Bible*, 132–50.

——. "Let the Reader Understand." In Silberman, "Orality," 135–45.

——. "Literary Relations among the Gospels: Harmony or Conflict?" *Studies in the Literary Imagination* 18 (1985): 17–32.

——. *Sacred Discontent: The Bible and Western Tradition*. Baton Rouge: Louisiana State University Press, 1976.

——. "The Word against the Word: Derrida on Textuality." In Detweiler, "Derrida," 5–28.

Schneider, Gerhard. *Das Evangelium nach Lukas*. 2 vols. Gütersloh: Mohn, 1977.

Scholes, Robert. "Cognition and the Implied Reader." *Diacritics* 5 (1975): 13–15.

——. Review of *Story and Discourse: Narrative Structure in Fiction and Film*, by Seymour Chatman. *Poetics Today* 1 (1980): 190–91.

——. *Textual Power: Literary Theory and the Teaching of English*. New Haven: Yale University Press, 1986.

Scholes, Robert, and Robert Kellogg. *The Nature of Narrative*. New York: Oxford University Press, 1966.

Schottroff, Willy, and Wolfgang Stegemann, eds. *God of the Lowly: Socio-Historical Interpretation of the Bible*. Translated by Matthew J. O'Connell. Maryknoll, N.Y.: Orbis Books, 1984.

Schüssler Fiorenza, Elisabeth. *The Book of Revelation: Justice and Judgement*. Philadelphia: Fortress Press, 1985.

——. *Bread Not Stone: The Challenge of Feminist Biblical Interpretation*. Boston: Beacon Press, 1984.

——. "The Ethics of Biblical Interpretation: Decentering Biblical Scholarship." *Journal of Biblical Literature* 107 (1988): 3–17.

——. "The Followers of the Lamb: Visionary Rhetoric and Social-Political Situation." *Semeia* 36 (1986): 123–46.

——. *In Memory of Her: A Feminist Theological Reconstruction of Christian Origins*. New York: Crossroad, 1983.

Scott, Bernard Brandon. *Hear Then the Parable: A Commentary on the Parables of Jesus*. Philadelphia: Augsburg Fortress, 1989.

——. "How to Mismanage a Miracle: Reader-Response Criticism." In Richards, *1983 Seminar Papers*, 439–49.

——. *Jesus, Symbol-Maker for the Kingdom*. Philadelphia: Fortress Press, 1981.

————. "A Master's Praise: Luke 16:1–8a." *Biblica* 64 (1983): 173–88.

————. "The King's Accounting: Matthew 18:23–34." *Journal of Biblical Literature* 104 (1985): 429–42.

————. *The Word of God in Words: Reading and Preaching.* Philadelphia: Fortress Press, 1985.

Seeley, David. "Poststructuralist Criticism and Biblical History." In *Art/ Literature/Religion: Life on the Borders,* edited by Robert Detweiler, 157–71. Chico, Calif.: Scholars Press, 1983.

Sheeley, Steven M. "Narrative Asides and Narrative Authority in Luke-Acts." *Biblical Theology Bulletin* 18 (1988): 102–7.

————. "Narrative Asides in Luke-Acts." Ph.D. diss., Southern Baptist Theological Seminary, 1987.

Shepherd, David. "The Authority of Meanings and the Meanings of Authority: Some Problems in the Theory of Reading." *Poetics Today* 7 (1986): 129–45.

Shuler, Philip L. "Questions of an Holistic Approach to Luke-Acts." *Perkins Journal* 40 (1987): 43–47.

Silberman, Lou H., ed. "Orality, Aurality and Biblical Narrative." *Semeia* 39 (1987).

Smith, Barbara Herrnstein. "Narrative Versions, Narrative Theories." *Critical Inquiry* 7 (1980): 213–36.

Smith, Paul. *Discerning the Subject.* Minneapolis: University of Minnesota Press, 1988.

Spanos, William V. *Repetitions: The Postmodern Occasion in Literature and Culture.* Baton Rouge: Louisiana State University Press, 1987.

Spencer, Aida Basançon. *Paul's Literary Style: A Stylistic and Historical Comparison of 2 Corinthians 11:16–12:13, Romans 8:9–39, and Phillipians 3:2–4:13.* Jackson: Evangelical Theological Society, 1984.

Spencer, Richard A., ed. *Orientation by Disorientation: Studies in Literary Criticism and Biblical Literary Criticism.* Pittsburgh: Pickwick Press, 1980.

Spivak, Gayatri Chakravorty. *In Other Worlds: Essays in Cultural Politics.* New York: Routledge, 1987.

Staley, Jeffrey Lloyd. *The Print's First Kiss: A Rhetorical Investigation of the Implied Reader in the Fourth Gospel.* Atlanta: Scholars Press, 1988.

————. "The Structure of John's Prologue: Its Implications for the Gospel's Narrative Structure." *Catholic Biblical Quarterly* 48 (1986): 241–64.

Stanzel, Franz K. *A Theory of Narrative.* Translated by Charlotte Goedsche. New York: Cambridge University Press, 1984.

Starobinski, Jean. "The Struggle with Legion: A Literary Analysis of Mark 5:1–20." Translated by Dan O. Via, Jr. *New Literary History* 4 (1973): 331–56.

Staten, Henry. *Wittgenstein and Derrida.* Lincoln: University of Nebraska Press, 1984.

Stempel, Daniel. "History and Postmodern Literary Theory." In Natoli, *Tracing,* 80–104.

Stendahl, Krister. "The Bible as a Classic and the Bible as Holy Scripture." *Journal of Biblical Literature* 103 (1984): 3–10.

Sternberg, Meir. *The Poetics of Biblical Narrative: Ideological Literature and the Drama of Reading.* Bloomington: Indiana University Press, 1985.

Sternberg, Meir, and Menahem Perry. "The King through Ironic Eyes: Biblical Narrative and the Literary Reading Process." *Poetics Today* 7 (1986): 275–322.

Stock, Augustine. *Call to Discipleship: A Literary Study of Mark's Gospel.* Wilmington: Michael Glazier, 1982.

———. "The Limits of Historical-Critical Exegesis." *Biblical Theology Bulletin* 13 (1983): 28–31.

Stout, Jeffrey. *The Flight from Authority: Religion, Morality, and the Quest for Autonomy.* Notre Dame: University of Notre Dame Press, 1981.

———. "What Is the Meaning of a Text?" *New Literary History* 14 (1982), 1–12.

Sturrock, John. "Roland Barthes." In Sturrock, *Structuralism,* 52–80.

Sturrock, John, ed. *Structuralism and Since: From Lévi-Strauss to Derrida.* Oxford: Oxford University Press, 1979.

Suleiman, Susan R. *Authoritarian Fiction: The Ideological Novel as a Literary Genre.* New York: Columbia University Press, 1983.

———. "Introduction: Varieties of Audience-Oriented Criticism." In Suleiman and Crosman, *Reader,* 3–45.

Suleiman, Susan R., and Inge Crosman, eds. *The Reader in the Text: Essays on Audience and Interpretation.* Princeton: Princeton University Press, 1980.

Talbert, Charles H. *Acts.* Atlanta: John Knox Press, 1984.

———. "Artistry and Theology: An Analysis of the Architecture of Jn. 1:19–5:47." *Catholic Biblical Quarterly* 32 (1970): 341–66.

———. *Literary Patterns, Theological Themes and the Genre of Luke-Acts.* Missoula, Mont.: Scholars Press, 1974.

———. *Reading Corinthians: A Literary and Theological Commentary on 1 and 2 Corinthians.* New York: Crosssroad, 1987.

———. *Reading Luke: A Literary and Theological Commentary on the Third Gospel.* New York: Crossroad, 1982.

———. Review of *The Gospel According to Luke (X–XXIV),* by Joseph A. Fitzmyer. *Catholic Biblical Quarterly* 48 (1986): 336–38.

Tannehill, Robert C. "Attitudinal Shift in Synoptic Pronouncement Stories." In Spencer, *Orientation,* 183–97.

———. "The Composition of Acts 3–5: Narrative Development and the Echo Effect." In Richards, *1984 Seminar Papers,* 217–40.

———. "The Disciples in Mark: The Function of a Narrative Role." *Journal of Religion* 57 (1977): 386–405.

————. "The Gospel of Mark as Narrative Christology." *Semeia* 16 (1979): 57–95.

————. "Israel in Luke-Acts: A Tragic Story." *Journal of Biblical Literature* 104 (1985): 69–85.

————. "The Magnificat as Poem." *Journal of Biblical Literature* 93 (1974): 263–75.

————. *Mirror for the Disciples*. Nashville: Discipleship Resources, 1977.

————. *The Narrative Unity of Luke-Acts: A Literary Interpretation*. Vol. 1, *The Gospel According to Luke*. Philadelphia: Fortress Press, 1986. (Vol. 2, *The Acts of the Apostles*. Sonoma: Polebridge Press, forthcoming.)

————. "Reading It Whole: The Function of Mark 8:34–35 in Mark's Story." *Quarterly Review* 2 (1982): 67–78.

————. *The Sword of His Mouth: Forceful and Imaginative Language in Synoptic Sayings*. Missoula, Mont.: Scholars Press, 1975.

————. "Tension in Synoptic Sayings and Stories." *Interpretation* 34 (1980): 138–50.

Tannehill, Robert C., ed. "Pronouncement Stories." *Semeia* 20 (1981).

Taylor, Mark C. *Altarity*. Chicago: University of Chicago Press, 1987.

————. *Deconstructing Theology*. New York: Crossroad, 1982.

————. "Deconstruction: What's the Difference?" *Soundings* 66 (1983): 387–403.

————. *Erring: A Postmodern A/theology*. Chicago: University of Chicago Press, 1984.

Taylor, Mark C., ed. *Deconstruction in Context: Literature and Philosophy*. Chicago: University of Chicago Press, 1986.

Theissen, Gerd. *The Shadow of the Galilean: The Quest of the Historical Jesus in Narrative Form*. Translated by John Bowden. Philadelphia: Fortress Press, 1987.

Thiemann, Ronald F. "Radiance and Obscurity in Biblical Narrative." In *Scriptural Authority and Narrative Interpretation,* edited by Garrett Green, 21–41. Philadelphia: Fortress Press, 1987.

————. *Revelation and Theology: The Gospel as Narrated Promise*. Notre Dame: University of Notre Dame Press, 1985.

————. "The Unnamed Woman at Bethany." *Theology Today* 44 (1987): 179–88.

Thiselton, Anthony C. "Reader-Response Hermeneutics, Action Models, and the Parables of Jesus." In Roger Lundin, Anthony C. Thiselton, and Clarence Walhout, *The Responsibility of Hermeneutics,* 79–126. Grand Rapids: Eerdmans, 1985.

Tiede, David L. *Prophecy and History in Luke-Acts*. Philadelphia: Fortress Press, 1980.

Tolbert, Mary Ann. *Perspectives on the Parables: An Approach to Multiple Interpretations*. Philadelphia: Fortress Press, 1979.

————. "Polyvalence and the Parables: A Consideration of J. D. Crossan's *Cliffs of Fall.*" In Achtemeier, *1980 Seminar Papers,* 63–67.

————. "The Prodigal Son: An Essay in Literary Criticism from a Psychoanalytic Perspective." In Crossan, "Polyvalent," 1–20.

————. *Sowing the Gospel: Mark's World in Literary-Historical Perspective.* Philadelphia: Augsburg Fortress, forthcoming.

Tompkins, Jane P. "An Introduction to Reader-Response Criticism." In Tompkins, *Reader-Response,* ix–xxvi.

————. "The Reader in History: The Changing Shape of Literary Response." In Tompkins, *Reader-Response,* 201–32.

Tompkins, Jane P., ed. *Reader-Response Criticism: From Formalism to Post-Structuralism.* Baltimore: Johns Hopkins University Press, 1980.

Tracy, David. *The Analogical Imagination: Christian Theology and the Culture of Pluralism.* New York: Crossroad, 1981.

————. *Plurality and Ambiguity: Hermeneutics, Religion, Hope.* San Francisco: Harper & Row, 1987.

————. "Reflections on John Dominic Crossan's *Cliffs of Fall: Paradox and Polyvalence in the Parables of Jesus.*" In Achtemeier, *1980 Seminar Papers,* 69–74.

Troeltsch, Ernst. *Gesammelte Schriften.* Vol. 2. Tübingen: Mohr, 1913.

Tuckett, Christopher. *Reading the New Testament: Methods of Interpretation.* Philadelphia: Fortress Press, 1987.

Tyler, Stephen A. *The Unspeakable: Discourse, Dialogue, and Rhetoric in the Postmodern World.* Madison: University of Wisconsin Press, 1987.

Tyson, Joseph B. "Conflict as a Literary Theme in the Gospel of Luke." In *New Synoptic Studies: The Cambridge Gospel Conference and Beyond,* edited by William R. Farmer, 303–27. Macon: Mercer University Press, 1983.

————. *The Death of Jesus in Luke-Acts.* Columbia: University of South Carolina Press, 1986.

Ulmer, Gregory. *Applied Grammatology: Post(e)-Pedagogy from Jacques Derrida to Joseph Beuys.* Baltimore: Johns Hopkins University Press, 1985.

————. "Op Writing: Derrida's Solicitation of *Theoria.*" In Krupnik, *Displacement,* 29–58.

Underwood, Horace H. "Derrida and the Christian Critic: A Response to Clarence Walhout." *Christianity and Literature* 35 (1986): 7–12.

Uspensky, Boris. *A Poetics of Composition: The Structure of the Artistic Text.* Translated by Valentin Zavarin and Susan Wittig. Berkeley and Los Angeles: University of California Press, 1973.

Van Aarde, A. G. "Plot as Vindicated through Point of View in Mt. 22:1–14: A Case Study." In Petzer and Hardin, *Perspective,* 62–75.

Van Iersel, Bastiaan M. F. "Locality, Structure, and Meaning in Mark." *Linguistica Biblica* 53 (1983): 45–54.

————. "The Reader of Mark as Operation of a System of Connotations." In McKnight, "Reader."

————. *Reading Mark.* Translated by W. H. Bisscheroux. Edinburgh: T & T Clark, 1989.

Van Tilborg, Sjef. *The Sermon on the Mount as an Ideological Intervention: A Reconstruction of Meaning.* Wolfboro, N.H.: Van Gorcum, 1986.

Van Unnik, W. C. "Éléments artistiques dans l'évangile de Luc." In *L'évangile de Luc: Problèmes littéraires et théologique,* edited by F. Neirynck, 129–40. Gembloux: Ducolot, 1973.

Via, Dan O., Jr. *The Ethics of Mark's Gospel—In the Middle of Time.* Philadelphia: Fortress Press, 1985.

————. "Narrative World and Ethical Response: The Marvelous and Righteousness in Matthew 1–2." *Semeia* 12 (1978): 123–49.

————. *Kerygma and Comedy in the New Testament: A Structuralist Approach to Hermeneutic.* Philadelphia: Fortress Press, 1975.

————. *The Parables: Their Literary and Existential Dimension.* Philadelphia: Fortress Press, 1967.

————. "Structure, Christology and Ethics in Matthew." In Spencer, *Orientation,* 199–215.

Vorster, Willem S. "Characterization of Peter in the Gospel of Mark." *Neotestamentica* 21 (1987): 57–76.

————. "The Gospel of John as Language." *Neotestamentica* 6 (1972): 19–27.

————. "Literary Reflections on Mark 13:5–37: A Narrated Speech of Jesus." *Neotestamentica* 21 (1987): 203–24.

————. "Mark: Collector, Redactor, Author, Narrator?" *Journal of Theology of South Africa* 31 (1982): 46–61.

————. "The New Testament and Narratology." *Journal of Literary Studies/Tydskrif vir Literatuurwetenskap* 2 (1986): 42–62.

————. "The Reader in the Text: Narrative Material." In McKnight, "Reader."

Walhout, Clarence. "Can Derrida Be Christianized?" *Christianity and Literature* 34 (1985): 15–22.

Walker, William O., Jr. *The Relationships among the Gospels: An Interdisciplinary Dialogue.* San Antonio: Trinity University Press, 1978.

Walworth, Allen J. "The Narrator of Acts." Ph.D. diss., Southern Baptist Theological Seminary, 1985.

Waters, Lindsay, and Wlad Godzich, eds. *Reading de Man Reading.* Minneapolis: University of Minnesota Press, 1988.

Ward, Patricia A. "Revolutionary Strategies of Reading: A Review Article." *Christianity and Literature* 33 (1983): 9–18.

Wead, David W. "The Johannine Double Meaning." *Restoration Quarterly* 13 (1970): 106–20.

———. "Johannine Irony as the Key to the Author-Audience Relationship in the Fourth Gospel." In *American Academy of Religion Biblical Literature: 1974,* compiled by Fred O. Francis, 33–50. Missoula: Scholars Press, 1974.

———. *The Literary Devices in John's Gospel.* Basel: Friedrich Reinhart Kommissionsverlag, 1970.

Weaver, Dorothy Jean. "The Missionary Discourse in the Gospel of Matthew: A Literary Critical Analysis." Ph.D. diss., Union Theological Seminary in Virginia, 1987.

Weber, Samuel. "Caught in the Act of Reading." In *Demarcating the Disciplines: Philosophy, Literature, Art,* edited by Samuel Weber, 181–214. Minneapolis: University of Minnesota Press, 1986.

———. *Institution and Interpretation.* Minneapolis: University of Minnesota Press, 1987.

Weeden, Chris. *Feminist Practice and Poststructuralist Theory.* London: Blackwell, 1987.

Weeden, Theodore J. *Mark—Traditions in Conflict.* Philadelphia: Fortress Press, 1971.

Welch, Sharon D. *Communities of Resistance and Solidarity: A Feminist Theology of Liberation.* Maryknoll, N.Y.: Orbis Books, 1985.

Wellek, René. *A History of Modern Criticism, 1750–1950.* Vol. 6, *American Criticism, 1900–1950.* New Haven: Yale University Press, 1986.

Wellek, René, and Austin Warren. *Theory of Literature.* 3d ed. New York: Harcourt, Brace & World, 1956.

West, Cornel. *Prophesy Deliverance!: An Afro-American Revolutionary Christianity.* Philadelphia: Westminster Press, 1982.

White, Hugh C., ed. "Speech Act Theory and Biblical Criticism." *Semeia* 41 (1988).

White, Hayden. "Michel Foucault." In Sturrock, *Structuralism,* 81–115.

———. *The Tropics of Discourse: Essays in Cultural Criticism.* Baltimore: Johns Hopkins University Press, 1978.

———. "The Question of Narrative in Contemporary Historical Theory." *History and Theory* 23 (1984): 1–33.

Wilder, Amos N. *Early Christian Rhetoric: The Language of the Gospel.* Cambridge: Harvard University Press, 1971.

———. "The Gospels as Narrative." *Interpretation* 34 (1980): 296–99.

———. *Jesus' Parables and the War of Myths: Essays on Imagination in the Scriptures.* Edited by James Breech. Philadelphia: Fortress Press, 1982.

———. "Story and Story-World." *Interpretation* 37 (1983): 353–64.

Williams, James G. *Gospel against Parable: Mark's Language of Mystery.* Sheffield: Almond Press, 1985.

———. "The Innocent Victim: René Girard on Violence, Sacrifice, and the Sacred." *Religious Studies Review* 14 (1988): 320–26.

————. *Those Who Ponder Proverbs: Aphoristic Thinking and Biblical Literature*. Sheffield: Almond Press, 1981.

Wimsatt, William K., Jr., and Monroe C. Beardsley. "The Intentional Fallacy." In *The Verbal Icon: Studies in the Meaning of Poetry*, 3–18. Lexington: University of Kentucky Press, 1954.

Winquist, Charles E. *Epiphanies of Darkness: Deconstruction in Theology*. Philadelphia: Fortress Press, 1986.

Winquist, Charles E., ed. "Text and Textuality." *Semeia* 40 (1987).

Witherup, Ronald D. "The Cross of Jesus: A Literary-Critical Study of Matthew 27." Ph.D. diss., Union Theological Seminary in Virginia, 1985.

————. "The Death of Jesus and the Raising of the Saints: Matthew 27:51–54 in Context." In Richards, *1987 Seminar Papers*, 574–85.

Wittig, Susan. "A Theory of Multiple Meanings." *Semeia* 9 (1977): 75–103.

Wolthuis, Thomas R. "The Narrative Plot of the Gospel of Matthew." Ph.D. diss., Duke University, 1985.

Wrede, William. *The Messianic Secret*. Translated by J. C. G. Greig. Cambridge, England: James Clarke, 1971.

Wright, T. R. "Regenerating Narrative: The Gospels as Fiction." *Religious Studies* 20 (1984): 389–400.

Wuellner, Wilhelm. "Narrative Criticism and the Fourth Gospel: Collected Papers of Wilhelm Wuellner, 1981–1983." Berkeley: Graduate Theological Union Library, 1983.

————. "Is There an Encoded Reader Fallacy?" In McKnight, "Reader."

————. "Where Is Rhetorical Criticism Taking Us?" *Catholic Biblical Quarterly* 49 (1987): 448–63.

Index

Acts of the Apostles, xx. *See also* Luke(-Acts)

Authorial intention: for Gérard Genette, 53; as immaterial signified, 64–65; for Jacques Derrida, 54; in narrative criticism, 8, 12, 34, 36–38; in New Criticism, 12; in reader-response criticism, 12, 77, 104; for Stanley Fish, 114–15; textual resistance to, 30–34, 53–54, 162, 174; transcendentalized, 172

Bassler, Jouette M., 84, 89, 90, 92; on Iser's implied reader, 87; Markan reader-response criticism of, 81–83, 87, 92, 97, 100

Character: definition of, 15; reliable, 5, 15, 74–75. *See also* John, Gospel of; Mark, Gospel of

Composition criticism: and deconstruction, 165–67; definition of, 4; and narrative criticism, 4–7, 10, 18, 34n8, 55, 57; and redaction criticism, 4n3, 5, 8, 18

Content: deconstruction of, 64–66, 135–36; in a gospel, 59–60, 61; in narrative criticism, 41–42, 44, 59–62, 66–67; in narratology, 44, 59–61, 67; in New Criticism, 9–10

Crossan, John Dominic, 111, 131, 137, 156; and deconstructive theology, 139, 149–50; and Frank Kermode, 141; on interpretation, 141, 142, 145; and Jacques Derrida, 138, 139, 141, 142, 144n15, 146, 148; on Jesus, 139–40; and language, 139, 140, 142, 143; and negative theology, 140, 148–50; on play, 142, 143, 146; and Roland Barthes, 141–42, 144–45; on Sower parable, 140–42, 144–45; and Yale deconstruction, 141

Culpepper, R. Alan, 43, 53, 63; Johannine poetics of, 45–50; Johannine reader-response criticism of, 93–95, 99

Dawsey, James M.: 53, 125; on Lukan reception history, 123–24; on Lukan style and point of view, 30–34

Deconstruction: and American literary criticism, xvi n12, 137n5; biblical studies in, 149; and composition criticism, 165–67; as critique, 134; definition of, 132–37; 145–48; and Gospel of John, 152–53, 160–69; and hierarchical oppositions, 133, 135, 136, 157, 161–62; and interpretation, 135–36, 137–38; and intertextuality, 133–34; and language, 132–33, 136, 157–58; and metaphysics, 133, 136, 145–46, 148, 150, 153; and narrative criticism, 165–67; and reader-response criticism, 108n1, 122n14, 159–60, 168–69; and religious belief, 150–51, 172–73, 174, 175; and Rudolf Bultmann, 150–51, 172–73, 174, 175; soft vs. hard, 136–37, 151–52; and source criticism, 164–66; and Stanley Fish, 131, 133–34, 135, 136; in theology, 150, 151n26, 175; at Yale, 137n5, 141. *See also* Derrida, Jacques; Logocentrism; Poststructuralism

Demythologizing: extension to critical text, 66, 129, 172–73, 174–76, 177; post-